the naked mom

Brooke Burke

the naked mom

MOTHERHOOD REVEALED

NEW AMERICAN LIBRARY

NEW AMERICAN LIBRARY
Published by New American Library, a division of
Penguin Group (USA) Inc., 375 Hudson Street,
New York, New York 10014, USA
Penguin Group (Canada), 90 Eglinton Avenue East, Suite 700, Toronto,
Ontario M4P 2Y3, Canada (a division of Pearson Penguin Canada Inc.)
Penguin Books Ltd., 80 Strand, London WC2R 0RL, England
Penguin Ireland, 25 St. Stephen's Green, Dublin 2,
Ireland (a division of Penguin Books Ltd.)
Penguin Group (Australia), 250 Camberwell Road, Camberwell, Victoria 3124,
Australia (a division of Pearson Australia Group Pty. Ltd.)
Penguin Books India Pvt. Ltd., 11 Community Centre, Panchsheel Park,
New Delhi - 110 017, India
Penguin Group (NZ), 67 Apollo Drive, Rosedale, North Shore 0632,
New Zealand (a division of Pearson New Zealand Ltd.)
Penguin Books (South Africa) (Pty.) Ltd., 24 Sturdee Avenue,
Rosebank, Johannesburg 2196, South Africa

Penguin Books Ltd., Registered Offices:
80 Strand, London WC2R 0RL, England

First published by New American Library,
a division of Penguin Group (USA) Inc.

First Printing, February 2011
10 9 8 7 6 5 4 3 2 1

 REGISTERED TRADEMARK—MARCA REGISTRADA

LIBRARY OF CONGRESS CATALOGING-IN-PUBLICATION DATA:

Burke, Brooke.
The naked mom: motherhood revealed/Brooke Burke.
p.cm.
ISBN 978-0-451-23233-5
1. Motherhood. 2. Mothers. I. Title.
HQ759.B775 2001
Y46.70085'2—dc22   2010040086

Set in Sabon and Gotham
Designed by Pauline Neuwirth

Printed in the United States of America

PUBLISHER'S NOTE
The recipes contained in this book are to be followed exactly as written. The publisher is not responsible for your specific health or allergy needs that may require medical supervision. The publisher is not
responsible for any adverse reactions to the recipes contained in this book.
    While the author has made every effort to provide accurate telephone numbers and Internet
addresses at the time of publication, neither the publisher nor the author assumes any responsibility for
errors, or for changes that occur after publication. Further, publisher does not have any control over
and does not assume any responsibility for author or third-party Web sites or their content.

To my family, David, Neriah,
Sierra, Rain, and Shaya.
You give my life purpose. This book is ours
and possible because of all of us.

To my man, my friend, my lover, thank you for
making me face myself. I am forever grateful for the
security and confidence you possessed to encourage
me to write this book and share the intimate details
of our lives. I adore you. You are my life.

To my children, you are my greatest
accomplishments. Thank you for educating me
every day, making me honest, and keeping me
grounded. You all make me want to be better.
Being your mom is the greatest I will ever be.
I love you more than words.

acknowledgments

THERE WERE TIMES when I doubted whether this book would ever see the light of day. I dissected every part of who I am during the year it took to write this. I second-guessed myself and what I believe in, and even doubted my ability at times to walk my own talk. On many days, I was unsure of what was relevant enough to reveal to the world.

There are many people to thank for keeping me on the right track, keeping me truthful, and encouraging me to share my experiences.

First and foremost, my partner, my love, David. Without him, I never would have had the courage or the freedom to share my journey. At moments of doubt, when I wondered if I was sharing too much, he sat beside me and listened to my thoughts and fears, and encouraged me to go for it all, as he always does. He is the support system that I always wanted but only dreamed of. Thank you for making me more, and being in my corner. You showed me true love and welcomed the concept of our ever-challenging blended family. You are my soul mate, my gravity. Somehow you always bring me back, and keep me where I belong. I am forever grateful to you for showing me a different way. *Je t'aime à la folie, mon amour.*

acknowledgments

The four dynamic, fantastic and special personalities that define my gorgeous children have allowed me to fully understand the concept of flexibility. Because of them, I know that I may never figure it all out, but I will keep learning and tweaking along our way. Their voices and fragile hearts and life's ups and downs have taught me so much and turned on lights in my darkest corners. I hope you will better understand my ways one day when you read this book. I always and only want the best for all of you, and all of you make me fight for nothing less. Thank you.

Mom, what can I say? You taught me about unconditional love and made me want to be a mother. Thank you for giving me that precious gift. I miss Armen and wish he could have seen who I am because of the life lessons you both taught me. Thank you. I love you.

Tamara Jones allowed my voice to come to life on paper. You made me feel safe to share all; you never judged me and you made me feel better about myself. Thank you for writing with me every day. You entered my sacred haven, delicately, kindly and compassionately. Thank you for making this experience so fulfilling. It feels like a sad breakup now that it's finished. I already miss our late-night talks, pity parties, and laughter. You are brilliant. Thank you from the bottom of my heart. I hope this is only the beginning. You were the right choice!

To my sister, Kim, my crash mat: Sharing our sucky moments together always makes them feel better. Thanks for reminding me that my tough road has led me to where I am. I am your fan.

As a woman, I value my girlfriends more than ever! You know who you are. Thank you for your virgin eyes during this process. Without you, I would go insane. Thanks for allowing me to make fun of myself, the bitch sessions, and your brutal honesty.

To my fabulous Glam Squad: Steven Lake, Marylin Lee, Steven Aturo, and Justin Ducoty—you guys allow me to pretend, escape, and never let anyone know how tired I really am. I am so lucky to play princess, share my intimate space, and trust all of you. You are the best of the best! XOXO

To supermom Lisa, my partner and friend. We breathe community healing; thank you for giving me a front-row seat. We always speak the same language. Thanks for your faith in me.

To Richard Abate, my literary agent. Thanks for pounding the pavement with me in New York, making this book happen, and giving me Tamara. I never imagined I would add "author" to my list!

To Tracy Bernstein, my editor at New American Library: Thank you for believing in this book, and giving me a place to share my triumphs and tribulations with women everywhere.

To my manager, partner, and dear friend, David Brady: Thank you for running my life and giving me mucho to manage. You are my Quan.

To the *DWTS* family: Thank you for changing my life and making one of my bucket-list dreams come true. I never imagined I'd go from carpool to the ballroom, from sweats to sequins, and make it home to tuck in my babies while dressed like a princess. What a gig!

And to every woman who picks up this book, and shares my journey: Make time to DANCE!

contents

introduction

Holding them close: (left to right) *David and me with Sierra, 8; Shaya, 2; Neriah, 10; and Rain, 3.*

L over, fighter, giver, taker, hero, villain, soul mate, bitch, spouse, daughter, sister, coach, seductress, ice queen, protector, chauffeur, chef, hostess, boss, trophy, caregiver, confidante, choreographer, director, playmate, maid, diva, martyr, negotiator, diplomat, nurse, gardener, cheerleader, hunter, gatherer, survivor, decision maker, counselor, vixen, fixer, dreamer, faker, mind reader, partner, accomplice, volunteer, drill sergeant, entrepreneur, juggler, clown, domestic engineer, goddess, witch, teacher, warrior, banker, concubine, geek, spy, dairy bar, mistress, referee, fashionista, dancer, femme fatale, peacemaker, nurturer, judge, jury, comedienne, shrew, lioness, actress, champion, bodyguard, CEO, role model, best friend, competitor, advocate, manager, rescuer, sprinter, courier, princess, saint, sinner, networker, homemaker, employee, slave, dictator, rebel, servant, healer, politician, magician, muse.*

How many different words describe you? A handful? A hundred? That's why I wanted to write this book, because I believe passionately that motherhood is so much more than the sum of its countless roles and dog-eared labels: This is about us. For us. Smart, sexy, soulful moms. Consider this an exposé of who we really are, when you shed the stereotypes and popular myths and the polished façades we all hide behind at times.

The Naked Mom is motherhood, revealed. It's not about being right or wrong. It's about being authentic. When you're raising four children, running a household, tending a relationship, building a multimillion-dollar business, and pursuing a television career, there's no room for pretense or posturing. I always knew I would be a mother, but I never imagined I would have this many children this fast, or that our lives would be full of changes and new challenges every day. But I was raised to take chances, to be strong, and to find my own way. When I think about myself as a mother, I suppose that's just what I've done. I don't believe in A-to-Z guides that spell out the "right" way to raise your children, or be a wife, or realize your personal goals. There's always going to be someone out there wanting to tell you exactly how to do it—that opinionated friend who thinks her way is the only way, another mother who's doing something better than you are. Modeling yourself after someone else will never work. I wanted to write this book to hopefully inspire women to share their experiences, to learn and live and laugh together. Motherhood is a community, and we should all reap its collective wisdom and joy. But at the same time, I hope you'll find your private dancer deep within, and let her guide you through the music that is yours alone. I hope that sharing my own missteps and triumphs will help you realize your own possibilities and discover potential you didn't know you had, or put aside long ago. The truth is, I've achieved more as a mother than I've ever done in my life.

This book won't tell you how to live your life, but I'll show you what really goes on behind the scenes in mine, and how I manage—on good days—to make it work.

Perfection isn't an ideal, it's an illusion. I just don't see life as an escalator, where ten easy steps will land you a perfect body, or perfect marriage, or perfect career. And this whole concept of defining success as the ability to balance everything? Makes sense if you're a circus seal, but not if you're a woman. Repeat after me: There is No. Such. Thing. As. Balance. I'm always asked in interviews how I balance everything going on in my life. The short answer is: I don't! If I strived for balance, I'd be disappointed every day. As a young mom, I was constantly chasing that goal, and when it (of course) eluded me, I would end up feeling inadequate. Clearly, I just wasn't doing "it" right, as if "it" could even be defined, much less contained and controlled. A decade of motherhood and too many missteps and mistakes to count have since given me the wisdom to let go of the stupid balance myth once and for all. Life serves up enough stress without lining up for second helpings.

That's why I couldn't fathom writing your typical handbook for modern moms. We're more complicated than that. It'll suck the soul right out of you if you buy into the popular how-to propaganda that portrays life as some giant jigsaw puzzle that you can solve if you're just clever enough or patient enough to fit together all the precut pieces. What I envision is more of a mosaic, forever shifting and changing design, color, and mood. You can take the same tiny stones and create a placid lake or turbulent sea. Once you start sorting those countless little fragments, a pattern will emerge. You have to take that much on faith, then let skill and imagination fill in the rest of the masterpiece.

Our lives are continually rearranged and take new shape. My own life is radically different today from what it was a year ago, when I sat in my office with a legal pad and a latte and first began thinking about what I wanted to tell you. My career is in a different place, my relationship has dipped and soared, and my four kids keep growing and learning and constantly changing. They educate and reeducate me every single day, and just when I think I've got them figured out, they change on me again! This whole process of soul searching has given me a chance to discover new things about myself, and to learn so much about myself as a woman, a mother, a lover. Having to examine my life and my choices under my own microscope was sometimes scary, but also exhilarating. I came to realize that what I wanted all along wasn't really balance after all.

It's fulfillment.

And that's something that's actually attainable, no matter who you are or what your circumstances.

So, no, this isn't going to be some step-by-step how-to celebrity guide that will spell out what you need to do to be like me. To paraphrase the late, great Judy Garland, why settle for being a second-rate version of someone else rather than a first-rate version of yourself? I hope, though, by sharing my journey and my experiences, you'll start reflecting on your own woman behind the scenes, and discover—or rediscover— who she is and what makes her uniquely wonderful.

What excites me most about these frenetic times we live in is all the opportunities we now have at our fingertips to connect with one another through social media. I know from my ModernMom.com community that women from all walks of life are eager to share their stories, to learn from each other, and sometimes just to see things from someone else's perspective. There's an undeniable sense of solidarity that enriches and entertains us, a wealth of wisdom, information, observation, and, above all, compassion that's instantly ours for the asking. Most empowering of all is the knowledge that there *isn't* one "right" way, that it's okay to find your own way, to define your own boundaries and discover your own philosophy.

As for me, I have to admit that I've always been a risk taker, whether I was staring down an eight-foot crocodile in a reptile pit while taping *Wild On* or setting out to stitch together a blended family from the tatters of my failed marriage. (Truth be told, the hissing croc has nothing on an enraged ten-year-old.) I sincerely believe that there's a purpose to everything that happens in our lives, good or bad. Mayhem is unavoidable. Still, it's a little intimidating to publicly admit some of those truths that we, as mothers, keep safely hidden away in our secret selves, never revealing that private dancer. Truths like "I love my children but I don't always like them," or "I'm too uptight to be the lover my partner wants."

One of the scariest parts of being a mother is also one of the most wondrous: not knowing what to expect next. That part rings even truer for me these days as my two older girls hurtle through those vexing and perplexing tween years. Add two toddlers and my soul mate, David Charvet, into the mix, and you have a house full of wildly different personalities, each person going through his or her own phases, at their own decibel level. Everyone has their own needs, desires, disappointments, and dreams. Their only common denominator? Me.

Been there, done that? Come inside, it's a big clubhouse.

So here's where we stand: We can either deal with the chaos or be consumed by it.

Women with even the slightest hint of a survival instinct obviously choose the former. But then what? It's not like there's some Emotional Merry Maids service we can call to dust, vacuum, and hand-polish the chaos away, preferably with a discount coupon for repeat customers. If only we could shovel it all into plastic bags, tie them up neatly, and leave them curbside. Accepting that you can't—no, really, you can't—may feel like a form of surrender, but I promise it's not. It's actually an important victory. Because the chaos is *always* going to be there, to some degree or another. Blithely ignoring it may be a tempting option, but that's ultimately as effective as the rhythm method in a rabbit hutch. I propose a more calculated approach: Dance through it. It's all about hearing the music, finding your footing, and moving gracefully. You're amazing; the world is a mess. Don't get confused.

Through my ModernMom.com Web site, blogging, tweeting, and good old-fashioned networking in the carpool lane, I've been able to build and tap into an amazing community of regular moms and celebrated experts. We vent, we comfort, we advise, we soul search, we coach, we share, we celebrate, and, when needed, we kick each other in the ass. It's a dynamic, 24/7 dangling conversation, and what I've learned—and continue to learn, every day—both sustains and inspires me. Technology didn't just give me tools, it gave me something of an epiphany: True fulfillment doesn't come from control; it comes from connection.

The Naked Mom explores the three personas that dwell inside us: the Woman, the Mother, the Lover.

The first section focuses on looking good and taking care of yourself. Moms are always too willing to put everyone else first and (falsely) claim that we're perfectly happy to forever be the last one on the totem pole. If you don't take the time to look good and feel good, though, it's all going to backfire on you sooner or later, and you'll become one more resentful statistic in the sad annals of *Roadkill Mommies: Steamrollered by Life*. We've all seen them, pitied them, and, yes, been them. But a little discipline, a bit of creativity, a lot of common sense, and a designer tote full of Hollywood's best glam tricks can fix that. (Hint: What do my hair and my favorite salad have in common?) So peel yourself off the pavement, already! You don't just deserve better—you deserve your best.

No doubt the toughest and best job of all is being a parent. "Mother" is easily the most revered word in the human language. It's an identity that is universally understood, yet interpreted uniquely by every woman who inhabits it. And regardless of whatever other responsibilities or aspirations we have in life, most of us would agree that nothing matters as much. But that passion, and the overwhelming love that drives it, can be dangerous if you don't know how to handle the hairpin curves and switchbacks that mark this road. Like any adventure, motherhood can be thrilling, and it can also be harrowing. No wonder we all occasionally lose sight of where we're going. It's time to pull over, cut the engine, and reconsider the road map you've been using. We've allowed social pressure, popular media, and our own insecurities to manipulate us into believing that "selfless" is the ultimate seal of approval for any mother. Check out that word again, and consider what it really means: the absence of self. That cannot possibly be a good thing, unless you plan to trade your sweats for sackcloth and go live alone on a very tall mountain for a very long time. Spare yourself the angst and altitude sickness, and strive for something more attainable and empowering: self-awareness.

I found that on live TV, of all places. I never expected that being a celebrity contestant on *Dancing with the Stars* would prove to be a turning point in my life, but it absolutely was. For the first time ever, I didn't believe in myself. I wanted more than anything to give up and limp away, but the love and support of my family pushed me forward, and I learned how to check in with myself, truly count on a partner, and to commit wholeheartedly to the challenge at hand.

We all know that good communication is at the core of any successful relationship, whether it's a business partnership, a romance, or the bond between mother and child. Knowing this and actually putting it into practice are two different things, of course. I remember too well the evening that I overheard my ten-year-old screaming something nasty at her younger sister. I was about to march in and ground her on the spot, when I suddenly realized something that made me literally stop in my tracks: She was imitating what she had learned from me. Like plenty of moms out there, I've been known to verbally lash out sometimes in moments of frustration and stress. Ashamed as I was to recognize my own bad behavior in my daughter, it did serve as a good reminder: Our kids hear everything, and they remember it, and it sticks. That night, I thought about my daughter's behavior for a while, then decided to talk to her about it. Our chat—and the effort I made to genuinely connect with her, instead of merely reacting to her—produced better results than knee-jerk punishment would have (which isn't to downplay the value of a well-earned time-out or grounding!). That day when I heard my own words from my daughter's mouth, I understood how ugly I sometimes sound. But I also realized that just stepping back and "checking in" with each other is vital when you're determined to give your heart without losing your mind. It's a technique I've been practicing in the "real world" as well as Mommyville, and it really does work.

Being a mother means having to learn the different, unique language of each member of your family, and to communicate with compassion. What motivates one child may crush another. We also have to learn how to receive messages as clearly as we send them. Having a blended family and shared custody with my ex-husband makes that even more challenging, and I have to remember to step back and just breathe sometimes, or the domino effect of an ill-considered remark or action can be devastating. My oldest daughter and I have started keeping a shared journal, and the insights for both of us have been amazing.

Most women give up a lot to become mothers, and the lover always seems to be the first part of a mom's identity to go AWOL. Does the libido always have to take one for the team? My answer is a definitive *"No!"* Sexuality and motherhood are not mutually exclusive. Many of the same traits that make you amazing as a mom make you amazing as a lover, as well: generosity, playfulness, devotion, patience, imagination, and intuition are just a few that come to mind. I think feeling sexy and sexual is a state of mind. Letting our erotic fantasies play out gives us a needed break from the give, give, give nature of motherhood. Behind many a sweet, wholesome mom, me included, there is a feral woman. A carnal self, a sort of secret slut. She is you, unfiltered, unedited, unapologetic.

Learning how to set a mood, play out a fantasy, and reconnect with your mate are ways to reclaim yourself as a lover. I'm happy to reveal some of my secrets in steamy detail, from the most outrageous place I've ever done it to my favorites list of erotic literature, hottest movie scenes, sexiest songs, and trustiest aphrodisiacs.

Chaos is such a mainstay in my life, I'm surprised it doesn't appear on my driver's license as my permanent state of residence.

We've all had these mornings: You wake up to discover that the ants have reclaimed the kitchen counter, your laptop and cell phone have carried out a suicide pact overnight, your mate has just remembered that he invited six vegans over for an important business lunch on Saturday, the baby kept you up all night but you need to be perky and on for a big meeting at the office, and your seven-year-old wants to know the facts of life right this minute. It's easy to fall into the trap of thinking we can be Supermom if we just had more time or energy. How often do we lie in bed at night taking mental stock of everything we *didn't* get accomplished that day, and adding it onto the next day's to-do list? The pace of our lives is already fast and furious; increasing the tempo is just going to make you more exhausted, not more efficient. We know from experience that the demands of raising a family change continually and sometimes dramatically. Needs are never synchronized, and trying to be everything to everyone all the time leaves no one— including you—satisfied. That's especially true if, like me, you're one of the millions of American moms trying to rebuild a family from the ruins of divorce. The painful knowledge that

I'm the one who wreaked this havoc doesn't make it easier to contain. But facing the toughest challenge of my life has taught me an elemental truth: You may not be able to choreograph chaos, but you can dance through it with something resembling grace. Finding your own rhythm means living inside each moment of your life, and learning how to tune out the noise so you can hear the music.

My purpose here isn't to suggest that I have all the answers—far from it. But I have had plenty of trial and error, under circumstances both ordinary and extraordinary. I hope that this book makes people laugh, because I certainly laugh at myself even in my most stressful situations. You have to keep dancing even when life seems to be getting the best of you.

And when I'm really lost, or frustrated, when I'm sick, or deflated, or feeling small and lonely, my own mom is still the one I run to. Her love fortifies me, and I strive to build that kind of bond now with my four children, so they might someday feel as blessed as I do. Mom is my ultimate superhero, the woman who made me want to be a mother, whose gift of unconditional love gave me the faith and courage to raise a family of my own.

If there is one gift I could wrap up prettily and hand to every woman on the planet, it would have to be confidence. Much as I would like to, I know I can't simply give you that. But maybe, by giving you my truth, you'll be able to find your own.

XOXO,

1

the mirror-ball trophy

Derek Hough and I survived plenty of blood, sweat, and tears to become the Season 7 champs on Dancing with the Stars.

I NEVER DREAMED that dance lessons would become life lessons, but that's exactly what happened when I first joined *Dancing with the Stars* back in 2008. The whole thing was supposed to be a lark. Performing as a celebrity contestant would provide a nice prime-time boost for my image, and what could be easier than dressing up in Cinderella gowns, learning a few ballroom steps, and being swept across the stage in the capable arms of a professional partner? Sounded like a sweet gig.

But somewhere between my first, tentative cha cha cha and my final, daredevil freestyle, this act of folly became the pivotal experience of my life, changing the very way I moved through the world. Long after the competition ended, I find myself still hungry to explore what commitment really means in our lives as women, and how our vulnerabilities define and shape us as both mothers and lovers.

Back to the first step, though. The closest I'd ever come to dancing before this was a misguided attempt to become a song leader in high school back home in Tucson. I made the squad, then promptly quit after the first practice. Just not my thing. I was a die-hard tomboy who preferred pigskin to pom-poms. I ended up playing football, instead. But fast-forward twenty years, and here I was, another Hollywood mommy yearning to become part of the *DWTS* phenomenon. What can I say? It looked like so much fun, plus, it was glamorous and sexy as all hell. I had just given birth to my fourth child, Shaya, and his sisters were eight, six, and eighteen months, so . . . Fun? Glamorous? Sexy? Sign me up! Really, how hard could it be?

Oh, if only I'd known.

For starters, *DWTS* turned out to be a seven-day-a-week job, for three solid months. That translates into ninety days of hard labor. I found myself rehearsing with my professional partner, Derek Hough, for eight hours a day, often more. And if I was expecting to be Cinderella, this blond boy dictator thirteen years my junior clearly hadn't gotten the Prince Charming memo! To say Derek was a taskmaster would be an understatement. That man was focused, and he was fierce. As for me, I was inexperienced, insecure, and awash with new-mom hormones. I was beyond needy, and Derek was beyond distant. We focused on the footwork, and tried to ignore the emotional missteps we were already making. This was, after all, a performance.

My son, Shaya, was barely four months old when taping began, and just the idea of being separated from him tore me apart. I had been an advocate of attachment parenting since the birth of my firstborn, Neriah, and I was one of those papoose mamas who basically wore all my kids. During my first marriage, we even slept together in a family bed. (Try undoing that later on! But that's a different story.) I had been hosting the extreme adventure travel show *Wild On* while pregnant, and I had kept up my demanding schedule after Neriah was born. She spent her infancy gallivanting around the globe with me, and had filled two passports by her second birthday. I was determined to prove that work wouldn't interfere with motherhood, or vice versa. So, with that template still in place, I decided to take Shaya with me to the dance studio every day. He loved listening to the music and watching all the action, lying belly-down on his little blanket. Sometimes I would scoop him up and take him for a spin around the floor, too. That probably didn't help the slow boil that Derek was doing over what he perceived as my inattention to his choreography, but I couldn't exactly expect a young bachelor to understand baby brain and its effects on my ability to remember the steps. Still, even Derek had to admit that having Shaya strapped to my front helped tremendously with one of our early routines, the quickstep, since your chests are never supposed to touch in that dance. And I have no doubt that the muscle memory of my baby pressed up against my heart calmed my nerves considerably when it came time for my live performances.

Needless to say, my lovely little rehearsal reverie with Shaya didn't last long. I'd been pretty spoiled by my previous TV gigs—*Wild On*, *Rock Star*, and even my stints doing red-carpet celeb interviews had all relied on hosting skills that came naturally to me. But *DWTS* was more than just a show—it was a competition. My ability to ad-lib wasn't going to distract viewers if I literally fell on my ass on live television. And that horrifying scenario, I might add, is a very distinct possibility when you're wearing three-inch spiked heels while quick-stepping across a polished stage.

CHA CHA CHA, CHIDE CHIDE CHIDE

I had worked hard to get back into shape after having Shaya—by the fourth child, I certainly knew the drill—so I was feeling reasonably fit and healthy by the time I showed up for my first dance lessons with Derek. But I soon found out that physical strength was only part of the equation: Learning how to waltz, rumba, and jive proved to be mentally taxing, as well. Because I had to give so much emotionally, and focus so intensely, bringing Shaya to work quickly became unfeasible. This job—and my teacher—demanded my undivided attention. Reluctantly, I realized Shaya would be better off at home, where Papa was holding down the fort with the girls. Having to pry myself apart from my baby no doubt added some resentment on my part to the disconnect Derek and I were feeling.

The funny thing is, Derek and I were faring well in the competition from the start, despite our personality challenges. Our scores were consistently high, and there were effusive compliments about my grace and the breathtaking beauty of the routines Derek was choreographing for us. I don't think anyone had a clue that what was going on backstage was more train wreck than tango. People don't realize that being cast on *DWTS* is like a prearranged marriage (without the sex, at least for me). You have to form a partnership with a complete stranger, trust each other instantly, and work through any problems quickly and decisively. As the competition heated up, though, so did the tensions between Derek and me.

No matter what show I'm on, I'm one of those people who will have a bad rehearsal and then come back to nail it on air.

The added pressure just makes me perform better. Derek didn't have any faith in that formula, and really, who can blame him? He didn't know me, and it wasn't just my reputation on the line. We would emerge from rehearsal and he would make it clear how fed up he was, ripping me up one side and down the other. He was a tough teacher, not big on positive reinforcement, and I didn't like feeling like a failure when, as far as I was concerned, I was working my damn butt off. The strategy for winning a fan-driven show like *DWTS* is to be good, of course, but you also have to be likable and relatable. Lack of charisma had sent plenty of dancers more talented than I was packing on previous seasons. If Derek and I didn't have natural chemistry, we were going to have to figure out fast how to fake it, and fake it well.

Derek was a Latin dancer who'd won a slew of championships on the pro circuit. I felt as if he were expecting me—a rank beginner—to match the gold standards of the professional partners he'd had. Didn't he see how hard this was for a novice? I felt extremely insecure for the first time in my career. Celebrities are generally a very guarded, carefully protected breed—you always have your entourage of people who make things work and help you shine, and thank God for them and the tight safety net they weave. But on *DWTS*, it's you alone being judged by millions of people, doing something you've never done before, and it's freakin' scary. Scarier than giving birth scary. Scarier than standing in a pit of crocodiles scary. (I've done the former four times, but once was enough for the latter, FYI.) The fear factor gets really amped up for me when I'm not the one calling the shots. I was used to being in control, and I liked it that way, but Derek was the one with the knowledge, talent, and experience we needed. I had no choice but to count on him. In hindsight, I'd have to say the crocodiles showed more mercy.

naked truth

"Hell, no, this will never work in America!" was my response in 2005 when I was asked if I might be interested in dancing on an American version of a smash British TV hit called *Strictly Come Dancing*. Who wanted to watch a bunch of celebrities learn how to foxtrot? Um, everyone, I guess, since *DWTS* is now the number-one show in America. Thank God for second chances! Mine came in Season 7, when I was the last star cast (rumor had it someone else had bailed at the last minute). Being the underdog definitely fueled my drive to win.

BREAKDOWN

At home, David could see that the show was taking a serious toll on me. I was utterly spent each night—my body screaming, my mind numb. Derek and I hadn't even hit the halfway mark, and I was a hot mess. I looked more like a guest star on *ER* than a cast member from *DWTS*. I had landed hard coming out of a flip on our jitterbug, and ended up injuring tendons in both feet. One foot was so painful I could barely put any weight on it at all. A physical therapist was making house calls each evening to keep me going.

Trouble was, I wasn't sure I wanted to.

I'd never really had to fight for anything before, and to be honest, I didn't think I had it in me. I remember hobbling up the stairs one night and literally crumpling in the shower. I started to cry and couldn't stop. I missed my life so much! I wanted to be with my baby and my three girls and the man who loved me more profoundly than I had ever experienced love before. I fell sobbing into David's arms.

"I can't do this anymore," I wept.

Work had always been something I relished, and I wasn't used to not enjoying what I did. It was obviously time to get out of this nightmare and move (okay, limp) on. And frankly, it would have made David's life a lot easier, too, if I just threw in the towel. Flying solo as Mr. Mom with a newborn, a two-year-old, and two squabbling young stepdaughters was no picnic. My injuries alone were certainly a justifiable excuse for leaving the show. But as he held me and comforted me that night, David made me see that I had an obligation to myself—and more important, to my two older girls, Neriah and Sierra—to suck it up. "The kids are fine," he assured me. Shaya was not being scarred for life, Rain thought all mommies danced on TV, and Neriah and Sierra were old enough to comprehend and be amazed that I was doing something I'd never attempted before. They saw me struggling, but they also saw my progress. The kids were so proud to see me all dressed up and dancing each week on the show (even though Sierra sheepishly confessed that she had been calling in to vote for the Disney heartthrob Cody Linley instead of me). Every night when I staggered home, all three girls would be waiting eagerly. "Mommy, Mommy, let's dance!" they'd beg before I barely got through the door. I couldn't refuse, no matter how tired or sore I was. We'd always have our dance. If I quit now, what was I teaching them?

"You can do this," David insisted that night I finally broke down.

I didn't feel like I had much courage left to summon at that point, but I reluctantly decided I would stick it out. I would probably get voted off soon enough, anyway. Derek and I had already stood together on the stage on elimination nights with frozen smiles, feigning relief when our names weren't called; it would have been an act of kindness to give us the hook, and I distinctly remember one night when I had to bite my cheek to keep from blurting out a bleepable curse of disappointment when I was voted through for another week.

NO AIR

In the dance studio, Derek was running on empty, too. The time I had to spend nursing my foot had meant he had had to choreograph our routine alone, with an invisible partner (though I'm sure that Invisible Brooke was far more compliant than I was). And just to make it even more daunting, we were heading into the semifinals, which meant we were looking at two routines to perform that week, not one. "Double dances, half the time to rehearse," Derek ruefully observed.

If there was a saving grace, it was that one of the numbers was the rumba. The dance of love. I'm a deeply sensual person, and I was sure this would be my dance, my magical moment. But Derek and I were still locking horns, and the cameras caught us bickering backstage that night. He was doing his usual "this is how it is" belligerent bit, and I was doing my usual "if you're not going to listen to how I feel" martyr whine, underscored by my still-hurting foot. We went onstage angry and disconnected. The song was called "No Air," and I remember that's how I felt out there, as if I couldn't breathe. Of course, we blew it. Adding insult to injury, the producers sent us to counseling because we were such a dysfunctional couple.

The counseling segment never aired, but our single session with a life coach actually did transform us as a team. The advice she gave us still resonates with me to this day, and has guided me through far more crucial challenges in my life than perfecting a rumba. "You have to check in with each other every day," we were admonished. "Even if it's only for seven minutes. You have to really listen, and really care. Treat each other with compassion. Ask how each other is doing. And if you're tired and having a lousy day, then say, 'I'm exhausted and having a bad day, but I'm here and I'm committed and I'm going to give all I have to give today.'"

Derek and I redoubled our efforts, but we also sat down and pledged to show each other compassion and respect. I'll never forget the grueling day when we were rehearsing in a studio in a seedy L.A. neighborhood. We were both exhausted after going at this every single day for two months. Derek is such a brilliant choreographer, but his creative juices had been tapped dry. And I wasn't recuperating from my injuries very well, because I couldn't follow medical advice to stay off my feet for a week—that would have meant leaving the competition, and I had already resolved not to do that. On top of everything else, I was feeling guiltier and guiltier with every hour I spent away from Shaya. He was so small, and he needed me so much! I missed my whole family beyond words. It was as if someone had physically carved away my core, and left this aching, gaping hole behind.

That afternoon in the ratty neighborhood, I ventured outside for a quick breather and happened to see a woman walking past with her small daughter. The mother stopped and bent down to swipe at her little girl's runny nose with a tissue. I stood in the parking lot and felt hot tears streaming down my face. *What gives?* I asked myself. Was this just pent-up nerves and frustration that we couldn't get our new dance down? But my tears had turned to full-out sobs, and I knew what the real problem was: That tiny, everyday gesture of a mother wiping her child's nose had undone me, because it made me feel so unavailable to my own children, so disconnected and sad and emotional.

I stopped sniveling and went back into the studio so Derek and I could resume choreographing our upcoming salsa routine. Suddenly, we looked at each other, and I saw his eyes well up.

"I can't do it," he said. "I don't have anything left and I don't know what to do. I'm having a really hard time putting this dance together."

"I can't help you, either," I replied carefully.

The naked honesty of that moment—both of us admitting we couldn't make it all right—made us genuinely connect as vulnerable, deeply human beings for the first time. We both just stood there in the studio and wept. There was nothing else to do. Finally, we decided to take a break and regroup. Over lunch, we made a promise to one another, and to ourselves: *Let's just pull it together. Let's be there for each other. We've come this far, so let's just do it and not stress out anymore and have fun. And who knows, maybe we'll be able to win this darn thing.*

That mirror-ball trophy was in sight, and we were just going to commit to dancing our best every single time we went out there. If all we had to give was a 3 instead of a 10, then we would give that 3 with every drop of passion we had in us. We would give that 3 wholeheartedly.

But my real turning point was yet to come.

CHRONICLE OF A DISASTER FORETOLD

In the semifinals of the ten-week competition, we were given the jive. The jive is incredibly fast-paced—a super-fun, high-energy dance. But it was also the most challenging choreography I'd faced to date. There was this one step right in the beginning of the routine that I kept screwing up. It wasn't that complicated, just a classic sort of kick-and-flick, where you lean back on one foot and kick with the other. I always wanted to lean on the wrong foot. Common sense should have warned me to stop early on in rehearsals to concentrate on the problem area, and correct it once and for all. I'm always preaching to my children about the importance of being confident in all your choices, so you can do whatever you're doing with conviction. I clearly needed to listen to my own inner doubts and address them when it came time to jive. I opted for denial, instead. And boy, did I ever pay the price.

Even when rehearsals go well, I'm the type of performer who's invariably a nervous wreck come show night. My mind just loves to play out all the worst-case scenarios. (I don't know how David ever did *Baywatch*—I would have envisioned the opening scene of *Jaws* every time the director told me to hit the water!) On *DWTS*, I would mentally flip through all the possible catastrophes: What if I forgot the steps? What if a heel broke? What if Derek dropped me? Each week, David would clear my dressing room minutes before I went on, then sit there coaching me to breathe from the center, calm myself, and purge the negative thoughts from my mind. Sometimes it even worked. The sports doctor who had been treating my dance injuries had also advocated the power of positive thinking, encouraging me to visualize an amazing performance before going out onstage.

Standing in the wings in my scandalously skimpy blue micro-miniskirt and sequined white bra that night, though, my imagination ran its usual little disaster movie. But this time, I bought into it instead of letting it go. With cruel clarity, I visualized myself forgetting the jive routine and embarrassing myself, and Derek, too. Not to mention my mother, who loved to watch me proudly each week from the front row. And my children. I'd probably have to start homeschooling them to spare them the public shame.

We heard our cue, and I felt Derek's hand in mine, leading us onstage as the band struck up our song. And, on silent cue from my imagination, I immediately lost that step I'd never felt sure of in rehearsal, the very one I had just visualized blowing. I felt a jolt of panic shoot through me. Try as I might, I just couldn't get back in sync with Derek. My worst fear was coming true! I tried to fumble through, but toward the end of the routine, I suddenly drew a complete blank and froze. I couldn't hear anything. I didn't know where I was. All I wanted to do was hold on to Derek. He tried to move my body into the right place, but I couldn't remember a single step. Then my long hair got caught on his costume. It was time to put a fork in us—we were done. Play the routine back on YouTube, and you may not think it was that big a deal; the fiasco was just a matter of seconds. But those seconds lasted an eternity for me. I was thoroughly humiliated. The judges shredded us. Len Goodman pronounced it "a disaster," while Bruno Tonioli expressed shock, and concluded that my "technique went down the toilet." Carrie Ann Inaba condemned me for an illegal lift she considered "disrespectful." Ouch. We ended up with the lowest semifinal scores in the show's history—7s straight across. We'd been pulling 10s.

No autopsy was necessary. I knew exactly what had happened: I had visualized failure, and it became a self-fulfilling prophecy. Naturally the producers ate it up, and gleefully told me that it was great TV. (Yeah, at my expense, I thought bitterly, and remind me never to enter the Indy 500.)

I braced myself for Derek's righteous fury. His supportive reaction surprised me.

"It's okay," he told me. "You're only human. You're not a pro. Now, pull it together, because a champion will go back out there and show them how it's done." Going back out there was the last thing I wanted to do, but we still had our salsa to perform. I knew I couldn't succumb to tears, or waste time licking my wounds. I was absolutely terrified. I had let my faith falter, with devastating consequences, and now I was going to have to let it go and rely on both my body and my partner. We went out there and danced our salsa with a vengeance, promptly reclaiming our 10s and redeeming ourselves.

As it turned out, the producers were right about my fumble being great TV, and the audience still loved us, too. My mortifying mistake had been one of those humanizing moments, and I was stunned to realize that people hadn't rejected me because of my misstep—they had felt compassion, and identified with me. We were voted through to the finals.

I realized the power of fear that night, and how easily it can take over when you stop believing in yourself, or in the forgiveness of others. Something clicked inside me. I was no longer just sticking it out on *DWTS*. This wasn't about the silly trophy or even the great publicity. It wasn't about what I owed, or what others expected of me. This was about a commitment to *myself* and a commitment to my partner. It was about giving whatever I could give, every day, because *I* deserved no less. I had to trust myself. It was time to think like an athlete instead of bellyaching and wishing I were home. I finally understood that perseverance is more gratifying than perfection.

I'm here, I made it this far, I may as well win, I resolved that night.

Not that it was all smooth sailing from there.

LEAP OF FAITH

It took every ounce of will I had to keep going. Whenever I wanted to quit, I asked myself not what millions of viewers would think, or what Derek or the producers would think, or even how David would feel. I asked how I would feel about myself.

For our finale, Derek choreographed a daring freestyle number to "The One That I Want," from *Grease*. By then, I had pulled a hamstring as well as my groin, and Derek had thrown out his back, so our rehearsals were more like *Dancing with the Gimps* than *Dancing with the Stars*. There was a move called the roly-poly, which turned us into a human carnival wheel, and one where I was supposed to jump up on the judges' table and then take a flying leap into Derek's arms. Trouble was, we couldn't rehearse that last showstopper, because Derek's back by then was so messed up, he knew he only had one catch in him, and we had to save it for our live performance. Waiting to go onstage that night, I remember praying as we waited for our cue: *Okay, God, I have no idea what's about to happen, but please, please, please just get me through this!* I was so afraid of letting my partner down when we were finally in the right place—in it to win it. I wanted that damn mirror-ball trophy now. For myself, for my family, and for Derek. We had all invested our hearts in this, and it had taken the support of each and every one of them to get me that far.

I'm not afraid of physical risks—on *Wild On*, I had jumped out of airplanes and swum with sharks without a second thought. But failure scares the holy cannoli out of me. Our freestyle had the potential to be fantastic or fatal. The band struck up our song, and off we went. The music seemed to fill my body and command each movement. Every step, every spin, every lift, and even the tiniest gestures felt sure, and totally exhilarating. Adrenaline pumping, I not only jumped off the judges' table into Derek's open arms, but did so with such exuberance that Derek very nearly dropped me. We ended up putting on a performance that brought everyone in the ballroom to their feet and racked up a perfect score. Still, I knew that hardly guaranteed us the championship. My competition was the NFL star Warren Sapp, a talented gentle giant whose fan base was enormous. For our final dance, we were allowed to repeat our favorite number from the season, and I had chosen the Viennese waltz, which we performed to John Mayer's beautiful ballad "Daughters." The song's lyrics about daughters growing up to become lovers and mothers resonated with me deeply. Understanding this, Derek choreographed the number so it would end with me reaching out to my own daughters in their front-row seats, cupping their little faces in my hands, and giving them a kiss. I'll always treasure that powerful, sweet moment.

The next night, as we all stood onstage waiting to hear who had won, I felt surprisingly calm as the lights dimmed. It honestly didn't matter to me at that point. I was just so proud of myself for seeing it through. I had never accomplished anything so difficult in my entire life.

When I heard them call my name, I was in shock. I remember hearing Derek scream, and everyone hugging. All the dancers converged onstage, and I was swept onto the shoulders of Corky Ballas, the famed ballroom dancer and coach who had raised Derek and competed alongside us that season. More than anything, I wanted to rush into David's arms and thank him for knowing when to push me and when to just hold me, but the pandemonium robbed me of that moment, and I couldn't get off Corky's shoulders.

I couldn't see it from the stage, but watching the show later, the cameras had zoomed in on David's face the moment after my name was announced, and captured a tear rolling down

dance lessons for life

Finding your rhythm is essential. It comes from within.
At times we must learn to dance through the chaos:

- Find your balance
- Never lose your footing
- Be flexible and change direction
- Listen to the music
- Fall down, get back up, and try again
- Learn how to work with a partner
- Trust your partner
- Take risks
- Lose yourself in the moment
- Stay open and be fearless
- Commit
- Feel free enough to take chances
- Follow someone else's lead at times
- Know how to dance a solo
- Stay open to learn a new routine
- Practice, practice, practice
- Try your best and give it your all
- Know it's okay not to be perfect
- Stretch your mind and body
- Enjoy the process
- Take time to hear the music, and celebrate the dance, because the song will be over before you know it

his cheek. We were so connected, it was as if we had both won. As the confetti rained down on me, and I hoisted the heavy mirror ball over my head, people probably assumed I was crying out of joy. Of course I was happy, but truth be told, they were tears of pure relief. It was over. I had made it.

The coveted trophy would end up rotating through each daughter's room before I placed it on my desk for good. When I look at it now, it isn't the victory that makes me smile. It's knowing how many steps I had to master, and what agony I endured both mentally and physically to do so.

Settling back into the "real" world, I wrote Derek a letter, trying to find the words to thank him for all the lessons I had learned from him, which would serve me so well long after the music stopped. I was only beginning to see how dance's many truths applied to my private life and its complicated choreography.

REBUILDING

Outside the ballroom, the mirror-ball challenge of my personal life has definitely been my struggle to create a blended family from the rubble of divorce. It's an ongoing dance, an improvisation with no steps to memorize and a tempo that can change radically and without warning. Sometimes, the tender beauty of it breaks my heart, and sometimes the harsh ugliness of it does the same. There are days when I feel inspired and idealistic, and full of energy to pour into this effort, and there are days when I feel crumpled and hurt and exhausted, unsure if I have anything left to give. But ultimately we let the music of life carry us, and we keep dancing on, the six of us, together.

Sierra was only three when her father and I separated, too young to actually process what was happening, but Neriah was not quite six, and the impact on her was like a full-body blow. Garth and I had never been shouters who had it out in front of our children; in fact, our inability to truly engage was the source of my unhappiness and frustration. The marriage felt empty to me, as if we were living two polite, parallel lives. Because she wasn't hearing or seeing us fight, I can see how Neriah must have felt completely blindsided by the divorce. No matter what we told her, she remained convinced that we would be a family again, that I would move back "home" and the life she had known would simply resume. David's appearance in my life—and, by extension, hers—infuriated Neriah from the beginning. I first introduced him to the girls as a friend over a casual lunch at a Cuban restaurant. I can't believe now how naïve I was to assume that the children would effortlessly return the affection and goodwill he had toward them. David didn't have any kids of his own yet, but after a decade of international stardom, his daddy clock had gone off, and he was eager to put down some roots and raise a family.

David and I had first met on a dance floor, ironically enough. It was a charity event at a seaside resort in Mexico. I was a single, twenty-two-year-old model, and he was the sizzling hot lifeguard who ran slo-mo across the sand on *Baywatch*. You couldn't miss him that night on the outdoor dance floor, handsome even in an asparagus-green jacket. Our eyes met and just locked. We ended up dancing together, then talking for what seemed like hours, then going for a long, romantic walk on the beach, then skinny-dipping (he still lies about that—I did too keep my panties on!). Then we went back to the hotel. Then—

Well, let's just say that our connection was so special that I kept the key to that room in a little wooden treasure box for eight years.

We went our separate ways, stayed in sporadic touch, and fell in love with other people. But we had mutual business acquaintances, and years later, when David heard that my marriage was ending, he reestablished contact and soon began courting me in earnest, convinced that destiny demanded we be together. I was emotionally numb at that point, but the romantic still deep inside me wanted desperately to believe that there is such a thing as soul mates, and I'd never forgotten the powerful connection I'd felt the first time I saw David. Nor had I felt anything like it since then. Still, I held back. David finally swayed me with a song he wrote and recorded just for me: "If I Don't Tell You Soon." I decided to take the leap.

In our early days as a couple, David shared the blueprints he had for the dream house he was planning to build in Malibu. He had originally conceived it as the ultimate bachelor pad—a Mediterranean-style villa with two master suites and three guest rooms. The project had consumed him since moving back to the States, and at first, I wasn't eager to be a part of it. I didn't really know where I stood, even after David altered the plans to reconfigure his personal playboy manse into a family-friendly home for five. (I had discovered I was pregnant with Rain not long after ground was broken.)

Over the next eighteen months, I watched David micromanage construction with an attention to detail that bordered on obsessive. He was in this 110 percent. The walnut floor was hand-distressed and inlaid with 250-year-old tiles reclaimed from a French chateau. When heavy rains flooded the newly dug basement, he spent twelve hours bailing it out. When the stone path was laid in the backyard, I found him on his hands and knees, sanding down any rough edges because he was afraid the children might cut their feet if they were running outside barefoot. I understood then that his commitment wasn't to a design, but to a dream, and that the life he wanted to create for all of us was meant to be safe, idyllic, and filled with memories that would become our shared history. I wanted that, too.

I still do.

The house is finished now, but with the addition of Rain, quickly followed by Shaya, we outgrew the place the day we moved in. Sierra and Neriah spend half their week here, and half at their father's, and we share holidays. One of my biggest smack-downs as a divorced mom came the first time the girls rejoiced about spending Christmas "at home" with Garth, in the house we had once shared. I was crushed to realize that my home base wasn't automatically my children's, but I had to accept that being the one to move out had cost me that claim. I was just going to have to get over it. Now, I allow myself to take comfort in knowing that my girls still find a sense of security sleeping in the bedrooms I created for them when I was a new mother.

Sierra was young enough to welcome David into her heart with the easy affection that makes her the family cuddlebug, and David is always ready to wrap her in a bear hug or wish aloud that she didn't have to go to school so they could spend the day together. But Sierra suffered repercussions from the divorce, too, and developed some mild obsessive-compulsive traits, which child psychologists have told us is a response to feeling out of control. The wrong socks can send her into full-blown hysteria.

Neriah is less outwardly emotional than her sister, and David makes a convenient target for her bottled-up anger. The two of them clash constantly, with fleeting truces, which always give me false hope for a lasting peace. I wish all their interactions could be as warm and special as the time David taught Neriah how to ride a bike, running alongside her as they both chanted, "Breathe, focus, balance, balance, breathe, focus, balance, balance . . ." Or as gratifying as the time when Neriah was starring as Glinda in *Wicked*, and turned to David to coach her. I have zero vocal skills, but David patiently shared his wisdom and experience as a performer with Neriah, teaching her how to project, and to sing from the gut instead of through the nose. They worked on her lines together, and when the curtain rose on that third-grade performance, David was as proud of her as I was.

But as promising as those moments are when the two of them really connect, at the end of the day, David and Neriah both boast strong, stubborn personalities, and they know exactly where to find each other's hot buttons. David's a stickler for manners, for example, and it drives him crazy if the children fail to politely greet anyone entering the room, or chew with their mouths open, or don't maintain eye contact while speaking to someone. Neriah resents his rules, and his right to impose them in our home, and she would rather escalate the drama than comply. I have to compassionately understand her loyalty and closeness to her father, and see how letting David into her life might seem, from a ten-year-old's perspective, like betrayal. Still, I can't count the times when the dinner table has become a battleground, with me trying in vain to make everyone like and respect one another. Sometimes I just feel like screaming out loud to the heavens: *What's it going to take???*

No advice books, counseling sessions, or friends who've gone through it can possibly prepare you for the dramas and disappointments of blending a family. I'm convinced that every Brady in the Bunch had to have been smoking crack. If only our lives could be like bright, indestructible LEGO sets where you just keep patiently snapping piece after piece together until you've created what you want, and then, if you take that apart, you just start all over again and build something new and, possibly, even better. But when I sat back and tried to analyze our situation intellectually instead of emotionally, I came to understand that we each harbored our own vision of our ideal family. Moreover, there was only a single common denominator in these different, and sometimes conflicting, dreams.

Me.

naked truth When David took me back to his hotel room that first night we were together in Mexico, I made him show me his ID because he looked so young. (He was twenty-one to my twenty-two.) Then I switched on the TV and discovered *Old Yeller* was on. David had never seen it. *Poor little French boy!* I thought. So I made him watch it. Talk about a mood kill. . . .

GIVE UP OR GO ON?

It's scary to admit this even now, but as the holidays approached in 2009, we were on the brink of losing everything. I wanted to be working less, David wanted to be working more, and neither the economy nor the entertainment industry was cooperating with the goals we had in mind for our life together. At one point, I found myself managing two TV shows, my Baboosh Baby business, and my fledgling ModernMom.com Web site all at once, with assorted endorsement deals and photo shoots sandwiched in between. I yearned for more time to spend doing what I loved most of all: being a mom. Competing on *DWTS* had cost me valuable early bonding time with Shaya, and he was paying me back with some rejection of his own—just because I was madly in love with him didn't mean he was going to instantly latch on to me with equal devotion. I was going to have to earn it. At two, Rain couldn't understand why I was paying attention to any of her siblings, anyway, because as far as she was concerned, I was her mommy and hers alone, and the others were just random pirates out to steal her gold. Once she learns to write, I think she's going to be surprised to discover her name isn't spelled R-e-i-g-n, because that's certainly the assumption! Luckily for us all, she's generally a benevolent queen.

Building and maintaining the Malibu dream house had strained our resources to the breaking point, and we had reluctantly begun talking about possibly having to rent it out. The financial stress was taking a serious toll on our relationship, too, and David and I basically stopped taking care of each other. We were resentful about our situation, and we didn't know yet how to love each other through a really difficult time. We made the mistake of focusing on our failures instead of our future. The tension on the home front was getting unbearable, and deep down, I think I knew that if we rented the place out and I packed up, I wouldn't be moving in with David again. I loved him, but I hated this. What we were living was a far cry from the fantasy we'd envisioned. Maybe it was time to accept reality, and give up the dream. I didn't feel any sense of resolve, though, or even bittersweet liberation. The thought of breaking Rain's and Shaya's hearts the way I had Sierra's and Neriah's saddened me beyond words.

Rain had changed the dynamic of our family-in-progress. After much preparation (including a viewing of *National Geographic*'s breathtaking documentary *In the Womb*), we had decided to let Neriah, then seven, witness her sister's birth. (She wasn't the only one: Both my mom and David's mom were there, too, plus David's sister, and, of course, David and Neriah. I half-expected the neighbors, my favorite Starbucks barista, and my glam squad to wander in and pull up chairs, too. Seriously, I should've sold tickets!) I had always been blessed with quick, easy deliveries, and luckily, this one was no different. Neriah lay beside me in bed during labor and rubbed my back. She helped David coach me to breathe and to push when the time came, and as Rain entered the world, we felt like a "real" family for the first time. She united us, this flesh-and-blood little miracle we all shared. Was that fragile bond now about to unravel before she even turned three?

Before we could make a decision about keeping the house or our commitment to one another, French television approached

David to star on a wildly popular show that would require him to go off and live on a primitive South African game reserve for three months. They were offering him a contract far too lucrative to even consider turning down. We would be allowed to talk to each other—cameras rolling—during brief Skype calls just a couple of times a week. Even though we were on the brink of a breakup, the thought of being alone scared me. I confided my fears one day to Lisa Rosenblatt, my good friend and business partner.

"You'll be okay," Lisa tried to assure me.

"I'm not going to be okay," I insisted. "I'm going to cry every day. I'm not going to be able to do this."

Lisa looked me in the eye and spoke to me in that firm, loving tone that comes with motherhood.

"You are a strong woman," she said. "You are stronger than you think. You are going to be fine."

David left right after New Year.

Fate had clearly forced our hand, dictating a trial separation. It felt like the time-outs I give to Sierra and Neriah when they're being especially hateful to each other; I send them to their separate rooms and forbid them to have contact. "Now you've lost each other," I tell them. Invariably, they end up begging for each other's denied company five minutes later.

I wondered if I would last that long. The reason I so quickly assumed I wouldn't be able to endure living without a man was because I never had. But I was surprised to find myself quickly embracing my alone time (such as it was—we all know there's no such thing as solitude, really, when you have kids! Mine would find me in the Bermuda Triangle). I liked to flop down in the middle of the bed I normally shared, flinging my arms out across the empty sheets, and closing my eyes to breathe in the quiet, slowly and deeply. I would let my mind drift. How did I envision my life playing out now? What could I do to make what I wanted to happen come true? I had come across the concept of a "bucket list" on a terrific mommy blog, and I was fiddling around with compiling one of my own, jotting down my wildest dreams, my biggest hopes, and my deepest yearnings. I used to do something similar every New Year, but this felt different. Some of the things on the list were heartfelt but impossible, like wishing my own mother could live forever, or that I could have one last chance to take my late stepdad on his dream vacation. Others were sweepingly idealistic, like convincing people not to ruin the environment. But the majority of the items on my bucket list were concrete, and within the realm of possibility, no matter how long a shot they might be. Into that category went things like appearing on *Oprah*, going on safari with my family, and hosting either *Dancing with the Stars* or *American Idol*, though the latter hinged on me being able to make Ryan Seacrest disappear. (And appearing as a fugitive on *America's Most Wanted* was *not* on my bucket list.)

Making the list turned out to be a blast, but more than just an amusing exercise, it was a chance to step back from the try-to-please-everyone mode of motherhood and focus on what I wanted—not for others, but for myself. This was a new type of self-awareness for me. Then the weirdest thing started happening.

Wishes on the list began coming true.

I'd heard some buzz in the industry that the *Dancing with the Stars* cohosting slot might be opening up. It's the most glamorous hosting job for a woman in the industry, and I didn't just want it—I longed for it. Having won as a celebrity dancer already made me feel like part of the *DWTS* family, and I would kill for the chance to work with Tom Bergeron. (Okay, maybe not *kill*, except maybe Ryan Seacrest, but as far as I knew, he wasn't going to fight me to the death for rights to the sheer, black-beaded Herve Leger tube minidress or the rest of the va-va-vavoom *DWTS* wardrobe.) Corny as it sounds, I actually started visualizing myself walking down the ballroom stairs as the announcer introduced me: ". . . and cohost Brooke Burke!" But daydreaming alone wasn't going to get me there. I began sending out feelers. The producers and network were going to start testing a lot of different people, which could mean they were going to rotate guest hosts. Word came back that I didn't need to worry about auditioning; they already knew me, after all, and were familiar with my work. I had hosted a slew of red-carpet interview shows before the Emmys and other big awards ceremonies, and I'd hosted the rock 'n' roll version of *Idol* on CBS, *Rock Star: INXS* and *Rock Star: Supernova*. I'd just started a stint as mommy correspondent on the popular daytime talk show *The Doctors*, and was shooting the third season of TV Land's midlife model-search program, *She's Got the Look*. Plenty of clips from my salad days on *Wild On* were drawing fans on the Web, too. It was flattering to know that I was already considered a contender to hold the bejeweled microphone on *DWTS* without auditioning, but I didn't want to sit back and just be a contender here; I wanted to be the winner.

I had already established a professional relationship with the head of ABC and the executive producer of *DWTS*, so I decided to reach out to them personally. This was no time to play the diva! I wanted them to hear how passionately I felt about this job directly from me, and I needed to know for myself that I had done absolutely everything in my power to get this gig. I offered to do a screen test.

It turned out to be one of the toughest auditions I'd ever had—they even threw in some intentionally uncooperative "celebrities" for me to interview to test my cool and my ad-libbing abilities. By the time it was over, I wasn't sure whether I had gotten the job, but I was sure that I had given all I had to give.

While the network was still deciding, I got a surprise call from David's producers in South Africa, inviting me to come visit him. Off I went with the two youngest kids. While there, we had our family safari. I checked lions off my bucket list. My manager was expecting to hear the news about *DWTS* while I was away, and I was supposed to call him on decision day. I picked up my phone, then put it back down again.

"I'm too scared to call," I told David that evening in our tent.

"Just do it," he urged.

"I can't. What if it's bad news?" I worried. We were having such a wonderful trip, and I didn't want it ruined.

I punched in the numbers, and my manager came on the line. Seconds later, I was screaming with joy and flinging myself into David's arms.

One of the biggest dreams on my bucket list had just come true.

I headed back to L.A. with just a couple of weeks to prepare for the show. David would end up spending another month in Africa. It was hard for me to believe how much had shifted in our lives in such a short period of time. We were no longer in danger of losing the house, and the very real prospect of losing each other had ended up renewing our relationship in ways both exciting and reassuring. David and Neriah had written to one another while he was gone, and he had shared pieces of his own childhood with her, recounting how much he had despised and resented his own stepfather when he had suddenly appeared on the scene. He told Neriah he loved her, but didn't want to replace her own father, or cause her any pain.

"He's changed!" Neriah told me one night as I was tucking her in. "He gets it, Mom. I feel like he really understands me."

I noticed a change in David when he returned home, too. The isolation of Africa had given him a chance to focus on his music once more, and he was ready to go back to the studio and record the new songs he'd written. He felt less pressured than before, and as a result, he was a lot more mellow. I was surprised when he became all emotional over the redecorating I had done in his absence. For the first time in our four years together in Malibu, he felt like I was going to stay for good, that I was throwing my whole heart and soul into this crazy, imperfect, breathtaking dance, and it didn't matter how often we stumbled or fell or missed our cues. We were in it to win it.

BACK IN THE BALLROOM

Being back on the ballroom floor, minus the anxiety of memorizing new routines, is flat-out thrilling. I feel such empathy for the contestants, knowing exactly what they're going through, and how much harder it is than it looks in those brief snippets you see on your TV screens. It's terrifying, even for seasoned performers. It's equally difficult for the pros, and I lived and breathed all of it firsthand.

My first season of cohosting, I found myself particularly drawn to the underdog, reality-TV mom Kate Gosselin. She was in the throes of a nasty divorce, and the tabloids were shredding her to pieces. I recognized the anguish behind her stoic façade, and my heart went out to her. I had barely been able to hold it together to compete on the show with four kids at home, and I lived within commuting distance of the studio. How on earth was she managing with eight young children clear across the country? On-screen, she tended to come across as cold and wooden, but when the cameras were off, she was genuinely warm and likable.

I knew Kate would never win, but I desperately wanted her to have just one breakthrough dance, one that would penetrate that armor she wore and give her the freedom to show her vulnerability. A dance that would make her believe in herself. She was always a bundle of nerves before going on, and I remember trying my best to calm her down. I urged her to just have fun, and to replace her fear with joy by pretending there was nobody in the audience, "except eight little ones lined up rooting for you." I'm not sure whether she ever felt like she got a mirror-ball moment, but I'd like to think she took my advice the night she got her highest scores and warmest praise from the judges. They're the same words I tell myself when I think I can't keep trying so hard to be so much for so many, when I feel spent but know I can't quit, because if you want to get what you want, you have to give all you can give.

"Think of your children," I told Kate, I tell myself. "They're the ones you're dancing for."

brooke's bucket list

- Sleep for eight hours a night, all week long, maybe even squeeze in an hour nap!
- Eat margherita pizza with jalapeños for lunch every day, drizzled with olive oil, and not gain a pound.
- Take my children on an open-water dolphin dive.
- Have the sex and romance that David and I shared in Saint-Tropez, prekids. We still have great sex, but oooh, that was one romantic trip!!!
- Dance the rumba with Derek one more time for a big charity event . . . and not screw it up.
- Win an Emmy.
- Spread the 4 Rs concept: Rethink, Reduce, Reuse, Recycle.
- Hit Rodeo Drive for a purse-shopping spree, unlimited budget.
- Do the milk campaign with my kids . . . Got Milk?
- Inspire women to embrace the woman behind the scenes and be who they are meant to be.
- Learn French.
- Appear on the cover of *Shape* magazine.

2

beauty, deconstructed

My DWTS glam squad knows all my secrets: (left to right) *Marylin Lee, stylist Justin Ducoty, and hairstylist Steven Lake.*

I GREW UP equating beauty with stupidity. That may sound hypocritical coming from the mouth of a television hostess, but I promised you the naked truth, and there you have it. My mind-set had nothing to do with media stereotyping, or radical feminist theory. I came by my bimbo aversion honestly, courtesy of my handsome playboy father.

My parents split up when I was still in diapers, and I never had much of a relationship with my biological dad. But come summer, my sister and I would be sent to Connecticut to spend a couple of weeks with him. Even as a child, it didn't take me long to figure out that he was all about the surface shine. If you had any doubt about my father's vanity, all you had to do was step inside his house: There was nothing hanging on the wall, save mirrors. "Why do I need art when I can admire my own beauty?" he would explain. No joke. The look-at-me obsession was reflected in his choice of girlfriends, as well. He knew when and how to play the charm card, and he seemed to have an endless supply of clueless women half his age. Whenever I arrived for a visit, there was sure to be a fresh blonde applying lip gloss in the rearview mirror of whatever flashy car Dad happened to be driving at the time. The girls were always stunningly gorgeous, and always stunningly dumb. They dressed in black cocktail dresses to go to the beach. They were perfectly pleasant, but had absolutely nothing to say. My father treated them horribly, with utter contempt. I remember the time that one of them was apparently annoying him with her mindless chatter, and he suddenly pulled the car over and ordered her to get out. The fact that we were in the middle of New York City—at least a two-hour drive from home—didn't matter one bit, and I remember wishing, hoping, wanting, *needing* that woman to just put my father in his place once and for all. Where was the backbone beneath that beautiful shell? She just whimpered and groveled, while Dad drove off. I was too young, and too scared, to say a word. At first, these cruel, sexist little skits he staged were merely confusing, but as I entered my teens, bewilderment turned to outrage, and I would beg my mom and beloved stepfather not to make me go anymore. I can remember sitting there seething with anger while these nineteen- and twenty-year-olds just beamed blankly at every rude remark and public put-down my father doled out. And then they came back for more! It was perfectly clear to me—if not to them—that he considered them nothing more than decoration. They served the same purpose as Dad's diamond pinky ring, but were valued far less. I absolutely hated the way he treated them. Even more, I hated the way the girlfriends put up with it, how docilely they let themselves be defined by someone else's perception. These women never added up to the sum of their perfect parts. By the time I was sixteen, I had reached the only logical conclusion: Pretty was pathetic.

That probably explains why one of my most enduring fantasies as a woman was to be desired by a blind man.

How ironic, then, that I've spent my entire adult life immersed in the world of beauty, from my early days as a bikini model, through my marriage to a famous plastic surgeon, to the TV career I have today. I never planned it that way—I was a hard-core tomboy who could name more NFL players than supermodels, and my first-choice career was to become a mechanic just like my stepdad, so I could build my own motorcycle someday. Then, when I was seventeen, I accompanied my college jock boyfriend to a go-see at a modeling agency in our Arizona hometown. The president of the agency asked if I'd ever considered modeling, and whether I'd be interested in doing a test shoot. "Let me think about it," I said. A few months later, I went back, put together a portfolio, signed with the agency, and booked my first job, modeling activewear for a catalog. I'll never forget the purple tights and black leotard; I looked like the scared reject from a *Flashdance* audition. Once I had stumbled into the industry, though, I found my niche and settled in happily enough. I soon graduated from velour jogging suits to string bikinis. The money was good, and if swimwear companies wanted to make me look hot and have me pose on some fabulous beach in an exotic paradise all day, then Brooke and the Art of Motorcycle Maintenance would have to wait.

Modeling was more vocation than aspiration for me, but I'm pretty outgoing, and I did honestly enjoy it. But I also knew, realistically, that I was never going to walk the runway in New York, appear in the pages of *Vogue*, or take Europe by storm. My face was girl-next-door natural, not haute exotic.

And my modeling card boldly claimed that I was five-feet-eight, which was a two-inch lie on my tallest day. I would have given anything to have the long, shapely legs of Gisele Bundchen, but I figured out how to work what my mama gave me instead. In my mind's eye, I was five-feet-eleven, and I spent hours at a time standing on my tippy-toes on photo shoots, trying to trick the camera into believing that, too. Bone structure notwithstanding, a fair amount of looking good comes down to a combination of confidence and illusion. Beauty stopped being stupid to me, and became something more intriguing: a career.

After ten years of toiling in the bikini trenches, I landed my first shot at the major leagues: a three-year TV contract hosting E! Entertainment's *Wild On* travel series. Now I would not only be wearing a bikini before viewers in 120 countries, but I would be doing things like participating in the world's biggest food fight, which involved three tons of tomato puree in a small Spanish village. (If you ever find yourself in that situation, wear goggles. Consider yourself forewarned. Those fruit acids burn!)

Since I had no hosting experience, I have to assume E! hired me for my sense of adventure, and if the producers were disgruntled when I told them a month into the gig that I was pregnant, they had the good grace not to show it. ("Brooke, your new boob job looks really good," my unknowing sidekick whispered to me one day.) I soon learned even more about how to emphasize the good and steer attention away from the not so great. As my pregnancy progressed, the camera shots got tighter and tighter. I wasn't Bikini Girl anymore. I was Bikini Top Girl. Looking back now, I can see why the producers were so supportive. My cup size was practically doubling with each episode.

Being in the public eye obviously means subjecting yourself to public judgment, and I've learned to take neither the fawning praise nor the vicious criticism to heart. When I was a finalist for my hosting job on *Dancing with the Stars*, total strangers actually spent time in Internet forums discussing things like the shape of my nostrils. Funny as that is, it also speaks volumes about how obsessed our culture is with physical beauty. No disrespect to the nostril analysts, but let me be blunt here: Looking good is not so much an art as it is a craft. Anyone can maximize their looks by learning about the techniques, the tools, and the fake-outs. I'll happily give up all the Hollywood cookies and share those with you. They're fun and useful things to know. Honestly, achieving beauty is something anyone can do. But what a shame to settle for that when there's a more elusive, yet far more gratifying, goal to be had. Which brings me back to the blind man, and why I so prized his imaginary approval.

It's because having beauty and *exuding* beauty are two entirely different things.

BUILDING A BETTER ME

Let's begin with the superficial. Who hasn't flipped through a magazine, or seen some star in a TV show or movie close-up, and thought, *Damn, why can't I look like that?* Me, too. Except I know that what I'm seeing is not real, and I can tell you from experience exactly what it takes to create those enviable images. Does anyone have real hair or real boobs or real teeth anymore? Not on my patch of the planet, babe. In the interest of career security and personal safety (did you really think I was going to call out the A-listers?), I'll just deconstruct myself here.

First, meet my glam squad, the pros I depend on to get me camera-ready for *Dancing with the Stars*—a process that requires an entire day and the skills of hair and makeup artists who know my every stray gray and Juvederm-starved laugh line, plus the sleep patterns of my four kids and who's to blame for the bags beneath my eyes that morning. And let's not forget the stylists who contemplate whether champagne is the new gold, or the nail technicians who see that my microphone hand is sporting up-to-the-minute My Private Jet instead of predictable old Ballet Slippers, or the seamstress who stitches me into my gown to hide the drive-thru sirloin burger I wolfed down on the way to work. (Easy, haters, it was bunless! And don't think I didn't notice the two pair of Spanx producers had waiting for me in my dressing room!) Then, of course, there's the hulking security guard on hand to make sure the loaner 10-carat pink diamond pendant around my neck doesn't accidentally-on-purpose disappear down my cleavage when no one's looking. Oh, and did I mention the detailing team that airbrushes my face, same as you'd spray-paint a car, assuming you want your ride to be a healthy shade of suntan? Airbrushing, for what it's worth, only sounds soothing—it feels like your head got stuck in one of those tornado booths at the fun fair. Then my eyelashes are glued on one by one, and as many as five hairpieces are clipped strategically around my head. My main mane guy, Steven Lake Louis, cuts and styles them separately first, which means when I have a six a.m. hair call, my hair can go ahead and get started without me! If you think those fat, glossy chignons that show up on the red carpet are the actress's own hair, then I'm sure Bernie Madoff has some stock he'd be happy to sell you from prison, too. Suffice it to say, come showtime, nothing has been neglected in my *DWTS* primp-a-thon: Even my toes have shimmer lotion on them before slipping into their $1,200 snakeskin Gucci platforms.

It would be hard *not* to look good after all that, LOL.

But, even more important, what the glam squad does is make me feel good about myself. I know when they're done that every feature I have is being played to maximum potential, and every flaw is being likewise downplayed. Grueling as the whole process is for everyone involved, it's also undeniably a rush when we're ready to go, and I enjoy the thrill every single time. Seriously, nothing is sexier than self-confidence! Without that, there's no way I'd be able to make it down the hallway, let alone out onstage before a live audience and 20 million-plus viewers at home. And truth be told, I'd rather hold on to that confidence forever than the rarest of pink diamonds. (FYI, they snatched that baby back before I even kicked off my shoes.)

DIY

At home, my beauty MO couldn't be more radically different. When I'm in my usual routine of ferrying kids to school and playdates, running errands and maybe squeezing in a Pilates class before procrastinating my way through the aisles of the grocery store, I'm likely to have my hair pulled back in a pony-tail, and at most a coat of mascara on my eyes. Depending on my degree of self-consciousness that day, I may or may not have brushed a heavy concealer over the brown "baby mask" spots on my cheeks. The melasma appeared when I was carrying Neriah, my firstborn, then worsened and moved around with each pregnancy. I've tried everything from medical lasers to acid peels, but so far, nothing has worked. I have no choice but to accept it and master the art of coverage. A spot spackling of the heavy foundation used to camouflage tattoos, plus a dusting of powder to keep the concealer from melting under the hot TV lights, does the job.

On my days off, it feels great not having to care what I look like, or what flaws are showing. I'm not one of those moms who puts on her face for a Saturday morning with *Go, Diego,Go!*, or carefully applies waterproof lipstick before taking the kids for a swim. I feel as sensual plodding around the house in David's yummy soft sweats as I do in the slinkiest designer gown. When I was asked in an interview not long ago to describe the moment in my life when I felt the most beautiful, I'm not sure they were expecting my decidedly unglamorous but very real response: It's when I wake up in the arms of the man I love, with sunlight pouring through the windows and my kids snuggling close. Nothing makes me feel more like a goddess, impossibly lovely and cherished.

Professionally, I'm lucky enough to have some of the beauty industry's leading experts at my disposal, and I'm constantly trying new products and playing with new looks. I may lack the deft hand of my on-camera makeup pro, Marylin Lee, but I can manage a pretty decent smoky eye with a few drugstore shadows. Take advantage of the free makeovers offered at department store makeup counters, then use the color diagram they provide you as a paint-by-number for your face. That worked for me back in the day when TV budgets didn't cover traveling glam squads.

I think I've gotten fairly savvy about what works and what's nothing but $120 worth of bullshit in a cool jar. I never go anywhere without my Shu Uemura eyelash curler, which my longtime pal and makeup artist, Steven Aturo, names as his all-time fave tool, as well. Curling your lashes even if you don't have time for mascara just makes your eyes look wider, more open and awake. I also never go anywhere without my little vial of China Rain, the scented oil I've worn for years and like to mix now and then with other fragrant oils (pikake is my current blend). A travel-size can of hairspray is good to keep on hand, too. Spray it on your hands, not directly on your hair, and then use your palm to lightly smooth over the flyaways or frizz you're trying to control.

Spending a good part of my life first in Tucson and now California has made me religious about using a strong sunscreen, and as my skin matures, I pamper it with topical serums, especially ones with B vitamins and vitamin C. And I'm a total eye-cream junkie, with a three-times-a-day habit. I always keep a tube in my on-the-go beauty bag to reapply and use to clean up raccoon eyes when my mascara starts to melt. Keeping that delicate skin around my eyes hydrated is something of an obsession for me. If you were to catch me waiting in line for my morning latte on the way to work at six a.m., you might wonder about the white patches beneath my sunglasses; I'm not recovering from eye surgery, I'm moisturizing with those stick-on collagen pads you can pick up at a beauty supply store.

You don't need to haunt the chic skin boutiques to score quality products. The same swanky potion taking up prime real estate at the high-end makeup counters can be found in the aisles of your local drugstore. Compare the ingredient lists and you'll see for yourself. Proof is on your face, not the label. Bottom line is, find products that work for your skin, and if you're not getting the results you want, change your line or your routine.

As a general rule, I steer clear of beauty gimmicks. Why should the oxygen in a spa facial cost more than the tank an EMT would use to revive you if you went into cardiac arrest on the street? Air is air, and I'm not sure my face is more worthy than my lungs. I'm equally dubious about those pedicures where little fish eat the dead skin off your feet, but I can't say whether they work or not, because I'm too grossed out to try. Do you really want to turn your beauty maintenance over to wildlife? What's next—hiring a flock of sparrows to peck your pores clean? Not that I'm dissing nature here. I'm actually a huge fan of homemade treatments. When you pick up a $55 bottle of salon conditioner, what spells "luxury" to you? The long list of chemicals, dyes, and preservatives? Or the familiar ingredients from nature that women have used to enhance their beauty since wise cavewomen first observed that Thor make fire, but mud make good face mask? Getting back to the basics is one of the beauty principles I rely on.

brooke's diy beauty faves

- Grab a jar of 100 percent pure coconut oil in the cooking section of the health-food store for maybe $5, and you've got the best hair serum you could possibly imagine. Apply it to dry hair (it won't be absorbed if your hair is wet). Starting from the ends, I work it into my hair, then clip it up in a bun and leave it on all day. Olive oil is my runner-up (just make sure you're not grabbing the garlic-infused bottle!). Either way, it's easy enough to put on a base-ball cap if you need to run out while condition-ing. Cute caps are also my godsend on plain old bad-hair days.

- When I'm really feeling the need for some deep conditioning, I treat my hair to some guacamole (hold the chips, of course). Mash a ripe avocado in a bowl with a tablespoon each of olive oil and mayonnaise, and add one egg yolk. Beat it until it's the consistency of apple-sauce. Dollop it onto your hair, massage until it's well distributed, and then tuck it under a shower cap or make yourself a quick turban out of plastic wrap. Leave it on for at least half an hour, but longer is always better.

- Like most moms, I'm perpetually sleep-deprived. For puffy eyes, I keep spoons in my

continued

freezer, and grab one to hold under my eye in the morning as I'm refereeing breakfast table squabbles. Or I brew some chamomile teabags, add a handful of ice to cool it down, give the bags a squeeze, and then put them over my eyes while I steal a few minutes to listen to the morning news shows.

◆ Nothing soothes aching muscles like a nice long soak in a bath with good old-fashioned Epsom salt. It even keeps the water warmer longer. I've been known to float jasmine flowers or gardenia buds from my garden in there, too. Almond oil is excellent for moisturizing, and if it's calm you're craving, try soaking with chamomile teabags, whole milk, and a couple of drops of lavender oil. If you dare, a bit of Kama Sutra oil and a small cheesecloth sachet full of rose petals could do the couples trick! Put the toy boats in dry dock and lock the door—no kids allowed!!

◆ Sand is the best natural, free skin exfoliant I know. Coat the skin with oil (coconut works well), take a few handfuls of fine sand, and gently rub the rough parts of your body. Rinse with seawater. No beach? Use sugar and olive oil.

◆ Want to get the most out of your hand cream? Put a thick dollop in your rubber gloves before doing the dishes. The warm water acts as a steam and your hands come out silky soft.

CLOTHES ENCOUNTERS

At the end of the day, the very best beauty advice I can give anyone is this: Pinpoint your best assets and learn how to showcase them. It's funny, and kind of sad, how we fail to see ourselves the way we really are. When a stylist friend came over to inspect my closet recently, she was flabbergasted by what she saw. "I'm really shocked. I was looking for all your shorts, and all the things I'd be wearing if I had your body. You don't have anything structured in here!" she scolded, rifling through my collection of long blousy (but trendy!) tops. It was a major wake-up call. I suddenly realized that, because I'd spent nearly half of the past decade being pregnant, I was still dressing as if I were. My clothes were all fashionable enough, but they tended toward the kind of soft fabrics and shapes that could be artfully draped or layered to camouflage a bulging midsection. Here I'd done all that work to get my figure back after giving birth, and my brain was still apparently stuck in beach-ball mode. I immediately bought a pair of cute black Alice + Olivia shorts to get myself out of the rut.

Too many women, especially after we become moms, forget how to dress well, even if it's just choosing the right jeans or the most flattering silhouette. Simply because you're not twenty-four years old and a size 2 anymore doesn't mean you forfeit the right to look hip and stylish. Take an opinionated, chic friend with you when you shop, and don't be afraid to change up your style and make a statement. It's fun to have a color scheme for the season—right now I'm all about fuchsias and violets I wouldn't have given a second glance to before. I'm usually a denim, black-and-white kind of girl, but it felt like time to take some risks. If you're unsure where to begin, pull out pages from fashion magazines with looks you admire, and create your own look-book, or just stash some tear sheets in your purse so you can pull them out for inspiration. Even better, you can go online and buy those actual pieces or some really great knockoffs. Splurge on your classic pieces and designer trends, but don't be shy about sprinkling in some inexpensive funky pieces. One of my favorite rings is a big square chunk of jade that cost $9.99 from Loehmann's. I wear it on my right hand with as much pleasure as I wear the diamond eternity band sparkling on my left. Once, after a long day on set, I had to go directly to a posh birthday party. I knew the crowd was all about who's who, who's wearing who, who's carrying who, and who can't afford who. In a pinch, I had to grab something off the rack in my dressing room. I went with boyfriend jeans rolled up to showcase my new YSL heels and a relaxed but sexy off-the-shoulder cashmere sweater the color of fog. The only thing missing was the right piece of jewelry to pull it all together. I politely asked my stylist if she would trust me enough to let me borrow a particular piece that had been pulled for that day's show. It was a fabulous twisted black beaded choker with a huge diamond cluster in the center.

She made the "oooh, risky" face and drew a deep breath. "Not so sure," she told me, before breaking into a grin. "After all, it was $15.99!"

I admit that for a moment, I wanted to take it off, but it looked great and I couldn't resist pulling one over on the name-dropping crowd. Judging from the envious looks and gushing compliments I got, they never suspected the truth.

naked truth Some of my hottest looks are cobbled together. Literally. Many of my fave shoes and boots—including the expensive designer ones—have been resoled or reheeled at least once. A great shoe-repair shop can make any old faithful look new again. Well, except for my beloved fuzzy pink bunny slippers, which finally got too threadbare to keep.

BEAUTY BOUNDARIES

Watching my three daughters develop their own senses of style is both a delight and a disappointment. You gotta let your kids fly their free flag, right? My youngest girl, Rain, has spent a good part of her toddlerhood watching Mommy get her makeup done, and I sometimes wonder what kind of message she's getting. I always make an effort to remind her how naturally beautiful she is, and that makeup is for dress-up and something fun to play with, but not something we need. But Rain apparently has decided already that she really needs lipstick, and a lot of it, because she swipes every tube I own and stashes them in her bathroom drawer. Sierra, my middle girl, could not be less interested in all the girly stuff, and she has to carefully check out the inside of any outfit before she wears it, to make sure it passes the comfort test. Neriah is a full-fledged tween fashionista who needs to be firmly reminded that fifth-graders have no business trying to look like Paris Hilton.

How far you're willing to go for the sake of beauty is a complicated question that I ask myself both as a woman and as a mother. When Neriah was little, I was mortified when she walked up to a stranger in a restaurant, eyed his prominent nose, and announced: "You know, my daddy could really fix that for you." Does being raised by a Hollywood mom and a famous plastic surgeon dad mean she's getting some cookie-cutter concept of beauty? I want my kids to be able to see character rather than flaw, to appreciate the unique beauty of imperfection.

During my marriage to *Extreme Makeover* surgeon Garth Fisher, everyone assumed I was his crash-test dummy or something, able to get nipped, tucked, lifted, lasered, filled, and lipo'ed at whim. Right, and I'm sure Jimmy Choo cobbles together new shoes for his mate on demand, too. It's not like I could wake up in the a.m., look in the mirror, say, "Honey, the girls just don't look perky enough today," and get a quick detailing. After I gave birth to our two daughters, the gossip columnists had a field day speculating that I got my body-after-baby in the surgical suite rather than the gym. I resented it at the time, since I've always worked hard to take care of myself, but the false assumptions were good for Garth's business, and people are going to think whatever they're going to think, so why waste the energy worrying about it? But for the record, it was crunches and cardio that gave me back the bikini bod.

My own views on plastic surgery are pretty straightforward. If there's something that makes a woman feel uncomfortable and insecure, and a cosmetic alteration would help, then why the hell not? I've talked openly about having breast augmentation in my twenties, and I started doing Botox before my thirtieth birthday—I swear by it as a preventive measure—so I'm not one to judge anyone. But I think the decision-making process is more important than the procedure itself. Be informed, not impulsive. I think it's about why and when to have it. Is it really going to fix my problem? Do the benefits outweigh the risks? Is it something I'm going to have to commit to long-term, and have redone as I age? Personally, when I'm forty-five, I don't want to be frantically trying to look like a twenty-five-year-old. I want to look like the best forty-five-year-old. Nothing is worse than being pulled too tight, too soon, too often. The women who top my most-beautiful list are the ones who age gracefully, women like Jaclyn Smith and Sophia Loren and Raquel Welch, whose stunning faces reflect wisdom and a zest for life—not desperation. If they've had work done, they've definitely done the right thing, in the right measure, at the right time.

Of course, we've all made our mistakes in the name of beauty. A knack for improvisation and a good sense of humor are the best way to overcome those disasters. The breakup haircut is usually the worst, not to mention the most common. Must be something about shedding your old self. That's what drove me to march into a salon one day, park myself in the stylist's chair, and announce that I wanted to chop off all my hair. Got rid of my boyfriend and my hair within a matter of hours. Super long to super short, just like that. I just needed drastic change that day and did it. Such a huge mistake! I have wavy hair, and any delusions I had about short being easier to maintain were just that—delusions. It required a lot more maintenance, and it didn't really suit my face or my career. I had to fill in with extensions until it grew out.

And then there was the drunken night involving two Playmates, a Hollywood tattoo shop, and Evil Mean Bunny. My two girlfriends and I loved bunnies and used to give each other little rabbit-themed gifts—it had nothing to do with the famous

Playboy logo. So, on this tipsy night, we all decided it would be fun to get matching bunny tattoos. We had the tattoo artist do a cute bunny face, but then it started looking very scary, like a bunny starring in a rabbit remake of *The Texas Chainsaw Massacre* or something. We hastily had the guy turn it around to look like the back of a bunny, instead, just ears and a fluffy tail. Mine was on the back of my neck. One of my girlfriends, who was freshly married, then had to go home to her Jewish husband, who flipped out and made her laser it off. You can't be buried in a Jewish cemetery if you're tattooed; it's against the religion. Years later, I was tired of being marked with a silly bunny, and started fiddling around with ways to alter the tat. I found this Celtic candle that came with a lovely poem about letting old energy go and new energy in. The design was really pretty, with what looked like a Star of David in the center, which my David especially loved. So bye-bye, bunny.

naked truth I was honored to grace the cover of *Playboy* twice. I agreed to pose after a long decision-making process, and with the full support of my family, including my husband. No regrets—it was the right thing for me to do at the time. But I wouldn't do it now; not sure I could deal with the carpool parents and school staff seeing me like that. As for my children finding out, I certainly hope I've raised them not to pass judgment on people, especially their own mother.

My other impulsive work of body art was not so easy to make over. About three months into my relationship with

Garth, I had his name inscribed in cursive on my foot. It was my surprise way of proclaiming my love, and, since I had marked my foot for him, we made a deal that he had to buy my shoes for the rest of my life—and I love beautiful, expensive shoes. After our marriage ended, I was eager to change that tattoo; I doubted that staring down at my ex's name for all eternity would be a healthy thing for me or for my new man. If you're thinking about a tattoo, the foot is a great place to get one, because it's so pretty and easy to cover up. If you're thinking about getting a tattoo, the foot is a terrible place to get one, because it hurts like all get-out. And it took me two sessions to hide Garth's name with a henna design. (And no, in case you're wondering, I did not test the shoes-for-life deal in our divorce settlement—I felt so bad about leaving that I waived spousal support altogether.)

My body art is discreet, and I don't think I'm going to look back at seventy and think omigod, what is this hip thing on my foot? Unlike boyfriends, though, children are forever, so I was eager to have my children's names inked on the inside of my wrist at a tattoo party we threw when David wanted to update his Chinese symbol with Rain's name to add another with Shaya's. We invited friends over, seared some ahi, put on great music, poured generous shots of good tequila, and had a renowned artist tattoo our guests (only the willing ones, of course!). Tattoo parties have become a kind of funky Hollywood trend. C'mon, I've been to stranger things, and I've been to worse.

I'm not nearly as liberal when it comes to body piercings. My ears are it for now. Erotic piercings? I think they're kinda fun, and I might enjoy them, but I don't have any. And for all the navel baring I've done in photo shoots, I've never even considered dangling jewels there. I'm totally opposed to it. That part of my belly is for babies. My belly button is my center, my intuition, and I would not stab something through my center.

naked truth During my pregnancy, my belly button looked like a giant nose! Once I drew two eyes and a mouth on my stretchy belly skin to make a giant smiley face. Like the poet said, Laugh and the world laughs with you, weep and you weep alone!

THROUGH THE LOOKING GLASS

Self-awareness was a key element of *She's Got the Look*, the makeover show I started hosting for TV Land in the summer of 2010. The program featured everyday women thirty-five and up vying for a $100,000 contract with Wilhelmina Models, a spread in *Self* magazine, and a chance to change their lives forever. Our mission was to find a diamond in the rough. It was all about second chances and rediscovery. My first lineup of contestants included a voluptuous bus mechanic from New York, a mousy Southern lawyer, and a businesswoman from Texas who was so gorgeous we all figured she would easily waltz away with the prize.

The competition posed a series of elimination challenges every week—learning how to work the catwalk, say, or how to take a great photo underwater. We constantly urged the women to step out of their comfort zones and conquer their fears. I shared the wisdom I'd gleaned from a lifetime in a highly competitive, highly subjective business: "There will *always* be a woman more beautiful than you. Constantly comparing or rating yourself is demeaning, and when you chip away at your self-esteem like that, you're not challenging yourself—you're destroying your most valuable asset." Transformation was what we wanted them to experience. Some were more willing than others.

When I sent the women off for their makeovers and came back eight hours later to check up, I literally couldn't find the lawyer. I wondered if she had gotten cold feet and ditched us altogether. Turns out she was standing dead center right in front of me. I wouldn't have recognized her in a million years. Gone was the dull hair hanging past her shoulders, the shapeless business suit, the matchy makeup that looked like it came in an all-in-one kit. Now she was a sexy mama with a sleek short do that called attention to her amazing cheekbones. The right shadow made her big blue eyes pop. Stylish clothes that fit her well revealed that she had a terrific frame. She looked great, and she knew it. Her whole energy was different.

The very first photo shoot the women had to do was a bikini shot on the beach. They were scared to death. "Don't hold on to your twentysomething body and feel inadequate," I cautioned them. "Really own who you are now." The best shots that day didn't come from the fittest women; they belonged to the ones who forgot the pounds or cellulite they were trying to hide and just owned their beauty regardless of their age.

The curvy mechanic was the one you'd probably least be able to picture as a classic model, but even in a tacky outfit and unflattering makeup, she carried herself from the beginning as if she were Naomi Campbell, and she made us believe it, too. There was something compelling about her comfortable-in-my-own-skin attitude, and by the time our pros showed her how to keep her bodacious girls in, she was absolutely sizzling. You just couldn't get enough of her.

And then there was our presumed frontrunner, the tall Texan with a rockin' body and flawless face. But all that surface appeal quickly evaporated when she came off as just plain arrogant. She was never able to take that unsightly wall down and connect with the audience or judges by letting her inner light shine through. To her own clear dismay, she got eliminated.

So who won? The bus mechanic, of course.

Because confidence trumps DNA every time.

naked truth I was such a tomboy when I was a little kid that I used to tear off my shirt and ride my bike through the neighborhood topless—it was hot in Arizona! My sister Kim was mortified. "If anyone asks, just tell them I'm your brother, Bobby," I told her.

3

body of evidence

PHOTO RICHARD HUME

Calendar girl—nothing like a bikini photo shoot to whip me back into pre-pregnancy shape!

THE ONLY THING that I truly have control over is my own body. As I mature, and my body changes, I really have to stay on top of things to adjust my habits accordingly and make the smartest choices for me. It wasn't always that way. When I was making my living as a bikini model in my twenties, I had a bodybuilder boyfriend whose muscle mass far outweighed his common sense. Guess I could've used more of the latter myself, because he had me convinced that it was healthy to obsessively measure every morsel of food before it went into my mouth, eat according to a strict schedule, and subsist on tuna fish, applesauce, and oatmeal mixed together, yes, in one disgusting bowl. I weighed myself first thing in the morning, and despaired if my size 2 jeans felt the slightest bit snug.

Today, I'm a crazed, carpooling mother of four with my fortieth birthday in (slightly unnerving) sight, and I don't even own a scale. I wear what looks best on me, I eat what tastes best, and I do what feels best. The result?

I'm in the best shape I've ever been in, and I've honestly never felt better.

(I'm also a lot more kissable. There just aren't enough Tic Tacs in the world to adequately mask tuna-oat breath.)

Of course, the years and the pregnancies have both thrown a few curves my way, but happily, I've gained more wisdom than pounds, because I've finally figured out an enjoyable, doable way to maintain my physique, keep my energy up, and savor the decadent moments in life. And if you think I stay fit by living on freeze-dried algae tablets, keeping a personal trainer on salary, or having some Beverly Hills doc discreetly vacuum out the fat, you've dialed the wrong celebrity. Hello? I live with a Frenchman! We have appetizer cook-offs before dinner. Red meat and red wine are consumed with gusto. We sneak downstairs to devour midnight paninis after making love (for the record, though, David is the one eating the grilled chocolate Nutella calorie bombs; I hold out for half of the turkey-provolone-Dijon special).

My approach to empty calories? Earn 'em or burn 'em.

You won't find me touting some silly fad diet, or miserably following a workout regimen that would make a marine whimper and cringe. My commitment isn't to any specific program or self-promoting guru. It's to myself. It's not a trend; it's a way of life. I don't think it's vain to admit that looking good makes me feel good. And when I feel good, that translates into the kind of confidence that serves me well whether I'm in the boardroom or the bedroom. I can't say this enough: Confidence is *hot*!

Caring for yourself means caring for your body, pure and simple. What if you applied even a fraction of the attention you pay to your child's health and well-being to yourself? We're all so accustomed to disregarding our own needs as moms, because having kids changes our priorities so dramatically. But motherhood changes your perspective in more subtle ways, too, and once you've left the delivery room, it's a shame to discard the self-awareness that pregnancy provides. Becoming a mother gave me a whole new respect for my body. I remember that intoxicating, profound sense of wonder with each of my pregnancies, and how good it felt to nurture myself in order to nurture that tiny life growing inside me. I wish we women could feel that loving, tender connection to our bodies all the time, instead of falling so quickly and easily into the usual trap of disdain and self-criticism.

So how do we stay committed to ourselves, how do we find the time and summon the energy to plan ahead, eat well, and exercise to give ourselves the best shot at a long and healthy life? The best place to start is to acknowledge that you deserve it. And you owe it to your children, as well, to set them up for a life of good choices and healthy habits.

FOOD FOR THOUGHT

Let's start with the most obvious source of a healthy lifestyle: food. I love to eat, but at the same time, I firmly—pun intended—believe that 90 percent of fitness is what we put into our mouths. I never use the "D" word: Diets are too often gimmicks aimed more at making someone else rich than making you fit. They're usually not sustainable over the long run in real, everyday life. Your goal shouldn't be to lose twenty pounds or six inches or three dress sizes; it should be to create a lifestyle that you can live by, and happily stick to.

David and I both love to cook, and as a card-carrying foodie, one of the best lessons I've learned in the kitchen is that flavor doesn't have to be fattening. We favor a Mediterranean-style approach, with an emphasis on grilled fish, chicken, and (yes) red meat, with lots of fresh veggies and seasonings to give it all zip. I'm not afraid of natural fats—I'll use butter over margarine—but I try to make sensible choices. Extra-virgin olive oil is a staple in our house, and we go through enough of it that I have to wonder whether we should just invest in a giant press and grow our own olive trees. (Do child-labor laws apply to olive squishing?)

Freshness is my number-one priority when it comes to eating right. I started reading labels many years ago, and honestly, the ingredients in processed foods totally turn me off. That isn't to say I never eat any—I'd be lying if I didn't fess up to drive-thru frenzies now and then—but I don't make a habit of stocking my pantry with junk. If there's crappy food in the house, I'm going to be tempted, and more likely to cave in and just mindlessly eat it because it's convenient. I'd rather avoid the impulse altogether than struggle to overcome it: If you don't want to get hit by a train, don't stand on the tracks, right?

Once in a while, I do like to shock my body and challenge myself to the extreme, by trying to eat only green or raw foods for a week, or even just restricting myself to nothing but lemon water to drink and as many bowls of my special Cleansing Veggie Soup as I want to eat for three days. By the time I'm done, I feel motivated to introduce only clean, healthy foods back into my meal plan.

And "plan" is the key word when it comes to meals. I do best when I fit five small, healthy meals into my day. Breakfast is absolutely critical—your body needs refueling, and skipping breakfast means you're starting your day by putting your energy reserves into overdraft. What mom can afford that? Even a quick bowl of oatmeal can give you a good jump-start. It's a surefire way to lose weight, and has worked for everybody I know who's tried it: Just replace your breakfast with a single bowl of oatmeal each day. It fills you up, and is a great source of fiber and vitamins. Flavor-wise, I'd much prefer a bowl full of my favorite oat-cluster cereal, but, like the healthy superfoods smoothie I call my "dirt shake," oatmeal is something I'm willing to eat because I know it's really good for me. I mix the oatmeal with hot water, then add a couple of spoonfuls of berries and a dash of brown sugar to make it more palatable. I keep berries in the freezer to jazz up my protein shake, too—they add a nice boost of antioxidants and natural sweetness.

On the days when I'm shooting *Dancing with the Stars*, I'm glad that I've conditioned myself to be disciplined and plan ahead, so I'm not tempted to graze at the huge free buffet of mouthwatering food that craft services sets out. We're talking barbecued ribs, vats of creamy mac 'n' cheese, biscuits the size of baseballs, and gorgeous dessert towers of miniature cheesecakes, tarts, and chocolate éclairs. Not exactly what the seamstress ordered when you've got to wriggle into slinky designer gowns for work, and unless hula dancing gets added to the *DWTS* repertoire, I don't think I could get away with hosting in muumuus. But no worries. It's not like I'm holed up in my dressing room feeling deprived and counting the calories in half a celery stick while resenting the number of lemon tartlets the suits in Ryan Seacrest's wardrobe can forgive. I'm too busy happily chowing down on my favorite southwestern salad—chopped, crunchy romaine lettuce with black beans, avocado, tomato, and grilled salmon, topped with tortilla chips (just a few!) and a green cilantro dressing that I love. It's been my standing order for lunch for two seasons now. It's one less thing I have to worry about on show days, and knowing I have something delish to look forward to removes the impulse to make rash, unhealthy choices just because I'm in a hurry and I'm starving. Making the salad my habitual *DWTS* working lunch has also trained my brain to send the message ahead to my stomach: No need to panic, we've got you covered! And that dessert tray is gonna show up on Ryan's butt sooner or later! (That was my subconscious. Really! Consciously, I wish Ryan only the best!)

brooke's green cuisine

GOING TOTALLY GREEN is sooo smart and healthy, but I have to confess that it gets too boring too fast for me. And yes, you might feel bloated and gassy for the first couple of days, but once you get over the hump, you'll feel great. You don't realize how sluggish processed foods and oversized meals make you feel until you've rid your body of them for a while. Treating life like an all-you-can-eat smorgasbord 24/7 is a ticket to a heart attack, not happiness! And what's with the towering mountains of food on everyone's plates these days? Enough, already! This is a green plan you can easily stick to for a full week.

You can eat anything and everything that's green, with the exception of green M&Ms and green tortilla chips (but nice try!). Fill your shopping basket with veggies like broccoli, kale, zucchini, cabbage, snap peas, edamame, leeks, spinach, different lettuces, celery, and cucumbers. And avocado! I'm an avo addict. They're super healthy, and they really fill you up, too. In the fruit aisle, stock up on honeydew melon, kiwi, green grapes, and some limes, which are great for making just about any flavor pop. Buy fresh mint, garlic, green olives, herbs, and olive oil to add some pizzazz, and don't skimp on the seasonings. I always pick up a jar of pesto, too (or you can always make your own out of fresh basil or even parsley). I'll add a little dollop to a salad of chopped cucumbers, avocado, and edamame. Don't forget the green tea, either—it's a great antioxidant, and a multitasker that becomes a refreshing iced tea on a hot day, or a soothing hot tea when it's cold outside.

Breakfast: I always start the day with a tall glass of lemon water. Then I make a shake from coconut water, with a scoop of a good protein powder and a handful of frozen berries. When I add Vitamin C Plus and one of those superfood "greens powder," it can get a little gritty, hence the "dirt shake" nickname. Using almond milk instead of coconut water will make it creamier, and a bit of honey will sweeten it up, if you like. Vanilla-flavored protein powders are also available.

Lunch and late afternoon meals: Anything fresh and raw from the produce category.

Dinner: I try to stay all-green for at least a few days, and have veggies for dinner (try drizzling kale with a little olive oil and baking it—so good even my

continued

kids eat it!), but by the third or fourth day, I'm ready to start slowly introducing other things back into my system. I start with a modest portion—the size of my open palm—of grilled fish, chicken, or lean beef to have with any green veggies of choice.

I also make a big pot of Cleansing Veggie Soup that I can have anytime. I try to give up coffee and drink tea or water instead, but my willpower isn't always that strong, and I don't beat myself up if I fall off the caffeine wagon. If I can't quit, I give myself points for just cutting down.

CLEANSING VEGGIE SOUP

1 onion, finely chopped

1 parsnip

3–5 cloves chopped garlic

3 bay leaves

handful chopped parsley

3 chopped leeks

½ head chopped green cabbage

4 chopped zucchini

several cubes chicken or vegetable bouillon

Boil first five ingredients in a large saucepan for 30 minutes. Then add the rest of the ingredients and simmer until the veggies are the texture you like. Add salt and pepper to taste.

SERVINGS: 10

The best way to stick to any eating plan is to design one that you can enjoy. Listen to your body and experiment with different foods to learn how your system reacts. Some people may be fine with acidic foods like tomatoes during the day, when they're upright, only to wake up with heartburn if they eat the same thing at night. Keeping a simple food journal or log for even one week can be enlightening. Jot down when you're hungry (and hungriest), what you ate, when you ate it, and how you felt later. You'll come to know what foods are best for you, and what to avoid. The key is to enjoy what you eat, and welcome what it does for your body. Shift your point of view until you've trained yourself to crave healthy foods, and think twice about turning your body into a dump site for preservatives, food dyes, hydrogenated oils, fats, and other harmful additives.

Self-discipline shouldn't be treated as a referendum on your moral character; it's just a matter of taking some clever short-cuts so you can stay three steps ahead of the pizza delivery guy. Stress, fatigue, and not enough time are the universal overeating triggers for parents in particular, and you can zap all three at once with minimal effort:

- Cut up veggies and fruits and stash them in see-through containers on a shelf at eye level in your fridge. You're more likely to reach for them if they're visible and all ready to go.
- Don't leave home without it: I pack a cooler that stays in my car. I keep it stocked with fruit, nuts, water, protein bars, pretzels, and other smart snacks to fend off those grumpy, irritable, *hangry* (hungry plus angry) moments, whether it's me or the kids

heading for a meltdown. A protein bar—I like Bill Phillips RIGHT nutrition bar—in my purse can prove to be literally an ounce of prevention.

- Eat more often. When you keep fueling your body, it becomes a well-oiled machine, and it won't kick into survival mode and start holding on to fats. Don't skip meals. Eat five small meals a day instead of three bigger ones, and nibble wisely in between. When you set yourself up to be hungry, you're bound to make wrong choices. Yogurt is a perfect light meal, and an apple and a handful of raw almonds are easy when you're on the go. At home, I like to salt my apple slices and fan them out across a pretty little plate. Food that looks appealing is always more satisfying!

- A quick stop at a grocery store salad bar will give you a customized salad that's healthier than what you get at most restaurants. Whole Foods is primo in my book!

- Drink lots of water. I love to boil fresh ginger to make a tea, which I like to pour over ice in a nice glass pitcher to keep on the counter and drink from all day. (Warning: I adore fiery hot foods, and unwitting friends with wussy palates have ended up with tears running down their cheeks from my ginger water! If you can't take the heat, either go easy on the ginger or opt for sliced lemons or cucumbers, instead, to flavor a pitcher of water.) A glass of water twenty minutes or so before any meal gives your stomach a chance to feel fuller from the get-go.

- Appetizers: Choose wisely here, and watch the portions. When you're in a restaurant, it makes sense to order an appetizer. No, that isn't a license to wolf down loaded baked-potato skins or batter-fried anything. Have a salad, or marinated vegetables. That first course can really help take the edge off your hunger, and once your entrée arrives, you'll feel full faster, which means you're less likely to be tempted by the dessert menu.
- If I'm trying to drop some weight and need something to tide me over between meals, I grab an underWAY appetite suppressant supplemental drink: no caffeine, sodium, or preservatives, and you get loads of fiber. Natural flavorings. I'm partial to acai-pomegranate myself.
- Ignorance is no excuse! Educate yourself. Learn what nutrients your favorite foods have, and what different vitamins and minerals do for your body. Do the math and see where you need to fill in the gaps on meeting daily recommended requirements, and where you're going overboard (carbs? sodium? sugars?). You can easily type anything into thedailyplate.com and it will give you a calorie count—free! An even more complete nutritional breakdown is free at nutritiondata.self.com.
- If you can't give up your Starbys run, avoid the ginormous double-chocolate, extra-whip, caramel frappa-sugarcoma and have antioxidant-rich green tea instead. Save yourself 500 calories (and five bucks!).

■ Finally, here's my little bombshell of admittedly unconventional advice: The very best thing you can do regardless of your food plan and goals is . . . cheat!!!

EAT!!!

Yes. Really.

I'm not encouraging you to go all Tiger Woods here; I'm advocating a brief, contained fling with your favorite forbidden friends, be it chili cheese fries, ice cream, or margaritas. Or all of the above mixed together (hey, nothing's too gross once you've survived the tuna-applesauce-oatmeal combo!). The only rule is that you've got just one day to indulge yourself. I don't schedule them religiously, but I know how to recognize that antsy, needy, PMS-y feeling that signals I'm in need of a Cheat Day. When I give myself permission to cut loose and eat whatever I want for twenty-four hours, I'm always able to start fresh the next day, because I've had enough pizza or tiramisu or deep-fried whatever to quell the cravings. And no, I'm not endorsing binge eating; I'm talking about having a serving of lasagna if that's what you really want for dinner instead of the grilled chicken, or having some tortilla chips and guacamole if you're dying for something salty and crunchy and pretzels just will not make you happy today. (When I'm at a restaurant and can't resist the basket of chips and guac, I ask the waiter to bring them out closer to when our entrées are going to arrive—that way, at least it's just one basket we're going through instead of two.)

cheat sheet ✐

HERE'S WHAT ONE of my Cheat Days looks like:

Breakfast: A fat bran muffin with real butter and raspberry jam to go with my first cup of coffee. Or maybe a bagel with butter and tomatoes. If I'm showing some restraint. Otherwise, I'm the one sneaking out of Starbys in baseball-cap-and-sunglasses disguise, with a latte and maple-nut scone in hand. I'll pay for that on the treadmill later. Or I can just start race walking to Brazil now. I hear the scenery is great crossing the Andes.

Lunch: Straight to the local chain drive-thru for a gloriously juicy, messy sirloin burger with grilled onions. I may skip the bun, just to be on the safe side, because starches are such a danger zone for me. If I'm not in a burger frame of mind, I'll dig into a margherita pizza with jalapeños and olive oil drizzled over the top—heaven with a kick!

Snacks: If I'm in an airport (always a good chance of that, it seems), then I'll follow my nose to the Cinnabon counter. Gooey, comforting, totally decadent. Hopefully the Starbucks counter is nearby, so I can score (another) nonfat latte to go with it. They really should put recumbent exercycles with seat belts on airplanes. If I'm at home and wanting something sweet, I'll reach for one of the miniature

continued

Snickers bars I keep in the freezer. I love caramel, and the combo of salty and sweet. Added bonus: freezing them makes them harder to eat, which means they last longer. You're not as likely to go for seconds.

Dinner: Big rib eye on the grill, with a pat of butter on top like the steakhouses do. Fried calamari hot from the deep fryer I got as a present ostensibly for David. A chewy, warm French baguette to sop up the steak's juices. A big bottle of Margaux.

Dessert: I banned white sugar from my life a long time ago, and don't miss it, but once in a blue moon I'll go whole hog and have homemade chocolate chip cookies. À la mode. With chocolate sauce on top. (When I say whole hog, dammit, I mean it!)

Midnight snack: Big bowl of cereal in bed.

WORK IT OUT

Everybody's pretty much gotten the memo by now that exercise is a *big* part of being healthy, whether you want to lose weight or not. I do it to feel good, release stress, and guarantee a little me time in every day. Fatigue is an unchecked plague among parents, and bodily strength is our best defense.

If you don't typically work out, start slowly. Walk around

the block if that's your beginning. Then walk two blocks the next day, or five. Whatever you're doing, the point is to always strive to kick it up a notch. That's what this is all about: challenging yourself, and rallying to take care of yourself.

As for me, I'm totally obsessed with Pilates Plus. If you're not already familiar with Pilates, the exercises are done using either a floor mat or a machine called the Reformer, and the emphasis is on centering yourself both physically and mentally to build core strength. It has deep roots in the dance world, which isn't surprising, since the focus is on flow and creating length—elongating your muscles, and keeping your back in line. It's head-to-toe body sculpting and cardio, all in fifty-five minutes. One of the things you learn how to do is to breathe properly, which not only helps you release stress but achieve a natural smoothness and precision to your movements. It's a killer workout, and adaptable for any level. I started Pilates when I was pregnant with my first baby over ten years ago. I was able to do it through all my pregnancies with no problem. Age and agility pose no obstacle; I've had sixty-five-year-olds working out alongside me. Today, I prefer the more intense Pilates Plus classes to solo workouts. The group sessions are so convenient, plus, you save money, and the peer support is an added incentive. Sometimes I'll round up a couple of friends to go along with me, and we challenge and encourage each other to make it more fun.

Ideally, I get to three Pilates Plus classes a week, and in between I'll hit the gym for forty-five minutes of cardio. I used to do the whole circuit-training, yoga-class thing, but I don't have ninety minutes or more to spend at the gym anymore, and I also find that my body responds best today to short, superintense, challenging programs. Pilates Plus fits that bill. I just need to push myself to the max and work up a sweat and know I'm going to be sore later. It's a good kind of ache, proof that I've worked really, really hard. And that it'll show.

Walking has become so much a part of my routine now that I consider it more recreation than exercise. For many years, I did my neighborhood hike with my babies; as they grew, the stroller got a lot heavier, and my workout got a lot harder! These days, my favorite hike is four miles, but half of it is uphill, so taking the kids is no longer an option. Besides, I have to admit that I crave the solitude; the ocean views inspire me, and I just feel refreshed and clearheaded by the time I'm heading home again.

I go through phases when I'm supermotivated and working out five or six days a week. Other times, that's just wishful thinking. Seriously, though, if I'm able to do whatever my family needs of me without a second thought, but can't manage to give myself just forty-five minutes a day, I am in big trouble in the self-worth department! Sure, there are times when I want to cave in to being too tired, too busy, or just not motivated, but I don't let myself. I consider exercise something I just have to do, kinda like washing my hair. "No" isn't an option.

What I do know for a fact is that the more I do it, the better I'll feel. Notice that I said *feel*, not look. That dopamine spike that exercise gives you is well worth the sweat and burn. I promise that once you get over the initial hump, working out will deliver so many benefits beyond a hard body—less stress, more energy, more self-confidence, a sense of accomplishment, self-commitment, and a better sex drive (not to mention better sex!!). On top of all that, just plain feeling good about yourself has an emotional domino effect; it will spawn so many other wonderful feelings.

BABY BUMP TO BIKINI BOD

The first time I got pregnant, I had no idea whether I'd be able to model again, but I wanted to become a mother so badly that I honestly didn't care if I had to trade my flat abdomen in for my beautiful baby. I resolved to take the best care of my pregnant body that I possibly could, not only for my baby (Neriah, that time), but for myself. As I mentioned, I started doing Pilates while pregnant. But I couldn't exactly throw all vanity to the wind: I did have some added pressure to look my best— I had been cast as the hostess of *Wild On* a month before discovering that I was expecting. I'm sure they hadn't anticipated having an Oompa-Loompa star in a hip show on extreme travel adventure, but they were gracious, and I was game.

Being married to a plastic surgeon probably made me more aware than most of the myriad ways a woman's body can sag, bag, inflate, deflate, scar, mar, or otherwise challenge our concepts of beauty. Garth believes stretch marks are a matter of genetics, but with my olive skin, I was determined to do everything I possibly could to prevent them. Even before I started to show, I slathered my belly, hips, and breasts with oil twice a day—cocoa butter works great, but I'd use olive oil if I didn't have anything else on hand. Rub it into your skin vigorously enough to create a little heat and friction, so it gets absorbed and doesn't just create an oily sheen on the outermost layer of skin. Post-pregnancy, Garth told me that wearing a sports bra while I slept would help support my swollen breasts and maintain shape. It doesn't have to be anything special; just a comfy, wireless cotton number from Target will do the trick. I also kept lubing my body after delivery. I followed this advice during four pregnancies, and I managed to avoid stretch marks altogether.

Contrary to the tabloid gossip columns, I did not regain my bikini bod by having a tummy tuck or any other kind of surgery. I stepped up my workout routine big-time, and visualized myself with the figure I wanted to stay motivated. That helped counteract the chicken burritos I craved while carrying Neriah, and the cheeseburgers I was pounding down with my second daughter, Sierra. The second pregnancy came with some added pressure: My 2003 swimsuit calendar had a hard deadline for me to turn my photos in to the publisher by July 2002. Sierra was born in April. You do the math, and I'm sure you'll arrive at the same answer I did: Giving birth plus ninety days plus bikini equals holy crap! Being hormonal, caring for a newborn and a toddler, and adding that kind of stress on top of it all was not a pretty picture. But pretty picture is exactly what I needed! I had had a healthy pregnancy, and gained under thirty pounds, but I needed to lose those pounds and tone up fast.

I went into overdrive. I started running, followed a strict meal plan (no sugars, very little starch, tons of raw fruits and veggies, grilled fish, and no more midnight paninis). I met with a celebrity trainer and developed a core workout that pushed me to the limit, but I was frustrated by how slowly the weight was dropping.

"You need to eat more," the trainer advised.

I looked at him like he was crazy. I probably told him he

was crazy, too, for good measure, using some hormonally induced adjectives that I won't repeat here.

"Just try it," he went on.

"This is not a time to be experimenting here," I retorted. "I need to be in Belize posing on a beach in a bikini in three months."

"You gotta trust me," the trainer insisted, explaining the science: If I switched to five mini-meals a day instead of three, I would kick up my metabolism by feeding my body properly.

Still dubious, I followed his advice, and to my surprise, the results of my hard work finally started showing up on my body. My belly got taut and flat again, and by the time I was shooting the calendar, I felt healthy, confident, and proud of what I had achieved. It wasn't perfect (thank God for retouching; I am not too proud to pay homage to the wonders of Photoshop), but it was pretty damn good.

By the time I had Rain, I thought I knew all the tricks. But then David's mother, Christiane, who's French, taught me the best one of all: belly wrapping. Christiane was astonished to discover that I wasn't binding my belly after giving birth; it's a common practice virtually everywhere else in the world, from primitive tribes in Africa to the fashionistas of Europe. Doctors had even reminded Christiane to bring her wrap with her to the hospital when she had David. A belly wrap is believed to help shrink a swollen uterus back down to size more quickly, reduce water retention in the belly, and help you lose inches fast. It also supports that unwanted baggy baby skin. The only problem, I found, was that the wraps were all hideously ugly and incredibly uncomfortable. Why hadn't anyone improved on such a good idea and taken it out of the medieval era?

Long story short: I decided to do just that, and founded a company I named Baboosh Baby (babooshbaby.com), adopting the nickname David and I had given baby Rain. After much personal experimenting involving prototypes from as far away as India and as close as Ace bandages from my local drugstore, I developed an effective wrap that was comfortable enough to wear all day and even sleep in. I gave them a sexy VS look and set up shop with my mother in her Santa Monica condo. I called the wraps Tauts, and sold them online. We had no business plan, no marketing strategy, and, in retrospect, a really dumb name (how were people supposed to know what it was or land on it quickly via search engines when I had neglected to put any clues—like "belly" or "pregnancy" or "wrap"—in the name?!). I served as a one-woman spokesmodel. Despite our beginners' mistakes as entrepreneurs, Tauts started flying off the shelves. We couldn't keep them in stock. We added other pregnancy and post-pregnancy products to our inventory, including a lightweight organic oil enriched with rosehip, kukui nut, and meadowfoam oils, scented with a delicate blend of lavender and aqua flora, which I found to be especially soothing and comforting when applied twice a day to stretchy, itchy skin.

Then I got to thinking: If the compression from Tauts could help shrink post-pregnancy bellies, could similar principles be put to work to enhance the effects of exercise? Turns out they could. Now we offer a Baboosh Body unisex exercise wrap, which fits around your middle while you work out to help melt away those muffin tops, love handles, and water weight. It's the best sweat I've ever had. I use it to maximize my workout; I never do cardio or hit the treadmill without it now. It's a good go-to solution when your high school reunion is in three days and there's a special dress you want to squeeze into. (Don't tell any of the Mean Girls your secret—let's just let them look like overstuffed bratwursts in high heels. Sweet revenge, LOL!)

When *OK!* magazine wanted to do a swimsuit spread on me last year—at thirty-eight, after having had four babies by now—I wore the Body Wrap during my Pilates Plus classes and didn't hesitate about sharing tiramisu for dessert when a friend and I went to dinner at an Italian restaurant a day before the shoot.

Speaking of photos, they can be a terrific motivator. Visuals have always inspired me. Seeing other healthy, beautiful bodies in magazines makes me want to take the best care of myself possible. I always read fitness magazines and blogs. I like to collect healthy new recipes, or try new workout routines, and I also think there's a lot to learn from what other people have struggled with and overcome. Try posting your ideal body images around your personal areas, and maybe even on the fridge if you're prone to snack attacks. Being reminded of your goals will help you stay on track.

FAMILY FITNESS

Every now and then, I'll come across an old family photograph with me as a child, sitting at the table at some festive meal, with a miserable expression on my face and tears rolling down my cheeks because I was locked in battle with my parents over some hated food that I didn't want to eat. I was forever trying to sink Brussels sprouts in my milk or slip overcooked, tough steak to our dog, Lucky, who was always happy to live up to his name. We had to clean our plates before having dessert, and oh, the emotional trauma I would put myself through just to get that sugar! I'm surprised I don't have eating issues today because of those dinnertime dramas.

Because my career puts me smack in the middle of a world that is way too focused on body image—I've seen women literally starve themselves in the deluded belief that they'll look attractive as hollow-eyed skeletons in designer clothes—I'm especially sensitive to what messages my kids are getting about body image. My heart lurches when my third-grader asks if her little belly is fat. "No, it's beautiful," I tell her, "it's perfect for you." When Sierra was four, she spent a whole year insisting on covering herself up completely. It would be 90 degrees outside, and she had to be wearing long sleeves, long pants, and shoes that didn't show her toes. It was so sad to see her refuse to go swimming because she didn't want to wear a bathing suit! At first, I figured she was stressed and acting out—I had just separated from her father—but I started to get worried when she didn't snap out of the phase. Then the real reason behind her embarrassment over her body came out, and it had been right under my nose the whole time: The nanny at Garth's house was very conservative, and also happened to be overweight. She dressed exactly the way Sierra now wanted to. I'm not sure whether she had disparaged her own body and Sierra had heard, or if Sierra was merely mirroring her self-consciousness, but the subliminal message—"my body is unsightly"—had been absorbed. I didn't make a big deal of it, but I began to insist that Sierra wear weather-appropriate clothing, and gradually, the extreme behavior abated. But what an important reminder I got from the ordeal; I realized what little sponges kids truly are, no matter how young. I'm very alert about how I see myself in front of my children, and I choose my words carefully. Our daughters watch the way we regard ourselves, and if I'm sitting at my bathroom vanity with my ever-present audience of little girls, I'm not going to look in the mirror and say out loud the words that might well be popping into my mind ("God, I look like shit—what's with the bags under my eyes and these wrinkles?"). Likewise, I'm not going to put on a cute outfit, frown, and ask their father whether I look fat. I want my girls to grow up confident in their own skin, appreciative of their unique beauty, and committed to being healthy, not a size 00.

Naturally, as a mom, I want to instill healthy eating habits in my children, not hang-ups. Educating my kids about how to provide the best fuel for their growing bodies is something I take seriously, but I also think it needs to be fun, or your kids are just going to hear *wahwahwah VEGETABLES wahwah . . .*

When I did my first season as mommy correspondent on *The Doctors*, I remember Dr. Travis Stork doing an episode about ways to encourage children to eat healthy, and he displayed this gorgeous rainbow made of fruits and vegetables. It was not only a great visual, but a smart way to show our kids easy, fun, and sensible ways to eat the colors of the rainbow. We turned it into a game at my house. "I didn't do orange yet!" Rain will exclaim, unpeeling a tangerine from the bowl of fresh fruit I keep on the counter or in the fridge, within easy reach of small hands. I love hearing a small voice ask me, "What's a purple food, Mommy? Maybe I'll try an eggplant," or, "What's yellow besides a banana?" When packing lunch boxes, I try to keep junk to a minimum and offer treats like apple slices with peanut butter or honey. Frozen grapes and frozen yogurt tubes make yummy desserts, and we like to make our own fruit juice popsicles. Sometimes we get artistic with fruit or veggie kabobs or English muffin pizzas.

I stock a drawer full of healthy snacks for my kids to go to when they've got the munchies: breakfast bars, nuts, pretzels, raisins, beef jerky (not the best choice for sodium, but Neriah loves it, and it's a way to get protein in her). Like all kids, mine go on kicks when they seem to want only one thing all the time. Letting them help you come up with meal ideas, shop, and prepare them is one way to break out of the nuggets-only rut. I love to cook, and genuinely enjoy involving my kids in the process. It's a great bonding experience. Rain knew how to crack eggs into a bowl like a pro when she was just two. When they have a role in preparing the food, the kids are much more likely to eat it. Experimenting with different cuisines is also a creative way to slip in some cultural education as a side dish, too.

I usually have good appetites in my house, but everyone gets bored now and then. Nagging doesn't fix anything, so I try to fire up my imagination instead of my temper when I'm at my wit's end. Even when I hear "I'm not hungry" before school, I can sneak in some smart calories by making a frozen fruit protein drink from milk, half a frozen banana, a spoonful of peanut butter, and a scoop of protein powder. No one turns down a smoothie for breakfast.

Getting my kids to exercise isn't an issue, since we're lucky enough to live in a warm climate and they're always running around outdoors. They know they can't park themselves in front of the TV or video games for hours; it's just never been an option. I can remember practically living on my bike as a kid. I love to see mine tearing loose now in the park, kicking a soccer ball, or climbing all over the jungle gym. They're good motivation for me, too, to put my latte down, get off my butt, and play! Don't just supervise—join in the fun! Jump into the pool with them and play Marco Polo, or challenge your kids to a race. I love a good bounce on the trampoline, myself. If you live in a colder climate, don't just stay inside and make hot cocoa while your kids play in the snow; get out there and start a snowball fight, or help build a snowman. Because there's only one way to get the body you've always wanted:

Just *move it*!

4

not guilty

Cheers to me-time!

I WAS GOING through a hellish period of my life several years ago, and I'll never forget the insight and advice I got from my makeup artist at the time, who was also a trusted friend. Whenever we were working together on a TV show or photo shoot, his job was to read my face, and stepping back from his pots and brushes one day, he knew that something was terribly wrong. I was at a difficult turning point, struggling to decide whether to stay put in a marriage that felt empty to me. As it turned out, this friend happened to be at a crossroads in his life, too: He had always been deeply spiritual, and now he was thinking about ditching an incredibly lucrative Hollywood career to become a monk. To go from Bentleys to Buddha, no looking back. While he was still in the process of weighing his options, Southern California's notorious Santa Ana winds kicked up, and brushfires began raging through the parched mountains and canyons. My friend's home burned to the ground, turning all of his belongings to ash overnight. He considered it a sign. Instead of pitching him into an understandable depression, the clean slate Mother Nature had just given him left my friend excited—

almost giddy, really. Anything seemed possible now. That day over lunch, we found ourselves in a soul-baring conversation, and I told him how torn I was over my faltering marriage. I had to acknowledge that two years of counseling and trying everything we possibly could to hold it together just wasn't working, and I felt awful. I knew I needed to let go, but I couldn't, because the prospect of hurting my husband and our two small daughters seemed unbearable. How could I be so selfish? Hearing this, my friend reached across the table to take my hand. He looked me straight in the eye.

"Brooke," he said firmly, "don't do guilt."

A lightbulb came on. I knew that he was right: Guilt isn't an innate emotion, like joy or sorrow. It's a learned response. A choice. And since it only exists because you conjure it up, logic tells you that it cannot exist if you refuse to give it life. Don't flip that switch.

But exactly how, I wondered, do you stop doing guilt?

I was thirty-two years old, and at a now-or-never moment in my life. I chose "now," and years later, I still grapple sometimes with the guilt over my decision to leave that marriage. I know, intellectually, that hell, yes, I deserve happiness, too. But emotionally, there's an unhealthy insistence that I pay for it. And pay, and pay.

Common sense tells you that you would cripple yourself if you got out of bed every morning, strapped a baby grand piano to your back, then lugged it around all day until the pressure and pain made you crumple. Yet we don't think twice about bearing the emotional equivalent of that weight every day, and we just keep piling on more and more. We start treating life like a job to tackle, instead of . . . well, a life to live. There's a difference. Really.

Sometimes it seems like the more women take on, the more we judge ourselves, and the more inadequate or unworthy we feel. Because our loved ones often seem to want more from us—more time, more attention, more effort—we conclude that we're not giving enough. That's especially true for moms. We're so hardwired to put our families first, that even having a selfish feeling—let alone actually daring to *be* selfish now and then—is considered nothing short of betrayal. We reinforce this by constantly comparing ourselves to Other Mothers (hint: there's that recurring theme again!), and we disparage ourselves for forever falling short. Guilt is a predator we feed by listening to the opinionated girlfriend who always knows best, or by letting our imaginations paint a perfect life behind the cheerful smile of the PTA mom whose efficiency blows us away. Sometimes we feed the beast tidbits, and other times we throw it T-bones. But guess what. Guilt is never satiated. The only way to slay this beast is to starve it.

DEATH OF A THOUSAND PAPER CUTS

Let's start small. Guilt usually does, with a flash here and a twinge there, until you're so accustomed to it that you accept it as a way of life. You feel guilty about sleeping in on a Saturday morning and letting kids gorge on sugary cereals and the Cartoon Network, as if everyone else in the country is feeding their children shredded wheat while discussing current events and deciding what community service projects they'll volunteer for today. Or you flog yourself for sending your second-grader to school with a jelly sandwich for lunch because you forgot to buy peanut butter, and even though you know she's not going to keel over from malnutrition in the middle of recess, you pile on some more guilt by convincing yourself that you're a loser, a failure, a total fraud. Because obviously all the Other (Better) Moms are sending their kids to school with homemade sushi in bento boxes the family lovingly lacquered by hand on a rainy afternoon. While drinking hot cocoa. With marshmallows. But you can't even make a stupid peanut butter sandwich. You leave the baby sobbing, "Mamma, mamma!" in the nanny's arms and hate yourself as you sneak out the door to go to work, where you promptly beat yourself up some more for procrastinating over the big project due Friday, not to mention the expense reports you should have turned in a month ago. Your coworker has three kids, and you only have two, but she obviously manages to juggle instead of struggle, so what's wrong with you? Then your best friend calls to vent about her alcoholic mother-in-law, but you can't talk and promise to call her back on the drive home from work. Come six o'clock, you're stuck in traffic, your brain is fried, and you just don't feel like having that conversation, so you accidentally-on-purpose forget to get back to your fuming friend. She's always there for you, though, isn't she? When you get home, your kids and your man instantly want your attention, your youngest has Velcro'd himself to your legs, and all you can do is yell at everyone to just give you five minutes to at least change your clothes, geez, is that too damn much to ask? You pop a tray of frozen taquitos into the microwave, and remind yourself that your family would be less stressed if you didn't insist on having a career. Your sister and her husband get by fine on one income by budgeting carefully.

Do you detect a pattern here yet? You're not just holding on to guilt, you're sending self-esteem packing so guilt can have its room. And then there's the added danger of playing the comparison game—it's like mommy Russian roulette. We all do it sometimes, even when we know better than to go there. It's bad enough when you measure yourself against friends, coworkers, or relatives, but I sometimes catch myself practically canonizing total strangers in the produce aisle because they seem to have it so together. I know I never keep such a thorough, running account of every little thing I do right, or do well, yet I can reel off my screwups and shortcomings in a heartbeat. And however ill someone may think of me as a result of them, I probably thought worse of myself when it happened. How do we become so adept at invalidating ourselves? If you're like me, your immediate answer to that question is probably, "I can't help myself."

Au contraire.

You started it, and you can stop it.

Once my spiritual makeup artist enlightened me about guilt being a choice, I tried to make a conscious effort not to "do" it. Guilt is toxic, and you have to think of it as an addictive drug; if you allow your system to absorb it, you'll only make yourself sick. One way to kick the habit is to acknowledge that guilt doesn't make you a better person; it pins you down and holds you back. It's actually kind of self-indulgent. *C'mon.* Let's get over ourselves already! Being a mom is the greatest blessing in my life, and shame on me if I waste a second of this extraordinary experience treating it like a contest I have to win.

Refusing to do guilt doesn't mean you go all Lindsay Lohan and start smirking in your mug shots. I'm not suggesting that denial is the key to self-preservation here. We're all going to make mistakes, both big and small, and we're going to fall short of expectations at times, our own included. When I do, I try my hardest to follow the three As:

- Be accountable.
- Offer apologies.
- Make amends.

Say you forget to tell the school that your son can go home with his best friend for a playdate, and you're in a meeting and have turned your cell phone off when the principal's secretary tries to call you to confirm, so your son misses out on the special afternoon he and his buddy had been planning all week. Yes, it's your bad. So admit that you messed up, and ask for forgiveness (which, by the way, acknowledges the wounded party a lot more than a mere "I'm sorry already, okay?"). Even though you can't undo the wrong, this is a case where you can, in fact, make amends. Offer to take the two boys to the park or a movie over the weekend. Fix what you can; then let it go. Don't turn the incident into an internal trial by a jury of one over your availability as a parent. Totally blanked out about your coworker's big retirement party? Send a nice card or note and move on with it. And something else about apologies: One sincere apology is enough. Overdoing it makes it about you, not about the person you wronged. Ask for forgiveness humbly, and when it's given, take it!! Resist the urge to throw the gears into reverse and back up over yourself.

Presumption is right up there with comparison when it comes to guilt's deadliest weapons. The best way to shield yourself is through simple, honest communication. When you start mentally sketching out entire scenarios of what someone else is going to feel or do as a result of your actions or inaction, chances are pretty good you're going to presume the worst. That's what I did when I realized that a beloved family tradition was becoming an ordeal. Every Friday evening, we used to celebrate Shabbat with David's parents at their home, which is about an hour's drive from us. His mother would prepare a delicious meal, and the house would be aglow with candles. I love the cozy warmth of sharing this religious ritual with the kids. But both David and I are usually exhausted by the end of the week, and Dante would have added a tenth circle of hell if he'd ever battled L.A.'s rush-hour traffic on a Friday afternoon. By the time the weekly feast was over, the kids were usually cranky and tired, too, and all four would end up falling asleep on the drive home. Much as we enjoyed the Shabbat gathering, we were also starting to sort of dread the obligation. David and I both felt horribly guilty about secretly wanting to beg off and hunker down at home, instead. His parents would be so hurt! Finally, though, it just got to be too much for us, and I gingerly broached the subject with David's mom. She couldn't have been more gracious and reassuring.

"Are you kidding me?" she exclaimed. "We love you and can see you another time. Do what's easy for you! You know what, let's do it once a month, and we can rotate houses if you want."

Speaking up—owning our feelings—ended up sparing David and me the nagging guilt that we had been so quick to heap on ourselves. Turns out we could have our challah, and eat it, too! And what a relief to respect and honor David's parents with our honesty rather than silently—and guiltily—resent them by sticking with a routine that wasn't working for us.

things a woman should never feel guilty about

- Hormonal rage
- The dream you just had
- Eating dessert
- Mani-pedi
- Book club (even if it's a smokescreen to drink wine with friends)
- Breast-feeding *or* supplementing with formula
- Having to work
- Crying for no reason
- Gaining five pounds
- Buying the second pair of shoes

When I think about it, a good deal of my mommy guilt revolves around things I can't do, or places I can't be. I'm the kind who would rather say no when I really mean maybe, just because I don't want to run the risk of letting someone down. Especially my kids! I don't know a single mother out there who hasn't wished she had a clone (preferably one with really great hair). With four kids, there's never enough me to go around. I do everything humanly possible to make sure I'm there for dance recitals, school events, and all the major stuff, but there isn't a whole lot left over for the electives. One thing that's helped me a lot is to involve my kids whenever possible in the process of prioritizing. Sierra, for example, was always begging me to be a room mother or Brownie leader, and I felt guilty refusing because I was already stretched too thin. But

things a man should always feel guilty about

- Questioning the sanity of your close relatives or friends
- Checking out the woman in the next car
- Complaining about the one stupid item you forgot when you just packed for a family of five
- Noticing the five pounds you gained
- Asking how much the shoes cost
- Saying you look tired
- Assuming his naps are a sacred ritual, but yours are a sign that you're lazy or pregnant
- Expecting you to cater when the guys come over to watch the game, but never thinking of returning the favor when you host your book club
- Saying you remind him of his mother
- Or ex-girlfriend
- Or anyone except Audrey Hepburn

every year, she would ask again. Her persistence made me feel even guiltier, because I could see that it was really a big deal to her. Finally, we sat down together and I told her she could choose a grade for me to be her room mother, and I would make a commitment. She decided fifth grade would be the golden year. That gave me two years' notice to make it work, and Sierra's anxiety is now anticipation. We both feel better.

brooke burke

THE WORLD'S WORST MOM

I can't be positive about this, because it's one of those taboo subjects that only the closest of friends usually dare to share with each other, but I'm pretty sure that most women harbor at least one shocking, guilty secret about their worst mommy moment. I don't mean the funny tales from the trenches about little Brittany answering the phone and telling a prospective employer that mommy's on the toilet. I'm talking about those heart-stopping moments when something unthinkable happens, and—justifiably or not—you blame yourself.

Mine came when my second-born was around a year old. Neriah was at preschool, and I was meeting two girlfriends for coffee at Starbucks. When I got there, Sierra was asleep in her car seat, but the parking gods were smiling down on us, and there was a space right out front. So I rolled the windows down enough to let air in, put one of those sunshades on the windshield, locked the car and zipped inside, figuring my friends and I could enjoy our coffee at a table outside right by the car, and I would let Sierra sleep. But after we had gotten our drinks, my friends settled in at a window table inside, and without thinking, I plopped down with them. We'd been chatting for maybe twenty minutes when I heard a car alarm start blaring. Glancing out the window, I could see a small crowd gathering, and heard people shouting. I suddenly realized it was my car at the center of this ruckus. I had completely forgotten about Sierra! My heart was pounding out of my chest as I leaped up and ran outside to find a justifiably angry mini-mob surrounding my car, trying to get in through a window to rescue my poor daughter, who was red-faced and screaming inside. To make matters even worse, she had thrown up on herself. I was shaking and crying as the onlookers screamed at me, *"What's wrong with you?"* *"What kind of mother are you?"* *"Someone should call the police!"* My girlfriend hustled me into the driver's seat with a stern command: *Get in the car and just go! Go!* Sobbing, I drove away, quickly turning down a quiet side street to pull over. I held Sierra and apologized to her and cried with her. I was terrified, and so humiliated and pissed off at myself for being so friggin' scatterbrained that I had left my child in the car. I could have been arrested for neglect. My children could have been taken away from me. My daughter could have even died. I felt like the worst mother in the universe. I didn't deserve to have children. Call it baby brain, or just sheer irresponsibility, call it whatever you like, but it was awful, and it makes me shake even today to recount it. I felt guilty beyond words. It's still a painful memory, obviously, but I eventually accepted that this was one of those times when the universe was sending me a wake-up call: I needed to slow down and pay attention.

Filing for divorce when I realized that my marriage to Garth was unsalvageable was the most agonizing decision of my life, and the guilt I felt about tearing our family apart far outweighed any relief I felt about making what I knew was absolutely the right, healthy choice. Seeing my children in such emotional pain, and knowing I bore responsibility for that, was and, five years later, still is pure torture. But I unearthed a major life lesson amid all that anguish, because in the fallout after the separation, I had to grow up and realize the difference, for the first time, between being my daughters' friend and being their mother.

When Neriah was born, the joy and tenderness I felt was intoxicating, and there was nothing I wanted more than to be with her all the time. We bopped around the world together while I shot *Wild On*, and when Sierra was born, I was equally attached. I have to laugh now when I look at my swimsuit calendars from that era, especially when I see this one sultry shot of me leaning up against a stucco wall in Mexico in my string bikini, with this come-hither look on my face. What the photo doesn't show is the two toddlers who were playing right at my feet, barely out of camera range. I hope the guys who bought that calendar got their money's worth imagining that the half-naked model was fantasizing about them, when she was really thinking: *Okay, whose diaper stinks?* No matter how exhausted I was, my girls could always light up my life just by reaching out their arms for me. They were my little BFFs.

That shifted with the divorce. Neriah was five then, old enough and sharp enough not to be appeased by reassuring platitudes. Both she and Sierra were confused, of course, but Neriah was also monumentally pissed. And I had no clue how to deal with her wrath. I'll never forget the time she was jumping on a trampoline and announced for the first time, quite matter-of-factly, that she hated me. It was like a spear had just been plunged straight through my heart. I reacted the way a friend would instead of a mother—I felt rejected, hurt, sad, and yes, angry. The more Neriah acted out, the worse I felt. Being hateful and mean certainly weren't traits I had instilled in her, and it shocked me to encounter them. At the same time, I did nothing to correct the ugliness. I felt as if I deserved it; I was guilty as charged. As this volatile stage dragged on, though, something scary happened: I found myself starting to distance myself from my own child. I loved her with all my heart, but I felt little bond with this nasty stranger who seemed to have taken over my wonderful daughter. I was having trouble staying close to my little girl, and I desperately missed the deep connection we had had until then. Thank God I had enough sense to seek professional help. I confided my awful secret to the therapist I was seeing.

"You're not her friend, you're her mom," he reminded me. "It's not about wishing your kids were certain ways, or hoping x, y, or z about them. You have to love them unconditionally regardless of what you get back. Neriah doesn't need you to be her friend. She needs you to be her mother."

Part of me wanted to blurt out what I really felt, which was, *Wow, that sucks. Are you sure?* But I think I grew up in that instant, too, because I realized that I had to learn how to do this, how to calmly say, "We don't use words like that in our family," and set up consequences when I was being trash-talked, instead of silently reeling, like a friend betrayed. We weren't a partnership; we were parent and child. My job wasn't to walk beside my child; it was to clear the path ahead of her, then follow behind to support her when she faltered. And I needed to offer myself the same wisdom and compassion. Yes, I had made a choice that broke hearts big and small, and yes, I needed to feel the shame and sorrow that engulfed me when I did. I needed to feel the guilt, too.

But I also needed to not allow that guilt to own me forever.

It can be hard to put things in perspective when you let yourself get swept away by the ongoing drama of family life, and that lack of perspective is another open invitation for guilt to take root. You know those days that just seem to spontaneously combust the moment your slippers hit the floor in the morning? I recently found myself in one of those emotional storms, and boy, was it a whopper. We were having one of those rushed, frantic mornings, so tempers were a little short to begin with. Neriah was dawdling and ignored a couple of prods from me to hurry up and get ready. "I *am* ready!" she insisted. I gave her the once-over: She was wearing short shorts, and her hair was unbrushed. (She had begged me not to make her wash it the night before after dance class, and I had given in on one condition: that she wear it in a nice, tight ponytail the next day to camouflage how dirty it was. She had agreed, but now it was a greasy, unkempt mess.)

"You're not wearing those shorts to school," I said.

"Yes, I am," she sassed back.

"Get upstairs and change your clothes and brush your hair *now*!" I hollered. She ignored me. It took another, even louder and angrier order to get her moving. The bathroom door was closed, and Neriah, assuming my order superseded house rules, barged in without knocking. Sierra let out a banshee scream, and sibling warfare was on. At eight and ten, the girls seemed to be fighting constantly, and viciously, and no amount of consequences or enforced separations had any lasting effect. Now, Sierra and Neriah were yelling ugly things at each other again, so I flew upstairs and started yelling at both of them, then Neriah stomped downstairs, encountering David on the way, and the two of them got into it, and then David and I started yelling at each other, and it didn't stop until I caught sight of poor, terrified Rain trying to run out the front door to escape us all. The ride to school was bristling with an angry silence. "I have had it with you guys," I told Neriah and Sierra. They were both grounded.

After dropping them off, I mentally started in on myself. I had screamed my throat raw. I was a terrible mother: I couldn't control my children, and I sure hadn't controlled myself. I was still stewing when I headed out to *Variety*'s annual Power of Women luncheon, which was honoring some of my fave celebrity moms for their charitable works. Jennifer Garner and Diane Lane gave inspiring, heartfelt speeches, and the more I listened, the more I felt the dark clouds over my head that day scatter. One woman began to describe her own day from hell in hilarious detail, from running out of coffee filters and having to use a paper towel to stepping in dog poo, to running late only to discover the car was out of gas. Then she shifted to a parallel story about what the day had been like for an impoverished mother in Haiti who woke up to three small children with empty bellies and nothing to feed them, whose bathroom was an open sewer in her shantytown, where the filth at her feet was human, not dog, waste. Dwelling on my own problems felt petty and selfish after that.

I still felt ashamed by my own behavior that morning, and the only way to get rid of that lingering guilt was to acknowledge it and make appropriate apologies. I called home when I had a few minutes. Neriah was out, but Sierra answered. I told her how bad I felt all day about the way I had handled myself that morning, and I apologized for yelling at her. I let her know I was ashamed of my behavior, while still holding my ground on her punishment. I reiterated my concerns about the horrible things she had said to Neriah when she could have just handed her her brush, instead.

I ended up calling a family meeting for the following day, and told the girls to write letters to each other saying what they admired about each other and how they should treat each other. The idea was to read those declarations aloud, and then we'd go around the table and all talk about what we felt we needed to work on—grown-ups included. I also asked the children to get a sheet of paper and write out what family means to them. We would tack it to the kitchen wall as a reminder to us all.

naked truth We never dare admit it, but like most mothers, I don't always *like* my children, even though I love them endlessly and unconditionally. Each one can drive me crazy at different times, or exhibit undesirable traits that I haven't managed to buff out yet. I don't buy the PC statement "I love my children all the same," because the truth is that I love each of mine uniquely. On some days, there are certain things I enjoy doing more or prefer to share with one child. It's different. I love them equally, but differently.

A TEACHER'S GOLDEN RULE

Wouldn't you know that Open House fell smack in the middle of our family drama? I might as well go to the school with "Dysfunctional Family" scrawled across my forehead with a scented marker (the kind the back-to-school supply list had specifically warned me *not* to get, of course). I decided the best move was to come clean and give the girls' teachers a heads-up about all the tensions at home. No doubt my failings as a mother were stressing out my children in the classroom, too, impacting their ability to grasp long division or learn everything they needed to know about ancient Egypt. Imagine my relief when both teachers expressed surprise and assured me that the girls were always sweet, well behaved, and in general, doing wonderfully. Once again, I had jumped ahead to assume the worst, and was doing all the prep work to serve myself another heaping portion of unnecessary guilt. I swallowed my suspicions about concerned aliens helpfully swapping my kids out for mellower clones at recess.

When Sierra's third-grade teacher got up to address the roomful of parents in her welcoming remarks, something she said resonated deeply for me:

"There are only two things I care about in the classroom," she explained, "and that's if the children feel cared for and loved. I can teach them anything if they feel cared for and loved, but if they don't feel cared for and loved, they shut down. Then nothing gets through."

Sage advice for nurturing not only your child but your child within, as well. I felt like it was another little message from the universe: To love my family as fully and freely as I wanted to— to be the mother I yearned to be—I needed to love myself the way I loved them. I needed to allow myself to make mistakes and learn from them, to forgive my own shortcomings, and to comfort instead of chastise myself when I felt hurt or deflated. I needed to not merely correct behavior but to model it, and be the kind of adult I hope my children will be someday. Of course, there would always be trials and tribulations, and more than enough evidence against me at any given moment, but ultimately, I was the one rendering judgment on myself. I was the one who needed to stop handing down all the guilty verdicts.

A LIFE WELL LIVED

When I was in my early twenties, my therapist invited me to participate in a special group-therapy session she was facilitating. I was nervous about baring my soul in front of strangers, but I was also curious, so I decided to attend. The way it was structured, the group was really like a therapeutic book club. We would meet in the office our therapist had in back of her home. I think this must be when my fantasies of someday having a fabulous rose garden began, because she had these lovingly tended rosebushes blooming along the pathway to her office. The flowers gave me a sense of tranquility before I even went through the therapist's door.

The women in the group were all older than I was—mostly in their forties, fifties, and sixties—but there's something tribal about a community of women, no matter how small, and I instantly felt safe in their circle. We were all supposed to read selections from a wonderful book called *Women Who Run with the Wolves*, by Clarissa Pinkola Estes, then use the collection of myths, tales, and essays as a jumping-off point each week to explore our own issues. One passage she wrote really puts guilt in its place by illuminating how vital our mistakes actually are:

"Though fairy tales end after ten pages, our lives do not. We are multivolume sets. In our lives, even though one episode amounts to a crash and burn, there is always another episode awaiting us and then another. There are always more opportunities to get it right, to fashion our lives in the ways we deserve to have them. Don't waste your time hating a failure. Failure is a greater teacher than success."

I ended up mostly just listening to my elders in the group; I was so young, I didn't feel like I had much to contribute. But I soaked it all in, and I learned. What I heard was the collective hurt of women filled with regret. Regret over chances not taken, dreams unchased, regret over creativity that had been stifled, confidence crushed, senses of self allowed to wither, unnurtured, and die out altogether. I felt such a sense of sadness as I listened to mothers and wives who wondered what might have happened if they had pursued a passion for painting and just taken that art class long ago, or had tried to launch the small business they once dreamed of running, or had left an abusive mate sooner. The list of what-ifs went on and on. I promised myself then and there that I would never live my life with a finger on the mute button. I wouldn't make their mistakes. I would follow my heart always.

Of course it didn't exactly turn out that way. I spent seven years in a marriage trying to be someone I wasn't, because I had somehow managed to convince myself that I wasn't entitled to think of my own needs. Ugh. I hate that word even now—"entitled"—it's just so gross!

Today, I understand what I couldn't foresee as a naïve twenty-something: When you become a mother, you become selfless. But less should not equal loss. Give all that you have to give, but include yourself in that bounty. Feed your heart, your soul, and your mind to the bursting point. Don't sit in a circle at sixty, lost and lonely, wishing aloud that you had sometimes put yourself first, but never dared because it made you feel so guilty. Guilt leads inevitably to regret.

During my second season cohosting *DWTS*, I found myself dishing backstage one evening with celebrity contestant Florence

Henderson. Besides being beloved by TV fans around the world as the iconic TV mom on *The Brady Bunch*, Florence had raised four children of her own. As we compared notes, she surprised me by declaring that one of the most important lessons she had learned as a mother was to "put yourself first."

"Come again?" I said dubiously. I drew an invisible totem pole in the air, and pointed to the bottom. "But I'm here."

"No," she insisted. "You're first. You have to take care of yourself first to take care of everyone else."

I could see her logic, but I had to wonder whether she had been able to pull this one off before her children grew up and flew the nest.

"How old were you when you realized this?" I asked suspiciously.

Florence smiled sheepishly. "Yeah." She shrugged. "You've got a point."

It's funny, but what I hesitate sometimes to do for myself I do instinctively and effortlessly as a mother. I've never been the helicopter mom, hovering obsessively over my kids. I want them to climb trees and ride horses and have adventures. When Shaya makes a mad dash for the rope wall, I'm going to say, "Sure, you can climb it, and I'll be here to catch you." If we have an accident, we have an accident. I want to give them enough room to experience life. And I know I have to nurture my own spirit in the same way, to be true to myself without feeling guilty about it, whether it's ditching the kids for a romantic weekend with David, or just slipping out for a solitary hike and saying "not this time" to the little ones begging to come along.

I had this great flashback not long ago to a fund-raiser I attended years ago, before I had my children. The speaker was a woman whose husband had recently died after a long struggle with multiple sclerosis. She didn't speak with bitterness or sorrow, though; when she told her husband's story, the widow's voice brimmed with pride and admiration. She recounted how he had lived with zeal in the face of this debilitating disease, wringing every precious second out of his life. Even as his body betrayed him, this man remained true to his heart. As I listened to this powerful story, I knew that I someday wanted to say about my life what this man, at the end, had been able to say about his:

"I was who I was supposed to be. I have no regrets at all."

embrace the bitch

Even nice girls need to let the dogs out.

*W*HEN I WAS hosting the model-search show *She's Got the Look*, a memo came down from on high one day while we were preparing to shoot a segment featuring the famous 1970s supermodel Cheryl Tiegs as a guest judge. I was in my dressing room getting ready, and was so floored by this particular mandate from Production that I had to read it out loud to the glam squad just to make sure I wasn't suffering hallucinations from an inadvertent hairspray high.

Cheryl Tiegs would be arriving on set shortly, the memo advised, but under no circumstances whatsoever was anyone to utter her name. Instead, we should all use a secret code name when referring to (you-know-who). Henceforth, (you-know-who) was to be identified strictly as "the Special Package." I briefly wondered when a former cover girl had become a cabinet member, and what exactly would happen if I should slip and call her Cheryl, or Miss Tiegs. "What are they gonna do?" I mused aloud, hoping my eyelash curler wasn't bugged. "Throw me in hostess prison?"

My petulance was fueled by jealousy, of course. I mean, what woman worth her Chanel sunglasses doesn't want to be cloaked in mystery? I appealed to the glam squad for some much-needed moral support.

"I want a code name!" I whined.

The glam squad jumped on the case immediately, and we spent more time than I'd like to admit brainstorming before finding a moniker that suited me.

Meet Burniass Bastaline. Or don't meet her, if you're smart. Because Burniass is the high-octane antidote to my chronic Nice Girl Syndrome—my in-your-face, talk-to-the-hand diva in charge of all selfish demands, withering put-downs, and unseemly outbursts of bad temper. If you want to use me, abuse me, or just plain tick me off, you'll need to go through Burniass first. Burniass is not merely my alter ego; she's my personal superhero, always on standby to fight even the dirtiest of fights and champion even the lamest of causes. Burniass takes no prisoners, offers no excuses, harbors no regrets, and never counts her groceries before using the express checkout lane.

You gotta love her.

And chances are, you've got a Burniass of your own tucked away. At least, I hope you do. Every mom needs an inner bitch.

When I blogged about embracing my inner bitch once on my ModernMom.com Web site, I was surprised by the allergic reaction I got from many of my readers. It was pretty clear that even in this era, when tags like "fierce" and "edgy" carry such cachet, women are still deeply conflicted about the whole bitch thing. For many of us, the ultimate disgrace growing up was to be labeled a bitch or a slut (and it was debatable which was worse). Being someone's bitch was even more degrading. I guess it would be more polite, and comforting, somehow, to forever replace "bitchy" with "grouchy" or "irritable," but it just doesn't feel the same to me, and we're not all living in a Barney cartoon.

I'd rather own my inner bitch than disavow her. To me, she's not a reaction, she's a reinforcement—of my presence, of my boundaries, of my commitment to being always true to myself.

The dicey part, of course, is knowing how and when to unleash her.

THE UNBEARABLE RIGHTNESS OF BEING

"So, babe," I oh so casually ventured one languid afternoon when David and I were reflecting on our relationship and how it has evolved over the eighteen years we've known one another. "What do you think have been some of my bitchiest moments?" (FYI, selective amnesia happens to be one of Burniass's best traits.)

"No way," David shot back. "I don't even want to tell you, because we'll end up in a fight." The guy's no dummy when it comes to ignoring live bait on a big hook.

His wisdom is well earned, having gone through a divorce and two pregnancies with me, when first heartache, and then hormones, forced me to finally get in touch with my long-silent inner voice and start using it. Loudly.

Weird as it sounds, I could never really express anger until I knew happiness. Not just anger, come to think of it, but any negative or volatile feelings. I had always been the self-appointed peacemaker in my kingdom, willing and able to put out everyone else's emotional wildfires while diligently containing my own. You know how firefighters sometimes set a carefully managed blaze to prevent a larger, more dangerous inferno from spreading? For most of my life, I did the same thing with my feelings. I was the human equivalent of a controlled burn.

As a kid, I was surrounded by shouters. My mother and stepfather, Armen, were often at each other's throats, and my older sister jumped into the fray as well. I learned early how to fly beneath the radar by observing rather than engaging. My detachment gave me the ability to genuinely see all sides of whatever battle was raging, and my empathy allowed me to pass freely between enemy camps at any given time. Armen was strict, and I understood that he was never going to be a demonstrative dad, but I knew he loved me in his own gruff way. And most important, I knew I could count on him no matter what. Now that I'm grown and he's gone, I look back and appreciate the lesson he unwittingly taught me about being a parent: Always be true.

As a mother, I'm determined not merely to pass this lesson along to my children, but to live it every day, and instill in them the emotional intelligence I wish I had had all along. But back then, I was always too busy trying to be perfect to understand that being authentic is the real key to fulfillment. If you want people to love you for who you are, you have to show them who you *are*, not just who you aspire to be. And to get what you want, you have to be willing to ask for it. Five years and two children into our engagement, David is still patiently working with me on that one; I have to remind myself on a regular basis that we share the same energy, not the same mind, and that he can't read mine. I think that's such a common mistake that couples make in a romantic relationship, to assume that your soul mate should automatically know exactly what you want and need. That amounts to a hit-and-miss approach to contentment, and you're going to end up disappointed and resentful when your secret expectations aren't met. (*Why didn't he know I wanted him to hold me when I was pushing him away? Why would he buy tickets for the game when I was hoping for a quiet night out with just the two of us?*)

I was so used to boxing up my painful or uncomfortable feelings that I had quite the stockpile in my emotional warehouse by the time I found a soul mate I could risk sharing all that with. I've made a lot of progress, but I still have to fight the temptation sometimes to quickly sweep aside the scary stuff and pretend it's not even there.

When Armen passed away the week after Christmas 2004, David and I flew to Tucson to help with arrangements. It was New Year's Eve. Sitting in the hotel after spending that first day taking care of things, I began feeling antsy, and suggested we go out to a bar that had been one of my favorite old stomping grounds. "What the hell, we should just get out of this room and go out," I urged. David shook his head and wrapped his arms around me. "No," he said, gently but firmly, instantly recognizing my impulse to run away from my emotions. On some subconscious level, I obviously believed I could physically flee the sorrow welling up inside me. "We're going to just stay here and get through this," David insisted.

After we returned to Malibu, David and I began finalizing plans to move in together; construction was nearly complete on the dream house he'd begun building before we found each other, and the pop-star bachelor pad he'd envisioned had been reimagined as a cozy family nest. Excited as I was about our future, between my divorce, the death of my stepfather, and this life-altering decision to start a new life with David, I was feeling pretty stressed. For the first time, though, I found that

I wasn't able to easily bottle it all up and shove the cork down nice and tight. On the one hand, I felt incredibly strong—I had left the safety zone of marriage to become a single mother— yet on the other hand, I felt more vulnerable than ever before. In my animalistic state of mind, I knew when I moved to the Malibu house that this was no longer my cave, and I needed to define my boundaries. To my dismay—and to David's—what came out, in machine-gun bursts, was pure, unfiltered anger. I became a major bitch. I would pick fights and ratchet up the drama until I could explode in a cinematic, "&!%#-you-I'm-leaving!" climax.

And damn, did it feel good! The sick thing was, it was such a release that it made me want to yell louder, and longer, and uglier. It would take some trial and error before I figured out exactly how to calibrate my bitchometer.

Once liberated, however, my inner bitch got down to business cleaning up all the messes my passive Nice Girl had a habit of leaving behind. One of my biggest problem areas had always been a reluctance to untangle myself from dysfunctional relationships—professionally as well as personally. After spending two years in counseling, diligently working to save my marriage, the admission that I couldn't had hit me hard. I felt as if I had failed at my most important role as a woman: keeping my family happy and intact.

"What do you need?" I remember my therapist asking me.

"I don't need anything, I'm good," I automatically replied, not even hearing how utterly ridiculous those words sound in, of all places, a shrink's office.

"Everyone has needs," he prodded. "If you made a list, what would it look like?"

I was stymied. I sat there, almost embarrassed by my own silence. I had always assumed that needs and wants were the same thing, and if you wanted something, you must be selfish or greedy, or determined to set yourself up for disappointment. When you think that way, of course, what you're really doing is counting on everyone else to figure out what makes you happy—and setting them up for failure, because if you don't know, how are they supposed to? Inevitably, you end up feeling frustrated and resentful, and the whole vicious cycle starts all over again.

I was in my thirties, but so emotionally dependent and immature that I didn't even know how to entertain myself! No joke. When I was dating, I would always wait to see where my man was going to take me, or what he had planned for us over the weekend, or which friends (always his) we were going to hang out with. But I wasn't anyone's sweet little it's-all-good girlfriend anymore. Now I was a grown woman, a mother, someone with a career and businesses to run.

"It's almost like teaching someone your name," my therapist patiently explained. "You have a responsibility to communicate in a relationship, to teach someone about yourself, to teach them what you want, to teach them what you need." I knew he was right: I had to identify what I wanted, and learn how to get those needs met in a healthy, grown-up way. Tentatively, I started my list: I needed time to myself; I needed romance; I needed to love completely and deeply; I needed respect; I needed to feel valued and appreciated. I needed to be a good mother, because that makes me feel good about myself. And I needed girlfriends. After always living through my man and neglecting that part of my life, I had discovered how vital those connections with other women are, how we sustain one another.

Not all my attempts at being assertive were successful, mind you.

On my first day of work cohosting *Dancing with the Stars*, a production assistant popped into my dressing room to ask whether I had any needs. *What gives, is that word stalking me or something?* I wondered to myself. I knew this was the moment where I was supposed to request cut-crystal bowls full of orange Skittles, or, like one actress I knew, demand that the faucets in my sink flow with nothing but Evian water.

"No, thank you!" I chirped to the waiting p.a. "I'm good!"

The p.a. left, and my glam squad emitted a collective sigh of exasperation.

"You need some needs," they said.

"I need to need some needs," I admitted, chagrined. (It takes a while for some lessons to sink in.)

I looked around the makeup room. Paint! The scarred, dingy walls pretty clearly needed paint! I *needed* paint! A nice Tiffany blue and dove gray would be perfect. I put that thought on hold as filming got under way for the season, then decided when I came up for air a few weeks later to have it done.

I proudly but politely gave voice to my need.

Back came a mortifying memo with everyone but my mom copied in, announcing that despite the fact that we were mid-season, Miss Burke had suddenly decided that she *had to have* her dressing room repainted Tiffany blue, which wasn't part of the union-sanctioned color wheel. The memo informed me that, since this was a midseason request and not part of sched-uled maintenance, I would have to pay for the paint job myself, using the network's contractors. The price quoted was jaw-dropping. You could build a room that size for less. You could build it and stucco it with orange Skittles for less. I decided it was easier to just un-need my need, wait for the new season, and then comply with the color wheel.

Burniass, however, made a private note to put in a standing order for daily skim lattes, extra hot. Maybe there was a way to make them flow from my bathroom faucet.

In my private life, defining what I wanted was far less comical and a lot more complicated. David and I had settled into our shared home and added first Rain, and then Shaya, to the clan, and what I wanted more than anything was for our blended family to be harmonious. I was at last able to acknowledge to myself that, despite my guilt over the divorce, I had a right to be happy, too; I had to decide what happiness looked like for me, and mount a determined campaign to get there. I made a commitment to myself to never dwell in gray again, to not float through that lost place or settle for just okay. "I'm good" wasn't the right answer when "I'm better" is what I longed to tell myself.

Passive, I had finally figured out, wasn't the same as peaceful at all. Tucking all those feelings away in their tidy compartments had only led to seething resentment, not tranquility. I can't count all the payback fantasies I've hatched in my imagination over the years. (Next time around, I should just direct slasher movies.) The same unwillingness to rock the boat had hampered my business relationships, too. Summoning my inner bitch, I began to cut loose people I had hired to help me who had either fallen short or flat-out taken advantage of my Nice Girl's eagerness to always accommodate. No more slacker sitters ignoring my kids or sly agents trying to sign me up for lucrative Vegas nudie revues. No more spending ninety minutes in traffic to get to my old Pilates studio for a workout because I didn't want to hurt my instructor's feelings by admitting that her class was inconvenient now that I had moved to Malibu.

David, too, learned to deal with my inner bitch, once he overcame the shock of discovering that the friendly little beagle he had wanted to fall in love with had the scary ability to morph into a rabid Doberman lunging straight for his heart. One night during a fight, I went into superbitch mode, hurling furious expletives at him and storming to the door with everything I could hastily stuff into my Louis Vuitton duffel bag. David stopped me in my high-heeled tracks. "I'm leaving!" I yelled.

"If you walk out that door, I mean it, don't you *ever* come back!" he shouted back at me.

I could tell he was dead serious. *Ohhh, shit*, I thought. My heart was racing and my horns were out, but I calmed myself down long enough to focus, again, on what happiness looked like for me. *Him*, I heard my heart answer, *it looks like him*. I put my bags down (but didn't unpack them right away—Burniass has her dignity). Knowing how to let the bitch out was exhilarating and empowering, no question about it. But knowing when to tie her back up was just as important.

Cheaper, too, it turns out.

That, I discovered one day in the carpool lane at my big girls' school. The school is in a quiet residential neighborhood, and there's a long-standing routine for dropping kids off and picking them up. Because there's no real driveway, you have to pull over to the side of the road and idle in line until one of the school's two guards motions you forward. It's very organized, and there have never been any problems.

One afternoon, the line was inching ahead, and I was waiting my turn when I heard the whoop of a police siren and saw a motorcycle cop behind me, red and blue lights flashing.

"Scoot up, scoot up, scoot up!" I heard him shouting. I rolled down my window.

"Excuse me, are you speaking to me?" I asked.

"Scoot up!" he barked again.

Since there was a truck right in front of me, following his order would have involved air bags and tow trucks and insurance adjusters, which I was pretty sure was not part of the "protect and serve" motto officers of the law were sworn to uphold.

"Where would you like me to go?" I asked. I could feel Burniass rattling her cage, itching to handle this one for me.

The cop stormed up to my car door and asked for my license and registration. He appeared to be about fourteen and a half, and if anything, I should have been asking to see his license. I opened Burniass's cage with an unspoken command, *All yours!!*

By now, Officer McClueless was writing me a ticket. He was so young and snotty, I was tempted to hand him one of the crayons forever rolling around on the floor of my car.

"You can't park here!" he bellowed.

"I'm not parked," I snapped back. "I'm in Drive and my foot is on the brake only because I'm talking to you. I'm in carpool!"

"Carpool?" he blustered, as if I had just uttered something in Tagalog.

"Yeah," Burniass piped up sarcastically, "there's a school right in front of you! If you have an issue, you should take it up with the principal, not me!" I was livid. Burniass let rip, and I could hear my voice now screaming at a uniformed authority figure—albeit a dim-witted one—whose accessories included handcuffs and a gun. This was not wise. *"How long have you been a cop?"* I demanded. This was especially not wise.

"Long enough!" he retorted, handing me the citation.

"Well, you're a (felony curse word) jerk!!" I yelled.

The cost of not knowing when to shut up? Two hundred and seventy-five dollars.

Siccing the bitch on someone who deserved it?

Priceless.

DON'T MESS WITH MY CUBS, EVER

Even though I fought the law and the law won, I would still argue that there are certain situations and certain people that simply beg for the full-bitch treatment. One way to jump to the front of that line with me—and with most parents I know—is to mistreat my kids in any way, shape, or form. You'll get teeth bared, claws out, and don't expect the courtesy of a warning growl first.

Let me explain first off that I'm not one of those mothers who thinks her little darlings can do no wrong. My offspring have done their fair share of wreaking havoc. If it can be spilled, knocked over, or mowed down by a pink Barbie convertible, then trust me, we've been there, done that, and I've been appropriately mortified and apologetic. When Shaya hit his terrible twos, his tantrums were so over the top that we once actually had to leave a zoo because we were disturbing the wildlife.

But let's be honest here: There are people who, for their own reasons, simply don't like children, no matter how well they happen to be behaving (or not). Then there are people who actually do like them, but only in carefully managed doses. And sure, I may not always agree or understand, but I will absolutely respect your right to cringe when my crew comes rolling your way. And I'll respect you even more if you keep the negativity to yourself. Scowling at a double stroller doesn't make it miraculously take up less of the sidewalk. (Almost as bad: The well-meaning strangers who stop to ask whether the kids are all mine. As opposed to what, rentals?) If you ever wonder what it would feel like to be shunned by society, just board an airplane carrying an infant or toddler. You might as well be carrying the plague.

Whenever I'm out with my children, I make a genuine effort to be considerate without being obsequious, but even those good intentions sometimes backfire. For example, Rain likes to go to the gym with me and just watch or color while I work out. She knows not to touch anything or bother anyone and it's all good: This is one routine we've got down pat. Last week, a woman was on the machine next to the one I was going to use, and I saw her shoot us a dirty look as we approached. "She's not going to bother you, is she?" I asked lightly as Rain happily settled into the corner with her crayons.

"Actually, she does," the woman huffed.

I was dumbstruck. Rain hadn't said or done a thing, but this woman made it clear that her mere presence was considered an affront. I don't know why, but I had the sense that something else might be going on with this particular woman, and I decided not to push the issue. I hastily scouted out another spot for us, and relocated as far away as possible, but my inner bitch was already reprimanding my namby-pamby Nice Girl for wringing her hands and presuming in the first place that we didn't have as much a right as the intolerant stranger did to a square foot or two of space on the planet. I had to wonder:

Why do so many of us have that knee-jerk need to apologize for existing when we have kids? I wish I had just settled in and done my thing without giving someone else the power to grant or take away my permission to do so. If Rain had acted up in any way, I could have—and would have—simply dealt with it then and removed her.

I was much quicker off the mark when some predatory paparazzi hounded my little girls one afternoon when I had taken them to the beach near our home. I had just finalized my divorce, and had begun dating David, which made me a juicy target for the tabloids. Sierra was only three, and Neriah was five, and they were pretty fragile from this big upheaval in their lives. We were sitting in the sand, just playing and enjoying some time to ourselves, when I spotted a truck parked off to the side. Two men were sprawled underneath it with huge lenses aimed our way. I was annoyed, but relieved that they were at least keeping their distance, especially since Sierra was with me. She has always hated having her picture taken, and the paparazzi terrify her. Sierra is so bashful that she'll burst into tears and run away to hide at her own birthday party if people start singing to her when it's time for cake. As we got up to walk home from the beach that afternoon, more photographers popped up out of nowhere and began swarming us. Sierra was scared and began to cry, and I could feel Neriah's grip tighten in mine, too. "Don't worry. It's okay," I reassured them. "Just keep walking and ignore them." The shutters kept clicking and the photographers kept shouting to get my attention. Neriah, who's always been outspoken, suddenly put her hand in front of her face and begged them: "Can you just leave us alone?" Her plaintive little plea pushed my mama-bear button hard. I wheeled on our pursuers.

"What's wrong with you guys?" I yelled. "It's one thing to harass me, but when a little girl asks for privacy and for you to leave her alone, at least have some decency and self-respect!" Of course, me twisting my face in fury and gesturing madly was like tossing a Double Whopper into a pack of jackals, giving them more to shoot, but silently letting my child's boundaries—and mine—be violated would have been even worse.

I remember more recently when another mother-daughter outing was turned into an ugly ordeal by a nasty manicurist, of all things. I try to give each of my kids some quality time alone with me every week, and Neriah was excited about our date to get mani-pedis together. We headed to a local nail salon that I had patronized several times before, and the owner escorted Neriah to her own station. She had a kind of sour demeanor, but Neriah was determined to break through the ice, and began trying, in her eager ten-year-old way, to engage her. "How long have you been doing nails?" she asked. "Do you like it? Wow, you're really good!" The woman was having none of it, and as Neriah chatted away, I caught her eye and tried to mouth a warning: *Don't talk so much!* Oblivious, she prattled on about how pretty the colors were, and how she wanted to do her nails in a pattern, one pink, one purple, one blue, like a rainbow, then put sparkles on top. (I was perfectly happy to pay any rainbow-sparkle surcharge, natch.) Suddenly I heard the woman hiss at my daughter: "Stop talking!" Neriah fell silent, and I could see her fighting tears. The owner wasn't through with her, though.

"One color only," she gruffly informed her crushed client. (Yes, she would have had to open three separate bottles, but what Neriah was asking for was far less complicated than, say, a French manicure.)

By now, my daughter was utterly humiliated, and my blood

was boiling. Neriah was being treated like a horrible imposition instead of the appreciative customer she had made every attempt, in her childlike way, to be. I was midmanicure, which made leaving, much as I wanted to, problematic.

"You know, honey, just forget it," I called over to her, with a protective edge to my voice that clearly signaled my growing irritation with the owner. "You don't have to sit there and be treated that way. Come over here with me. I'll be happy to do your nails for you when we get home, and it'll be more fun. This isn't supposed to be a bad experience."

Props to her, Neriah maintained her composure and summoned her dignity. "It's okay, Mommy," she answered maturely. "I'm okay. This is fine. She can finish and I'll just choose one color." I could tell that she was miserable, and I doubted that the owner would have ever dared to treat a grown client so roughly. When we got ready to leave, I gave Neriah money for a nice tip. (I know, I know, but don't you ever fool yourself into thinking that displaying classy behavior to a vulgar person will somehow magically transform them?) The woman glared at me, and shoved the bills back into Neriah's hand. "I don't accept tips from rude people," she sniffed.

"You have *got* to be kidding me," I intervened. At that point, Burniass swooped in, smelling blood. "I will never return to this salon," I loudly informed the owner—and every other customer who had watched the whole episode unfold. "And I refuse to allow you to teach my child not to act appropriately even when she's been treated rudely, because two wrongs do not make a right." With that, Burniass threw the tip back in the woman's face and stormed out the door.

"Boy, she sure was a mean lady," Neriah said when we were safely outside.

"Yeah, she certainly was," I agreed.

And therein lies the difference, I'll tell her someday when she's older, between being a bitch and just acting like one when you have to.

R-E-S-P-E-C-T

It's funny how that instinct to rush instantly to the defense of our children turns into self-doubt or hesitation when it's time to protect our own tender psyches. Like a lot of parents, I admit I'm far more inclined to overreact than underreact when it comes to shielding my young. But the reverse is true when I'm the one in a tough situation. Too often, I pause, I waver, I second-guess, worried about that thin line that society has drawn between heroine and harpy when it comes to a woman fighting back. Sexist stereotyping has done a number on us all over the course of generations, and even when we know that it's ridiculous and grossly unfair, we're still culturally programmed to rein in the rage. For many of us, it takes a conscious effort to reroute those circuits and immediately push back when we need to.

I always strive to bring a positive energy to whatever situation or relationship I'm in, both privately and professionally. And responding to others with compassion is an ideal I try to live up to—perhaps that harsh woman at the gym was in a bitter custody battle, and her reaction had nothing to do with Rain herself, or maybe she was in a foul mood and just needed a wide berth that day. When I champion getting in touch with your inner bitch, I don't mean to suggest for a minute that you should stop being kind, or gracious, or good-natured. You can be all that, and assertive, as well. It's not an either-or proposition. Just consider the possibility that "doormat" doesn't have to be the default setting for a Nice Girl. Maybe what we need is a slogan to inspire us: *"Nice girls kick ass, too!"*

I could have earned a merit badge in meekness for the way I mishandled a situation involving my daughter's Girl Scout troop. When the time came for the big Girl Scout campout, I offered up our backyard. We have a huge, flat grassy field that's perfect for pitching tents under the stars. Neriah was overjoyed when the invitation was accepted, and immediately began planning our night together in a tent. When the big day arrived, though, I was told that I couldn't join Neriah that night because only "official" troop mothers were allowed to participate. Not random, unofficial ones watching forty tents go up in their backyard. I was a lender, not a leader. If they let me join them, then everyone else's parents, grandparents, and Facebook friends would have to be allowed, too, just to be fair. "Really?" I asked in disbelief. I got chapter and verse of the Official Campout Rules recited to me, with special emphasis on the statutes concerning Attempted Tent Invasion by Uncertified Parental Units Seeking Unauthorized Bonding Experience with Their Official Scout Children. I beat a hasty retreat, fearing pepper spray might come next. Neriah was bitterly disappointed, and I have to say that I was, too, as I wistfully looked out across the little tent city from my balcony that night. And I have to say that the Official Leader Mothers sure didn't seem to have a problem bending the Official Campout Rules the next morning when they came up to the house and asked me to pop their trays of cinnamon rolls in my oven because they couldn't get their camping stove to work. I just bit my tongue and played Betty Crocker.

It wasn't until months later, when a friend of mine asked to accompany her anxious daughter on her Girl Scout sleep-out, and got a similar rebuff, that I saw what a big mistake I'd made by not deploying my inner bitch that night with Neriah's troop leaders. Unlike me, my friend didn't just think, *Oh, well, rules are rules*, and swallow her anger. She fought them tooth and nail, right up the Girl Scout food chain, until she prevailed. If I had done the same, I wouldn't have let them ban me from my own backyard and rob me of a memory-making experience with my daughter.

Interestingly enough, the friend who found her way into the tent also happens to be a very powerful CEO whose confidence and strength in the boardroom has gotten her unfairly branded a "world-class bitch" in her industry, while men exhibiting the same qualities are described in glowing terms as "strong, visionary leaders." The tired old double standard still seems to prefer women to be sweet and warm as a fresh-baked sugar cookie no matter what. I've been told that I have a tendency to sound cold and abrupt when I'm in executive mode running my babooshbaby.com company, and sometimes I fret that businesslike is getting misinterpreted as bitchy. That said, I'm not changing my approach, because quick and efficient serves me best in the office. But I do try to counter that brusque vibe by giving the Nice Girl equal time to praise my staff, and express appreciation to everyone whose efforts make a difference in my life. (Note from the Nice Girl: Don't just say, "thank you," be generous, and be specific!!)

As it turned out, the whole campout fiasco left a bad taste in our mouths, and I wasn't surprised when Neriah and Sierra dropped scouting not long after that. I think Neriah, especially, felt let down by them, and even though I'm usually strict about the kids following through with their commitments, there was a good lesson in empowerment by walking away from this one: I definitely want my daughters to grow up strong enough to know that it's okay to cut their losses.

That incredible power surge you feel when you finally allow yourself to just let the dogs out can shock not only you but everyone who thought they knew you, as well. Long before I unleashed my inner bitch, I got a sneak preview of this weird euphoria courtesy of a man I was seeing years ago. (You'll never get them to admit it, but men most definitely harbor inner bitches, too! They just have better PR and call themselves warriors.) Anyway, this guy and I were heading off on vacation together, and were trapped in a row between the Passengers from Hell on the airplane. Two parents traveling with a hyperactive hellion of a little boy. As soon as we were airborne, they basically commandeered the cabin, turning the aisle into their playpen, changing the toddler's soiled diaper on the seat, and yakking back and forth, loudly, across other passengers (Mom and Hellion were in one row of two seats, and Dad was a couple rows back, but too lazy to get up and come to his wife's seat to talk). Obnoxious doesn't begin to describe this crew. We weren't very long into the flight when the woman, leaning across our space yet again to holler back at her spouse, looked down at us and smiled brightly.

"So do you have any kids?" she wanted to know.

"I'm not interested in conversation," my companion responded icily. She stared at him in slack-jawed dismay, but sat down and shut up.

I died a thousand deaths. I couldn't believe my friend had been so incredibly rude! I felt hot tears of embarrassment starting to course down my cheeks as I turned my head away to look out the window. What was wrong with me that I even wanted to be with such a monster? At the same time, I had to admit deep down that I felt enormous relief that Mrs. Obnoxious wouldn't be in our faces the whole flight. He had shut her down fast and final. Still, I was waiting for him to apologize to me for making a scene.

"God, that felt good!" he said instead. He was almost giddy with excitement. "It took me five years of therapy to be able to finally do that. I can't believe I did it!"

I didn't fully understand until years later, when I experienced that same exhilarating rush of relief when I really let it all hang out for the first time during a fight with David. The sensation was almost physical, as if something heavy had been holding me underwater for a dangerously long time, then let go, and suddenly I was buoyant and could breathe. There was just this euphoria. I wanted that feeling to last and last. But realistically, I couldn't go around staging mock explosions all the time just for the thrill of it. Not all circumstances warrant a shock-and-awe strategy. You don't need to blow up the whole fireworks factory when simply waving around a sparkler or two will suffice.

I'm at my best when my Nice Girl and inner bitch combine their unique strengths and sensibilities to create a happy medium. When I treat myself to a massage and the overly chatty masseuse is getting on my nerves, I'll say something along the lines of, "Pardon me if I fall asleep. I'm just going to check out and enjoy this experience." If she doesn't take the hint, I'll give myself the green light to get bitchier.

My inner bitch is way more efficient than I am, and I count

on Burniass to yank me out of the quicksand when my lifelong aversion to conflict mires me in indecision. I had known for some time last year that the nanny I hired in a pinch when I got the *Dancing with the Stars* hosting job was not a great fit. She was busy planning her wedding, for one thing, and the multitude of errands and obligations surrounding that got in the way of caring for Rain and Shaya on a regular basis. She was, in short, a scheduling nightmare, and I was overpaying her to boot. (I knew that going into the deal, but I was desperate, and I naïvely thought that the premium pay would reap premium service.) I found myself always scrambling to accommodate her, when what I should have done was fire her, quick and clean, so we could both move on. But my Nice Girl absolutely dreaded that drama, so instead of confronting the nanny with my needs and her shortcomings, I took the passive-aggressive route, and tried to sort of nudge her out of our lives. I thought that telling her we couldn't really afford her anymore would provide a diplomatic exit, but she countered by negotiating to work fewer hours, for less money. I stupidly agreed, assuming she would look for and land another full-time gig soon, anyway. That was mistake number two. Or number fourteen. I really don't know; I made too many to keep count in this dysfunctional relationship.

I'm not a big shopper. (Stick with me here; this is actually relevant.) With four kids and an erratic work schedule, I find that it's easiest to just hit the stores a couple of times a year and get everything they need in one fell swoop. I had just finished my winter swoop when a friend tipped me off that my nanny had secretly taken pictures of my car crammed full of bags, and was busy showing them to people, sniping that I had cut her pay while going on out-of-control shopping sprees for myself. The breach of confidentiality (not to mention the lie) was unforgivable. I'm fiercely loyal to the people in my life, and expect no less in return. Betrayal is a capital offense with me. I didn't have to think twice about going full-throttle bitch on this one! I called and fired the nanny immediately, and spelled out why. That she would later ask me for a letter of reference tells you something about her chutzpah, but I have to grudgingly admire it, too: She had no qualms about asking for what she wanted; to be assertive, you gotta be fearless.

As parents, one of the earliest lessons we teach our children is to respect us, and when they don't, there are immediate consequences. Demanding the respect we deserve out in the world isn't such a clean transaction, since we really have little control over the impact our actions will have on any given offender. Sometimes, as I knew when I confronted the paparazzi on the beach, you know from the get-go that you'll have all the impact of a gnat against the windscreen of a fighter jet. The biggest idiots will never get it. But that doesn't mean you should resign yourself to silence and let it pass if a principle you hold dear is at stake.

Once, I was waiting to board a plane in London when I darted into a bookstore with Rain to grab something to read. Rain spotted the rack of postcards and asked me if I would please buy her one. "Yes, you can choose one," I told her, "but remember: If you get one, you don't ask for more, or you lose the one you got." I implement that rule with my kids as soon as they're old enough to understand, to help keep greediness in check. Rain decided to test the boundaries that day, and immediately grabbed two more postcards and announced that she wanted those, too. When I refused, she began to howl, and I took away all three postcards. She continued to make a scene, flinging herself onto the filthy floor. I reprimanded her in a sharp voice.

"When you treat your child like that, they feel you don't love them," a bystander smugly informed me. (Leave it to me to attract a cheap Deepak Chopra impersonator while fighting over postcards.)

Nobody likes to have their parenting skills second-guessed by strangers, and unless the child's safety is at risk, no one has the right to interfere. That kind of meddling definitely merits a thorough bitch-slapping.

"This is not an issue of love," I told the British busybody. "We're fine. This is none of your business." I grabbed my sniffling daughter and marched off, but I was so thoroughly peeved that I turned on my heel and went back for more. Deepak was about to get the Double-Dip Bitch Special. I made a point of getting up in his face, to give him a taste of feeling his personal space violated the way mine had been.

"Shame on you for equating discipline with lack of love," I hissed before stalking off again. I was so angry, and so bitchy.

And so, so right.

6

dancing through the chaos

My dressing room is usually a zoo on show days. Wish I could power-nap like Shaya.

As I mentioned earlier, interviewers are forever asking me how I manage to "balance it all" as a career woman and celebrity mom. Balance? Really? I consider myself lucky just to get through any given day without losing my mind (not to mention a child or two, my car keys, diaper bag, studio ID, and every lip gloss I've ever loved). The closest I ever come to balance is holding the bow position for two minutes in yoga class. Balance is bullshit. End of story.

I was the first one in my circle of friends to have a baby, and I felt pretty alone out there in the mommy wilderness back then. My TV career was just launching, and I didn't have the time—or much inclination—to explore the mommy-and-me circuit in my community. And the extraordinary wealth of information we instantly have at our fingertips today was mostly a futuristic Internet dream a decade ago. So I basically did what millions of new mothers before me had done: I winged it. I followed my maternal instincts. I also followed the principles of attachment parenting, which emphasized the importance of forging an unbreakable bond by never separating mother and child for any extended period until they're past the age of five. I was pretty free-spirited, and I have to say I'm not entirely sure I'd make the same choices today that I did then (like heading into the jungles of Belize with an infant for a *Wild On* episode, for example). But what I was doing felt right for my daughter and me at the time, and looking back, I think that living in our own little bubble may have spared me a lot of the angst that I see so many devoted moms going through when they buy into our society's Big Balance Lie. Maybe you've fallen into the trap yourself at some point, and find yourself chasing the elusive supermommy dream, assuming that the only reason you keep falling short of the ideal is because you're not doing something—everything—"right." You're convinced that other moms brilliantly manage to tend their children, their marriages, and their careers, while preserving their own strong sense of identity, and that you could, too, if only you had more time, and more energy, and more help, and more discipline, and more money, and more fiber in your diet, and more highlights in your hair. . . .

Sorry. You know as well as I do that it doesn't work that way. Reality bites. It also pukes on your favorite blouse, flushes keys down the toilet, hits its sister, and turns you into a pariah on airplanes. And guess what. Balance doesn't fix any one of those things.

So if balance is your measure of success, don't bother looking for me under "supermom." You can, however, look for me in the stairwell at my Modern Mom office, where you will find me trapped with a feverish baby, because I didn't have a sitter to watch him early enough to meet the painters who never showed up anyway, and I didn't have the right key card for the elevator, so I took the stairs, but only after shutting the door on my toe, which is now bleeding, and the door to my floor is of course locked, so now I have to hobble back down six flights to the parking garage, where I hope I can sweet-talk my car past the gate because I grabbed the wrong purse and don't have my parking pass and I think my wallet is at home, too, and while I was rummaging in my (wrong) purse, I discovered Len Goodman's gold coin, which they're frantically looking for right now on the set of *Dancing with the Stars* because a toss of that coin is how they determine who dances in which order on the show, and maybe this whole fiasco of a day is the result of bad karma because I accidentally stole Len's precious coin.

But that was just my morning. The rest of that particular Saturday got worse—exploding tire, bad Mapquest directions, iffy neighborhood—and finally ended with me giving poor sick Shaya a dose of baby Tylenol before bed that night, only to go on Twitter an hour later and discover the medicine was being recalled. (Shaya was fine, but I could've used something for *my* throbbing head at that point.)

Suffice it to say, chaos is not merely the occasional storm that passes through my life. It's more like my entire ecosystem. And I've learned to thrive in it, because I know by now that trying to conquer chaos is an exercise in futility, and an exhausting one at that. It's best just to dance through it. *What's that supposed to mean?* you're no doubt wondering. *That I'm supposed to put on a tutu and pretend everything's not falling to pieces around me? Does this plan of yours require prescription medication??*

None of the above. Dancing through the chaos doesn't mean you ignore it all and just pirouette off into lollypop land. It means you follow your own inner rhythm and figure out how to maneuver gracefully through the bedlam. It's about taking the noise in our lives and finding the harmony there. It's about taking a deep breath and reminding yourself that everything's going to be okay. As moms, our days can sometimes seem like a giant obstacle course designed by an evil genius, where you're never sure what's waiting to trip you up, explode in your face, toss you around, or bury you alive. The only way to get through it all unscathed is to know when to duck, jump, defuse, or deftly sidestep. Panic and defeat are simply not options when you're raising a family.

There are times when I've wished I could just curl up in a ball and cry my eyes out, but there are little people who would find me and wouldn't understand. As mothers, we can't always deal truthfully with our emotions as they hit us; we have to hide the scary stuff, put on a brave face, and keep dancing.

Take that god-awful day when I was locked in the stairwell with a sick baby and bloody flip-flops from the gash in my toe. When Shaya started wailing, I wanted to join right in. Instead, I put aside my growing suspicion that the universe had it in for me that day, and tried to regain my equilibrium. If there had been a soundtrack accompanying that day, I'm sure the music would have been jarring—loud, fast, and dissonant. What I needed to do was tune to a better station internally, one that would carry me through the day more gracefully. When I took a moment—and a couple of good, deep belly breaths—to focus on my inner music, the cues I picked up made it clear that I needed to take it slow and easy, conquer one step at a time. First, I needed to get out of the stairwell. I carried Shaya back down to the ground level, and tried the knob. Victory! The door was unlocked. *Okay, huge sigh of relief, at least we're not trapped. On to the next step.* I headed over to my mother's house nearby to get the right key card (she manages the babooshbaby.com business from our Modern Mom offices). *No big deal, plus Shaya enjoyed the nice surprise visit with Nana; one more little disaster undone, what's next?* When the painters didn't show up, I decided not to waste even more of my morning trying to track down the supervisor by phone to ream him out; easier and more gratifying to just hire someone better first thing Monday morning. We could survive a few more days without that fresh coat of hot pink on the walls.

By now, I was feeling more in control with my one-little-crisis-at-a-time rhythm. I headed home to drop off the baby and get ready for the big script meeting we have every Saturday at noon at *Dancing with the Stars* to prep for Monday's show. The producers and network executives all attend, and it's important to be there and fully present.

Once I had Shaya settled down with the nanny (David was filming overseas), I was running a little late. I took David's car and hit the gas. I also hit the mother of all potholes, and a tire promptly exploded. David's car is low profile and all tricked out, which means that towing it is a big, expensive ordeal involving a flatbed truck. *No options here, just resolve it quickly and calmly.* As I got that process under way, I realized that the only way I was going to make that network meeting was if I called and played the damsel-in-distress card, which I am sooo loath to do. *False pride isn't going to get me where I need to be.* "Don't worry," my producer assured me. "We'll send someone to pick you up now." *Not the big deal you imagined.*

Once the meeting was over—and the Len Goodman gold coin was back where it belonged—I was famished. And carless. This time, my nanny drove to the rescue. It was only two p.m., and it already felt like this day would just never end. "I need comfort food!" I announced. All I wanted right then was a big bowl of the amazing chicken noodle soup they make at the Rainbow, a famous rock 'n' roll lounge on Sunset Strip. We pulled up, and . . . there was a big closed sign on the door. No lunch on Saturdays. Between the pothole and the chicken-soup deprivation, Sunset Boulevard was starting to get on my last nerve. On and on the day went like that, just one smack-down after another. I was Wile E. Coyote in boyfriend jeans.

Still, when I look back now and ask myself what went *right*, I have to give myself some props: I didn't collapse in a heap; I coped. I coped the best that I could: I solved what was solvable on my own, I asked for help when I needed it, and I was quick to let go of what didn't matter. Everything may not have turned out perfectly, but it turned out okay. And okay was good enough that day.

HURRICANE WEDNESDAY

I didn't get the memo about hump day. For my family, midweek doesn't bring a sigh of relief, knowing that we're all settled into our respective routines and it's all downhill coasting till the weekend. If only! For us, complete chaos is so predictable on hump day that David and I have given it another name altogether: Hurricane Wednesday. It's like this big, new energy system that comes rolling into the house every week like clockwork.

Under our shared-custody agreement, Wednesday is the day that my two oldest daughters decamp from their dad's place and come back to Malibu. I know even as I sit in the carpool lane to pick them up after school that the transition won't be smooth and easy—for them, or for the rest of us. I used to want these homecomings to be a certain way—all warm and cozy with everyone sitting down to dinner and lovingly catching up with each other—and I was always disappointed. The canvas of our life is much more Picasso than Norman Rockwell.

With various after-school activities, we usually don't get home until five-thirty, and even though little tummies are starting to rumble ominously, everyone's too hyped up to sit right down to dinner. Typically, Neriah will be asking me the same question forty-two times and clamoring to show me something important *right now*, and Rain will be screaming because she's worked herself into such a frenzy of joy and jealousy about seeing her big sisters yet having to share me again; Shaya will upstage Rain's drama with a terrible-twos tantrum, sending Sierra into anxious, mother-hen mode in an effort to bring him down. Our menagerie of pets will doubtless be underfoot (or on the lam—be advised that bearded dragons have a fugitive streak), and there I'll be, dead center in the eye of this hurricane.

My automatic response used to be to try to micromanage everyone, but all that really did was add to the chaos rather than diminish it. I had no choice but to accept that I wasn't going to be able to instantly calm "it" down.

But I could calm myself down.

I've come to appreciate that my peaceable kingdom fantasy is just that—a fantasy—because, hey, I've got four kids and my *life is* chaotic, not just this day or this moment or this dinner hour. And as appealing as the notion may sound, when push comes to shove, I honestly don't want to tune it all out and be some detached observer. I'm in the game, not in the bleachers.

So the real solution, for me, has not been learning how to

manage the chaos, but to manage my own expectations, and to stop setting myself up for disappointment. To do that, I have to make a conscious effort to keep compassion, not control, at the forefront. I need to look beneath the surface and remember that Sierra's annoying clinginess is because she's been missing me, or that Neriah's loud voice and impatience reflect how desperate she is for Mom's attention after going without for the first half of the week. They're starved for mommy time, and whatever I may want from them has to take a backseat to what they need from me. They're basically transitioning between two separate lives, and that's not easy.

Judging from the amount of e-mail I get at Modern Mom about this touchy topic, I know that other divorced families can definitely relate. Even when coparenting is amicable, which I'm thankful is the case with the girls' dad, it's draining. Taking everyone into account on both sides—parents, steps, siblings, and the kids themselves—the shift we undertake in our two households every week affects nine people altogether. That's nine people whose needs, schedules, and feelings need to be taken into consideration. Nine people who aren't going to feel the same thing at the same time and respond in the same way. Somebody is bound to feel anxious, or annoyed, or disrespected, or pressured, or left out, or crabby, or just plain discombobulated. As moms, our impulse is to swoop in and try to fix everything, for everyone (especially the kids), and to just somehow buff out all the rough edges.

Whether you're divorced or not, surely you know by now that if you try to run your family like a synchronized swim team, you're going to drown.

Knowing that the chaos of my Wednesdays is a given, I've

taught myself some moves to not merely get through it all but actually enjoy it for the carnival that it is. Some strategies are simple and obvious, like throwing together a make-ahead dinner that I know everyone likes, or sending the kids outside to blow off steam before we eat, or even just putting on some soft, easy-listening music to channel a more mellow ambience. Those little things can have noticeable impact.

But honestly, the biggest gift you can ever give yourself as a mom is permission. You have to allow yourself to find your own way, define your own boundaries, and shape your own philosophies, without holding yourself hostage to the ideals of that nonexistent "supermom." Stop beating yourself down, and start building yourself up, instead. Compare notes with real women, and consider them your inspiration, not your competition. Tap into that collective font of wisdom and experience we've all accumulated and use it to customize routines, coping skills, or chaos busters that work specifically for you and your family.

One of the tips I picked up not long ago in the Modern Mom community really resonated with me, so much so that I've resolved to make it part of our routine on Hurricane Wednesdays. It's all about reconnecting. As wives and lovers, women know how important it is to reconnect with our mates, whether it's through a regular date night or special weekend getaways (I'll have a lot more to say about that in a later chapter). But as mothers, how often do we apply the same logic to our relationships with our children? By reconnecting, I don't mean just routinely asking, "What did you learn in school today?" I mean putting everything else aside and offering your child your full, openhearted attention, which means truly listening and responding, instead of merely directing behavior. Maybe, because that mother-child bond is always there, and so inherently strong, we sometimes forget how important it is to hit the refresh button now and then.

I've been feeling the need more than ever to reconnect with my two oldest lately as they start to push away from shore and head for adolescence. Those prepubescent hormones are on the rampage, and nothing flips me out faster than a snotty attitude. Even as the girls test their boundaries, I know they need a sense of security and consistency now more than ever. Thanks to another custody-sharing mom's suggestion, I'm making an effort to stop off somewhere with Sierra and Neriah every Hurricane Wednesday before we tumble through the front door and the chaos consumes us. Even if it's just for twenty minutes, we need to be able to sit down and enjoy a light snack or cup of hot cocoa together, to give them a little breathing space between leaving one family life and jumping into another. It's a good opportunity for me to catch up on school projects, or find out whether someone's in a funk because of some friend drama, and to just hear all the news they're eager to tell me. And they love having some time of their own with me before they have to share Mom's attention with two younger siblings again.

There are lots of ways to reconnect with your kids. Once, instead of just taking Sierra to her horseback riding lesson and leaning against the fence to watch her, I signed up for a lesson myself. I rediscovered a joy I'd left behind in my own childhood. It gave Sierra and me something private and special to share.

Neriah and I found our own sweet spot, too. We both love to write, so we picked up *Just Between Us*, a beautiful mother-daughter journal created by Meredith and Sofie Jacobs when

puppy love

WHEN WE TOOK our German shepherd puppies, Thunder and Velvet, to obedience school, David and I may have gotten even more from the trainer than the dogs did. "Puppies need consistency," she told us. "They need to know you're in control. Don't give a command unless you're willing to back it up. They'll always push you and test you, but they really want to please you. Always let them know if they do something you like, and let them know if they do something you don't like. They respond best to positive reinforcement and rewards, even if it's just speaking to them in a loving tone or giving them an extra pat. The puppies need to know how to behave in the house, when they're outdoors, when they're around other people on a walk, when they're in the kitchen, and so forth. They've been taught proper behavior for different places, but they need reminders. You must reward good behavior and carry out consequences when they misbehave. If you don't follow through, they will think they don't have to listen, and they won't. You must read their personalities and know that they are different and respond to different things. Understand that they have good days and bad days, and make appropriate adjustments. Most of all, you need to be totally consistent or they will not respect you." David and I exchanged guilty looks: This was exactly what we should be doing with our two-legged pups, too. Forget camp, I'm sending my kids off to the canine academy this summer!

Sofie was nine. The only rules are that you can't get mad about what's written in the journal, and no entry can be discussed unless the person who wrote it is willing. It's a free space, just for us, to be who we are. It's our way of committing to one another, and carving out time just for us. "Let's go work on our journal," Neriah will suggest, and I know it's an invitation into her world. We explore and discover things about each other. Neriah and I are able to bond in such a powerful way through the written word, and we have so much fun doing it, too. I'll fill in a page, or several pages, and leave the journal on Neriah's bed for her to read, and she'll respond and do the same for me. It's a tender way to reveal our innermost thoughts, feelings, and fantasies, without fear of judgment, and it gives Neriah a chance to share things right away when the emotions are fresh and she can't wait until I'm available to give her my undivided attention. If your child is more visual than verbal, I don't see why the same concept couldn't work by exchanging drawings instead of words. The exercises are creative and thought-provoking, or you may be inspired to just come up with your own. One day, we might be just listing our ten favorite songs or foods, and the next time, we might share our worst fears or fantasize about what we would do if we could do one crazy thing without fearing any consequences.

DISORDERLY CONDUCT

I'm a closet neat freak. I mean that literally, because my closet is the only oasis of order in my house that I get to keep just the way I want, without having to compromise, nag, beg, threaten, or negotiate. It is a lovely little walk-in Zen zone of labeled shelves, tidy bins, and neatly arranged hangers. I wouldn't mind living in there. That's the Virgo in me.

Maintaining a semblance of order is important to me not just aesthetically, but emotionally, as well. If I can just stay on top of the little things, everything seems to run more smoothly, and that means fewer missteps and meltdowns for both the kids and the grown-ups. It can be as simple as setting the breakfast table the night before and asking what everyone's going to want so we're not making decisions in the morning and losing twenty minutes in the process, or pouring a marinade over some meat and sticking it in the fridge before I head out the door, so all we have to do is pop it in the oven or throw it on the grill come dinnertime.

Clutter makes me anxious, and one way I try to keep it contained is to park a large basket in the rooms where toys seem to congregate, so everything can be tossed inside and carted back to the playroom when it's time to clean up. But I also know where to pick my battles on that front, and force myself to stop short of a clean sweep sometimes to ask whether I'm really about to make things better, or actually worse—always a possibility when toddlers are a factor! David and I would love to have a pristine, romantic master bedroom, for example, but ceding one small corner to Shaya's collection of Matchbox cars means that I can get dressed and put on my makeup in the morning while he's peacefully occupied within sight and earshot. And that little chunk of me time is worth spending every night in a miniature car dealership. Unless you're channeling *Mommy Dearest*, there's always going to be a mess somewhere when you have kids. So set reasonable expectations to begin with, and err on the side of generosity when you have to compromise. Yes, letting an eager three-year-old crack eggs or stir batter when you're cooking is going to slow things down and make a mess, but why pass up an opportunity to giggle with a little girl who's got flour on her cheeks and sugar on her lips? I keep the roll of paper towels within reach of even the tiniest hands in our house, and my kids are highly experienced in the art of spill containment. I'm not the kind of mom who skips the arts and crafts because I can't bear the thought of sweeping glitter up off the kitchen floor or picking bits of Play-Doh out of the dog's fur. I want my kids to have the freedom to explore and screw up and get their hands dirty. Every mess can be cleaned up.

I do a lot of my shopping online, which saves me plenty of time, money, and gas. I had no idea how easy and efficient it was until my friend and Modern Mom partner, Lisa Rosenblatt, turned me on to cyberspace's vast twenty-four-hour strip mall. Sometimes I get excited when I see the stacks of boxes waiting at my front door; then I remember it's paper towels or school supplies. I handle a fair amount of household business electronically, too, but I kind of hate to read on the computer, so I can't claim to be one of those admirably green people who lead a practically paperless life. When I'm done with something, I flip it over to the blank side and put it into a scrap stack that the kids can pull from to draw on. But paper still has a way of accumulating, so I have to go on box patrol every so often and scoop up all the mail, computer printouts, and miscellaneous papers from the various counters and desktops where they migrate. Granted, the box may then sit in the mudroom for weeks or maybe months before I tackle it, but at least the clutter's out of sight! Eventually, I'll sit down with a big garbage bag next to me and sort everything in the box into "to-do" and "file" piles. If I can't get to the to-do pile right then, I stick those papers in a separate bright folder that goes in my bag so I can pull it out and work on it when I'm waiting in a dentist's office, or stuck in an airport, or just sitting in the carpool lane for ten minutes before school lets out.

Then there are the times when I just say screw it all, and dump the whole box in the garbage. Boy, does that feel good! If it sat around already for a few months and the world didn't screech to a standstill, I figure it can't have been all that important in the first place.

With the kids, I do a closet clean-out twice a year to get rid of everything that doesn't fit or that they don't like and won't wear. If it's still in good shape, it either gets handed down to a younger sister or given away. Instilling neatness in the kids is an ongoing process that takes vigilance and occasional "shock therapy" on my part. If I reach my exasperation point and feel like the girls aren't taking care of their belongings or are getting spoiled, I'll march into their bedrooms with a big box and announce that everything's going. That never fails to snap them back into best-behavior mode by the time it's half full. We're also big proponents of the get-something-new-donate-something-old approach. We celebrate both Christmas and Chanukah in my household, so letting go of gently used treasures is doubly important to keep materialism at bay. I made it a tradition several holiday seasons ago, when I gave each of the older kids a box and asked them to fill it up. Their first stab, the boxes got filled with broken toys, electronics that didn't work anymore, and only the ugliest stuffed animals.

"You have to give away something that will make someone happy," I insisted. Now they actually get into the spirit of it, choosing toys, books, and clothes that they *do* still like, but want someone else to have a chance to enjoy while they're still in good shape.

I'm not immune to the hoarding instinct, myself. Shoes are my downfall. When I joined the cast of *DWTS*, I knew I was going to have a lot less time on the home front, and I wanted as much of that precious time as possible to be spent enjoying my family. So I went on a rampage, determined for my own peace of mind to get everything organized before the show began taping. Anything we didn't use was either tossed, donated, regifted, or handed down to a sibling. When I got to my own closet, though, I took one look at the hopeless jumble and knew it was time to call in an expert. My stylist dispatched her assistant, Kayla, to the rescue. The goal was to get rid of everything I wasn't going to wear or shouldn't be wearing, and to organize what was left in a way that would make it easy for me to put together whatever look I needed in a minute.

It took Kayla four days to pull everything out and sort through it, then rearrange it in fabulously logical order. I prefer open shelves to lots of drawers, so I can easily spot the Stitch's jeans that go with my classic Missoni tops. Dresses arranged by season, occasion, and color mean I never have to hunt for the pale yellow Chloe number with maroon butterflies that always puts David in a romantic mood. When I'm packing for vacation, I know now that all my summery beach dresses are neatly rolled up in their own bin, and that swimsuits have their own home, as well. Kayla even put little labels on all the shelves, so now I'm trained to keep graphic tees in one stack, arranged by color, and solid tees in another. Getting my closet that organized also took some hard-core purging ("But that black Barely Brooke bikini was my first calendar shot!"), but I soldiered through. Really, how many white tank tops or black yoga pants do you need? The excavation also uncovered some long-lost favorites that had been hidden or had fallen behind something else, like the classic black Chanel evening bag that's fifteen years old now but will never go out of style. And the pair of cowboy boots from my old country-bar stompin' days in Arizona—you'd pay five times as much in a Rodeo Drive boutique now for boots as perfectly beaten up and worn in as those. Definitely keepers.

Yep, everything was going just fine and dandy with the closet face-lift until I found the box Kayla had stuffed with shoes to donate. *Whoa, not so fast, sister! Getting organized is one thing, going crazy is another. . . .* I promptly stole several pairs back. Hey, I don't care how ugly and out of fashion my purple and green silk Pradas are, I still love them! Seriously, what was the girl thinking?! Despite the contraband shoes, my closet rocked when we were done, and I can't tell you how much time and frustration I've saved by not having to search for what I want to wear. We put together five outfits for day time and five for evening, complete with accessories right there on the hangers, so I always have instant ready-to-wear options when I'm not in the mood or don't have the time to think about what I want to put on.

naked truth I hide in my closet when I need a good cry. (It's the only space that's all mine.)

CHILD LABOR

Even though I'm lucky enough to hire pros to help me with housecleaning, I consider it a blessing, not an entitlement, and I don't want my kids growing up lazy as a result. They're expected to help clean, and to earn some of the toys, electronics, and privileges they enjoy. And anyone who's there to help our household run more smoothly—whether it's a nanny or a housekeeper or a gardener—is to be treated with respect and appreciation. I still shudder when I think of one diamond-encrusted Hollywood brat I know who thought she was so cool she had to wear sunglasses to dinner in a nice restaurant. I run into her sometimes shopping on her own in the Beverly Hills boutiques, flashing Daddy's credit card at the age of fourteen and dismissively handing her bags to her driver to carry. No way are my daughters skipping down that yellow brick road! Once, Neriah bopped home from a sleepover with a slip of paper listing the chichi shops where, she announced, I should buy her clothes from now on. Guess again, Paris Hilton.

It's not just neatness, or common courtesy, or a touch of humility that I'm after: Establishing order in our lives, to me, doesn't revolve around some rigid system of white-glove inspections and unbreakable rules. This is our home, not a military academy. I do demand that the kids make their beds, keep laundry off the floor, and (pet peeve) not shout from room to room if they want me. (By the way, if you slam a door, you lose the door. Mommy has a screwdriver, and she knows how to use it.)

Order, to me, is about keeping a flow of positive energy in

the naked mom

our hectic lives. I admit that the control freak in me yearns to have everything done perfectly, but that would mean wasting an hour or more of time I don't have to spare—not to mention a couple of gallons of ga$—running around town until I found the perfect elegant silver paper and black velvet bow to wrap a hostess gift, instead of just sucking up my disappointment in the first shop and deciding that maroon and gold will work just fine.

Figuring out a system to run a household efficiently isn't a one-size-fits-all undertaking. Some people want a playroom where blue LEGOs go in one container and red LEGOs go in another, while others are happy just to have the LEGOs not go in their foot. It's tempting to look at a gorgeous magazine spread and imagine that the chaos in your life will vanish if you just replicate what they've done. But you have to be realistic, and match the solution to your lifestyle. Flip through a variety of articles, Web sites, and books on organization, and pull the tips that seem like the best fit for your household. But before you dive in to reorganize everything in a spring cleaning frenzy, ask yourself a few key questions:

- What's the easiest way for us all to meet our various obligations, pursue our various interests, and achieve our various goals?
- How do we, as a family, collectively create an environment where each individual can thrive?
- What are the most critical problem areas? If I made a list of what I wanted to achieve in those areas, and what it would take to accomplish each of those things, how many would be doable in a week or within a month?

171

I happen to be a very visual person, so my own system relies heavily on corkboards, behavior charts, and calendars or planners. My ultimate survival guide is the big weekly tear-away calendar that I keep on a counter in the kitchen. In the laundry room hallway on the way to the garage, I keep a corkboard with all time-sensitive reminders and permission slips, as well as a key hook that's too high for Shaya to reach (he's in his steal-and-hide phase). I stock up on school supplies at the start of the year and semester breaks, and keep a container full of anything I can think of that will spare me those frantic nine p.m. Target scavenger hunts for the missing components of a third-grade diorama due the next morning.

With the kids, I get out the colored markers, stickers, and glitter glue to make a behavior chart. Everyone lists not only their chores but also the behaviors they're working on ("no eye rolling," "sleeping in my own bed," and so on). They also get to choose a few prizes they're working toward (I try to keep a lid on materialism by suggesting fun rewards like family dance night in the living room, or going to a favorite park). We do a daily evaluation and talk about what we need to work on as well as what they're already good at. That daily check-in is the most important part of the process, because it not only encourages positive behavior and self-awareness in the kids, it holds me accountable to acknowledge what they're doing right and heap on the praise instead of mostly scolding them for what they do wrong. Each child accumulates points for tasks completed or good behavior, and we tally them up at the end of the month. I also love to see a little face light up and beam with pride when I award random points for something they weren't expecting ("I noticed how great you were at keeping Shaya entertained while we were running errands this morning, thank you!").

As for consequences, it depends on the offense, obviously. Wet towels on the floor or lights left on mean going to bed ten minutes early, and complaining about what's being served for dinner is a free ticket to go to your room without any. Sometimes, the natural consequences of their own actions motivate them to change their behavior: More than one daughter has learned the hard way that fussing over what to wear in the morning might mean driving to school in her underwear and getting dressed on the way.

bulking up

SOMETIMES IT SEEMS like we have a birthday party to go to every weekend. I look for toy-of-the-year awards and buy a dozen of the same thing in each of my kids' age ranges. Then we prewrap and label them so they're ready to go. (Not that they're sexist, but I don't think boys in my fifth-grader's class really want to decorate their own jewelry boxes!) Likewise, when I come across a great hostess gift like the pretty decoupage vases a local artist makes, I buy several to wrap and stash.

Speaking of getting dressed, I can't forget my biggest disaster-relief tip for families on the go: Always have a change of clothes for everyone packed in an emergency bag in the car. Remember to switch out the kids' spare clothes seasonally, or you'll find yourself trying to redress a carsick six-year-old in the size 4 tee you packed six months ago. And don't forget a spare shirt and pants for yourself. Especially when traveling. If I sound overly emphatic on that point, it's just a traumatic flashback to the time baby Neriah did a projectile number on me on an international flight. Of course I had a complete change for her in the carry-on, but I hadn't considered the possibility that I would need one, too. All I had was my emergency overnight bag. I ended up going through customs in my pajamas.

CHILL OUT

I totally envy my daughter's bearded dragon. Spike is a master escape artist, and when life at Chez Charvet got to be too chaotic for him, he once bolted and disappeared for good. Or so we thought, until the gardener called me outside one day a full year later. There was Spike, alive and seemingly well, and (or so he thought) blissfully by himself on a patch of dirt beneath our house. Can't say that I blame him: Under our house is *way* more peaceful than inside it. I scoped out his hideaway thoughtfully, not so much wondering how to get him out but whether I could wedge myself in.

What mom hasn't dreamed of running away at some point? Just for a weekend, or even a day, or maybe a couple of hours? Or hell, yes, I'll even take twenty minutes! Carving out some me time is hands down the most difficult thing to do when you're a mom. Face it, we always put our own needs last, anyway, and by the time we get to those, we can usually only cram in what's absolutely necessary, like getting a mammogram. Maybe you make yourself little promises to keep going—if I just get through this big project at work and the twins' birthday, I'll treat myself to a facial, or a girls' night out with my friends.

But chilling out shouldn't be the reward for how well you function, it should be part of *how* you function. And you'd be surprised by how much you can benefit from showing yourself a little compassion and the occasional random act of kindness. You can't dance through the chaos unless you learn to let go sometimes. You have to be willing to trust, and surrender to the strength of others, to laughter, and to the oh-so-human need to sometimes have space to yourself.

On my first day of work as the cohost of *Dancing with the Stars*, I remember feeling so excited as I pulled my car into the studio lot, but as I walked past security and down the hallway to my dressing room, the excitement turned to anxiety. It wasn't like me to be so nervous, and at first, I couldn't figure out what the deal was. Then it dawned on me that the jitters were a form of muscle memory from when I would walk this very hallway as a contestant on *DWTS*. I needed to turn off my internal oh-God-not-the-jive-again alarm. I thought I had it pretty much under control by the time I was introduced to the studio audience for the first time, but Tom Bergeron must have sensed my apprehension as I took my place onstage next to him. He put his hand on my shoulder and looked me in the eye.

"I'm right here if you need me," he said.

I instantly relaxed. I needed a partner to dance me through that momentary chaos, and there was something very beautiful and comfortable about being able to count on someone when I needed it. I'll always be so grateful to Tom for that compassionate gesture.

Tom also gave me another priceless gift when I joined the *DWTS* cast, sharing his own preshow ritual for clearing his head before going onstage. Clear your dressing room so you can meditate for twenty minutes, he advised me. That was going to be a challenge for me: My dressing room was usually a three-ring circus. My kids would often be there, spazzing out and clamoring for my attention, while my mom tried to engage me in a conversation about weekend plans, and my glam squad hovered around putting the final touches on my hair and makeup. Friends I'd invited to the show would drop by and want to catch up. The sound guy would come in to get me miked, my producer would be popping in with last-minute notes, and David would be gazing earnestly into my eyes, urging me to take deep, calming breaths. It was all pretty obnoxious. Sometimes Randy Jackson would wander across the hall from *American Idol* just to survey the scene and shake his head (whether it was dismay or pity, I can't say). The *Idol* bodyguards who routinely line our shared hallway would also creep closer to my door in a maneuver clearly devised to ensure that the craziness stayed contained within my borders.

Tom was right; I totally needed to chill out before doing a live performance. So I pushed aside my worries about coming off like a diva and politely issued a new mandate: The little sitting area adjacent to my makeup room was going to be off-limits to everyone from here on out, so I could have my own retreat and just sit on the sofa and get myself in the zone. I don't always get twenty minutes, but even ten or five help. It's become a calming ritual now.

Ritual plays an important role to center my family as well as my professional life. As I mentioned earlier, David's mother hosts Shabbat dinner for the extended family some Fridays, and the beautiful, warm intimacy of that meal—the candles glowing, watching my children participate in the religious traditions—is like a soothing touchstone no matter how insane my schedule has been.

My posse of girlfriends can also be counted on to bring the stress level down when I need to lighten up. My dear friend Cyvia Lewis is adamant about giving herself an occasional girls' night out or spa weekend away from her hectic life as a mom and makeup artist. One evening after the show, I watched her heading off for a night on the town with the gang from *Dancing with the Stars*. I envied the way she could claim some fun for herself without feeling guilty about leaving her husband to handle the kids. "You inspire me!" I called after her. She turned around and laughed. "You inspire me," she replied, "to get my ass home!" Cyvia even went off for occasional girls-only getaway weekends. I had always begged off from the overnight trips, but finally agreed when we arranged one at a Four Seasons just forty minutes from my house. I snuck out of the house during my littlest ones' afternoon naptime, and got to the hotel in time to enjoy a late lunch with Cyvia and my good friend Denise Richards. We ordered wine and felt totally decadent. We gabbed about men, exes, life, and everything under the sun except kids. Then we headed to the spa, where I went into total wet-noodle mode, taking a steam bath and bubbling away in the Jacuzzi before getting the most amazing massage. I could feel the tension lifting off my shoulders and floating away.

I retreated to my room, lit some scented candles I'd brought (they're as essential as my toothbrush when I go anywhere!), and flopped into bed, where I promptly fell asleep for eight delicious hours. That was the most therapeutic thing of all! We play musical beds in my house, and a night of uninterrupted sleep is pretty much an impossible dream. (I know moms who live for their "sleepcations"—they either hit a hotel for a night or just wait for the kids to be away at Grandma's or a slumber party, then they climb into bed at eight p.m., and turn the lights off early just to sleep for eight or ten hours. I don't care what the experts say, you can, too, catch up on your zzzs!)

I woke up in my hotel bed 110 percent refreshed after my girlfriend getaway day. I ordered a pot of coffee, and spent a lazy morning in bed reading a stack of fashion magazines while watching *Good Morning America* instead of *Dora the Explorer*. I know it probably sounds pretty mundane, but it felt wonderfully self-indulgent. I'd almost forgotten how nice it is just to enjoy your own company once in a while. I finally roused myself enough to hit the hotel gym for a workout, then met my friends for a lovely poolside lunch before checking out. I was home by two in the afternoon. My mommycation had lasted barely twenty-four hours, but that short interlude really revived me when I needed it.

Even if you can't get away for a quick battery recharge, you can still treat yourself to a mini "staycation" at home. Conspire with a friend to trade playdates so each of you ends up with a few hours alone (or, if your kids are old enough, arrange for sleepovers). Promise yourself ahead of time that you will not use your kid-free hours to run errands, do chores, or catch up on any work. Keep a bucket list of things you dream of doing, and include some alone-time fantasies in there, even if it's just "get a facial" or "go to a chick flick and eat a tub of hot buttered popcorn in the middle of the afternoon." Maybe you're more adventurous, and skydiving is on your bucket list. If there's an airport and skydiving school within driving distance, all you need is one free day to make that fantasy a reality. Go for it! Or take yourself to the beach without having to worry about watching or entertaining the kids. If you yearn for girly pampering and a day spa is beyond your budget, create your own. I love making my own natural hair conditioners and face masks with everyday ingredients like olive oil, avocados, eggs, and oatmeal. The point is to just step back from the noise and demands of your everyday life, and indulge yourself for a few hours. And if that's totally impossible, then retreat to your favorite chair, or the guest room, and just put your feet up and daydream for a few stolen minutes.

Stealing those minutes sometimes takes a bit of ingenuity. I think cars have some weird vibe that causes chaos to instantly increase about tenfold. Everything that drives me crazy drives me craziest when I'm driving. The clutter, the noise level—magnified inside that big metal box. But I've discovered a secret weapon: the Silent Game. My kids love it. "Ready, set, go!" I call out when I feel like my head is going to explode. I turn off the radio, and the kids instantly fall quiet, competing to see who can stay silent the longest. The first one to utter a sound loses. Sometimes the game lasts fifteen minutes, and sometimes only five. But sometimes five minutes of peace is all I need.

Grabbing unexpected moments when they present themselves is the mommy equivalent of redeeming a lottery ticket. I remember one evening when David and I decided to forgo the family supper scene and just feed the kids and get them tucked in so we could enjoy a quiet dinner à deux. Everything was going as planned, and I uncorked a nice bottle of wine to breathe while David put Shaya and Rain down for the night. I'd bought a beautiful steak, and I tossed a fresh salad while I was waiting. And waiting.

And waiting.

Finally, I tiptoed upstairs, and found David sacked out in Shaya's room. Sound asleep. At first, I was annoyed, and I briefly contemplated waking him up. He was ruining our romantic dinner! Then I realized that the house was perfectly quiet. Hmmm. Not only that, but I could slip into my jammies, pour myself a glass of that nice wine, put my delicious dinner on a tray, and eat in bed while watching a sappy chick flick. *Poor David needs his rest, I should just leave him be.* I swear my compassion had nothing to do with the prospect of sprawling out in the middle of our bed and having it all to myself for a night. Forget disappointment—I was my own dream date!

Life is full of unexpected curveballs. You can step aside when you see them coming, or take a crazy swing and aim for the bleachers. And if you strike out and fall on your ass, which is bound to happen once in a while, the best thing you can possibly do is just sit there in the dirt and laugh. The ability to laugh at yourself is often the most graceful way to glide through an awkward situation. When I raced out of the house one day and got to the market before realizing I was barefoot, I found David's gym bag in the truck and put on his size 12 sneakers. I looked like a clown. But why worry about someone else laughing at me, or the paparazzi getting off an embarrassing shot, when I could snap a picture myself with my phone and tweet it to 1.7 million followers right away? Humor trumps humiliation.

My mom, Donna, with me and my big sister, Kimberly.

My first bikini shot.

Next stop, the orthodontist.

Desperately seeking hair products in junior high.

Neriah, 3, cuddles baby sis, Sierra, 1. If only they could always get along so well!

Buddha Brooke—feels like I've been pregnant all my life.

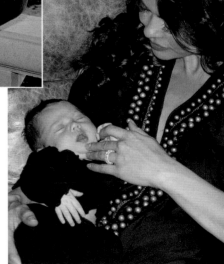

And baby Rain makes three.

My two favorite hotties.

Pure mommy bliss.

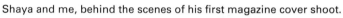

Shaya and me, behind the scenes of his first magazine cover shoot.

Sex and the city:
romancing in New York.

Vintage Brooke and David, love
at first sight in Mexico, 1992.

Getting older,
getting hotter—
I love the scruff!

Chilling in Mexico, 2009.

Setting sail in Sardinia,
summer 2010.

Four kids, fourteen bags, seven airplanes and twelve meltdowns—
our first European vacation together as a family.

The highlight of my career was when I became a sesame seed bun.

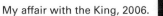

My affair with the King, 2006.

With Gilby Clark, Dave Navarro, and Tommy Lee on the set of *Rock Star: Supernova*. Too bad I can't sing and I'm about ten tattoos short!!! I always dreamed of being a drummer though.

The apple doesn't fall far from the tree.

Derek Hough, me, and
Tom Bergeron backstage.

Tom and I waiting for our cue to go live.

Rain sneaks into the *DWTS*
audience and hijacks the
mike, hoping to introduce
Miley Cyrus.

Diamonds? Check. Fake lashes? Check.
Sleeping baby? Check. Bucket of toys?
Check. Multitasking at work with Shaya
and Batman.

Nothing is sweeter than family time.

Girl power! Hanging on the beach in Malibu with my daughters.

Laughing to myself—and standing with my legs really close together—was also all I could do the time I paraded onstage at *DWTS* and spotted Cyvia sitting in the front row. Her lips were moving in a slow, exaggerated fashion, and I realized she was mouthing something at me:

I see your black thong!!

(All righty, then! We'll just make a mental note about backlighting onstage and the sheer panel in this black Herve Leger dress, and hope that 20 million viewers at home aren't pointing at their TV screens right now shouting, "I see London. I see France . . . !")

Back to you, Tom!

But my fondest chaos moment of all came on a recent family vacation. We were in a restaurant, and Shaya proceeded to throw his twelfth tantrum of the trip. Everyone was glaring, Shaya was not going to be placated, and I reached that point where I just couldn't take it anymore. I left the table to go outside for some air. When I came back a few minutes later, eight-year-old Sierra got up and came over to my chair and began to massage my shoulders.

"Everything's going to be okay, Mommy," she soothed, assuming her little yoga pose. "Just breathe."

naked truth I like to jump on the beds with my kids when we're in hotels. Pillow fights and splashing in the bathtub are also permissible when we're not at home. It's good to break the rules once in a while! Because I'm the mommy and I said so, that's why.

digital fox

I'm raising my own geek squad. Rain is already a budding hacker.

I WASN'T BORN a geek, but I've become a true believer thanks to the persuasive powers of a chicken. Not just any run-of-the-mill drumstick, mind you. Chickie was a tiny, $5.99 yellow plushie who happened to be the most beloved possession of my friend Lisa's eighteen-month-old daughter, Chloe. Chloe fell asleep every night with her little fingers wrapped around one of Chickie's soft, dangly legs. If any of your children have ever had an attachment to a toy, then you will appreciate Lisa's absolute panic the day Chickie flew the coop. Losing your child's favorite toy isn't like misplacing your car keys or cell phone. It's like misplacing a family member—like Nana being in the backseat, and then an hour later, she's slipped into a black hole in the universe. You can't just say, "All gone!" and think a juice box is going to fix it.

Lisa painstakingly retraced all her steps that day, trying to imagine where Chloe might have dropped Chickie. She conducted scorched-earth sweeps of any vehicle, diaper bag, hamper, sofa cushion, or appliance where Chickie might conceivably hide. The family dog was interrogated, but no evidence of fowl play was found and no charges could be brought. To make matters even worse, Chickie's manufacturer had gone out of business; the Baby Style store where Lisa had originally bought the bird had shut its doors for good. (With two toddlers of my own, I was such a regular there that I could have kicked myself for not thinking to pick up some backup Chickies for Lisa on one of my forays, not that my hindsight would do them any good now. But . . . lesson learned about buying stunt doubles for treasured toys.)

Needless to say, the tragic Chickie affair put Lisa's entire household in a state of turmoil for the better part of a week. Chloe was inconsolable, Lisa was frantic, and as a good friend and fellow mommy, I ached for them both. Lisa also happens to be my business partner at Modern Mom; she and her husband, Demand Media founder Richard Rosenblatt, are considered Internet royalty. I mention this because they're the savviest surfers I know (Lisa cofounded iMall—the girl knows how to find stuff!), so when it came to searching cyberspace for another Chickie, they left no window unopened. Lisa even tracked down the vendors who had bought up the closed store's leftover inventory. No Chickies. In the plushie world, this bird was extinct with a capital *E*.

Lisa traipsed into our shared office at Modern Mom, defeated and forlorn.

"What am I going to do?" she worried.

We did what we always do best as moms running a company: We went downstairs to see what munchies we could mooch off Demand Media's free snack café (chocolate pretzels—yum!); then we brainstormed together and drafted a plan of action. Extreme circumstances, we concluded, called for extreme measures. We decided to send out an all-points bulletin across Mommyville.

As the representative mom voice of Modern Mom, I was blogging about parenting issues regularly anyway, and I also had a fabulous flock of fans—over 1.2 million of them—following me on Twitter. I logged on to my computer and sounded the alarm:

"ATTENTION, ALL MOMS! We have lost Chickie. . . ."

We figured that someone out there probably had a gently used Chickie their child had outgrown or wouldn't miss, and could sell to us, or maybe a mom in another state knew of a store in her town that still carried the toy and would be willing to ship. We attached a photo to our blog appeal, set up a special Chickie e-mail account for responses, and waited. I tweeted a PMHOGC! (pulling my hair out going crazy!) plea for good measure.

It didn't take long.

Hundreds of people replied. Kindhearted strangers combed the Internet and sent us possible leads to new Chickie suppliers (no luck). One proud husband boasted that his wife could sew anything, and he offered to have her stitch together a new Chickie for us (sweet, but we couldn't help but notice she would be doing the work and *he* would be getting the credit . . .). People suggested all kinds of substitutes—how about this duckie, or a fluffy baby owl? Would a cute little penguin do? Other moms who had survived similar ordeals offered advice on dealing with the trauma of an AWOL attachment toy. The support and encouragement were overwhelming.

Then, three days later, the FedEx man arrived at our Modern Mom office to deliver not one but two packages containing Chickies from families who were kind enough to part with theirs. Chloe was overjoyed, Lisa was grateful and relieved, and I was touched beyond words. I realized for the first time that what we had built wasn't merely a business but a vibrant community, and that the true power of social media wasn't about how quickly or broadly we could connect, but how meaningfully. These weren't hits on a site; they were friends. There was nothing virtual about this Modern Mom village of women—and dads!—eager to bond via computer to pool their knowledge and experience, share triumphs and missteps, laugh, vent, cry, and just enjoy the company of fellow travelers on the sometimes lonely road of raising a family.

I may be the de facto mayor of our ever-growing community, but I'm also an enthusiastic citizen, and I've relied on the collective wisdom of my cybervillage many a time to help me through a crisis of my own. I'm sure many of you are used to doing it all yourself, and never asking for help. I used to be that mom, too, but not anymore. Sharing info mommy to mommy has become my most valuable source of support. This is literally where all my chickens come home to roost!

SLEEPING WITH MAC

I was resistant at first. I've always been wary of change, to tell the truth, and as far as I'm concerned, anything that lends itself to one of those *For Dummies* manuals cannot possibly be fun. But before I even knew what was happening, I was sleeping with Mac. Just to clarify, I'm not the fickle type—my heart doesn't start racing with anticipation whenever a hot new gadget or app arrives on the scene. Technology seduced me on my own terms, slowly but insistently, with a clever prompt here, a coy suggestion there—I'm always motivated by the desire to make my life as fun and easy as possible. My mistakes were never ridiculed and my screwups never mentioned beyond a gentle, *"Did you mean . . . ?"* (If only men could be programmed so easily!)

I knew I'd fallen hard when I started seeking out my laptop for secret midnight rendezvous while my unsuspecting man slumbered beside me. At first, I told myself it didn't mean anything, that I just had to sift through my e-mails, and the best time to catch up on my Modern Mom workload was while the rest of the house slept. *Oh, God, I hope this doesn't ding or beep and wake anyone up!* I thought as I answered a bunch of interoffice e-mails from my Modern Mom staff. My fear was short-lived. Within minutes, replies began pinging into my inbox. I had to smile when I realized what was happening: We're all parents at Modern Mom—not guys in business suits sitting behind desks cranking out canned "mom content"—and like me, my co-madres were using the witching hour between kids crashing and Mommy turning in for the night to catch up on things.

Running my babooshbaby.com business and the Modern-Mom.com Web site, I've definitely gotten my geek on these past few years: Now I blog, text, tweet, link, stream . . . and wring all I can out of the Internet. I don't want technology to take over my life, but I'm not going to miss out on ways to simplify it. If the Internet is going to save me time, save me money, and make me more organized, then I'm logging on. The ever-changing technology and constantly updated choices of new gadgets, applications, shortcuts, and so forth can be intimidating, to say the least. And not always ready for prime time, as I learned the time I got all excited about voice-recognition software and dictated a business letter to my computer, only to have the salutation mysteriously transcribed as "Dear Sausage Breath." Glad I proofread that one before hitting the send button. I may not be able to spell "algorithms" without spell check, but I know what they are and what they can do for me. You don't need a computer science degree to make technology serve you like an impeccably trained cabana boy—the beauty of it is how user-friendly technology has become, and how easy it is to shape until you have what you want. It's like a virtual lump of Play-Doh, and you just gotta get your fingers in there and start working it! Whether you're shopping, paying your bills, or socializing, there is no question that technology provides the best tools in today's world for making life more efficient. That holds true for running a business or running a household—or both.

The most exciting part for me was when I kicked it up a notch, and began to appreciate the power of social bridging, which is all about making one platform feed the other: Your tweet about the cool kitchen gadget you just found on sale can drive traffic back to the foodie blog you created to share recipes and ideas, which in turn can provide a link to a virtual pal's great home-based custom-cupcake business. Symbiosis is the first law of cyberspace. Social media is the ultimate word-of-mouth: If you're looking for a job, or house-hunting in a particular neighborhood, announcing your search on your Facebook page or even in a round-robin e-mail to all your friends and contacts can put their friends and contacts on the lookout for you, too.

The Internet offers far more to moms these days than frantic Google-thons trying to print out everything there is to know about wallabies for a hysterical fourth-grader's *huge* project due the next morning. My laptop (or, more recently, the iPad I got for my birthday) goes with me everywhere, in a cute black case on wheels. At home, it's usually on the breakfast counter that serves as Mission Control in our kitchen. I'm always going to ehow.com for quick answers or how-to videos on everything from how to grill an artichoke to the best way to get glitter glue out of my favorite sweater. I go online to shop in bulk for household staples and school supplies, and even get great discounts by setting up regular deliveries (and if you check for super-saver discounts on your favorite shopping sites, you can often get the swag sent to your doorstep for free). I'm not just looking for products online, though; I'm looking for kindred spirits, too, to offer helpful advice, food for thought, or just a pat on the back when I could use one. Think of it as having all the smart, generous friends you could ever wish for, constantly available, twenty-four hours a day, and they never get sick of your neediness. Where else can you rant, rave, or just have a good therapeutic cry without having to make an appointment or provide proof of insurance? You can go straight to the source now when you want the 411 on something. Planning your first family vacation in eons and obsessing over the possibilities? You can find entire blogs about popular destinations, with advice from folks who've been there, done that and are ready to share the down-low about everything from how to minimize your time waiting in lines at Disney World to where the port-a-potties can be found in the Grand Canyon. Wondering what Paris has to offer for tweens? Do a search for expats living in the City of Light—trust me, there'll be plenty of groups to choose from—and get your answers from locals.

The moms I've never met but *know* in my alternate universe have become my go-to resource, and I've enjoyed sharing what I've learned along the way with them, as well. Without ever actually meeting, they know me in a way that's fun, interactive, and far more personal than any TV talk-show interview or feature in a celeb magazine. I'm able to break through the wall of traditional media and actually engage with my audience. No script, no talking points, no publicists or stylists or producers. Just me. When I say something online, anyone can respond with their own question or comment, and I can choose to elaborate, explain, or just chat back. ("Is this really you?" people always ask. "Prove it!") I like having some control over my own story out there in the public arena. I can instantly shoot down rumors (no, LOL, Carrie Ann Inaba and I didn't bitch-slap each other over gowns to wear on *DWTS*—we have different styles, and actually alert each other when we come across a gown or jewelry we know the other will like). And I can also inadvertently start rumors, as I discovered one night when Lisa and I decided to polish off a bottle of cabernet and post a blog, in that order. It seemed like a great idea at the time. Giggling like fourteen-year-olds, we posted an item hinting that I might be expecting baby number five. Unfortunately, *nobody* looked at the April 1 date, and before I knew it my manager was getting inundated with media calls, and my prank was reposted as hot breaking news by gossip columnists from here to Zimbabwe and back. I knew I was in the doghouse when my indignant mom called me first thing that morning: "Brooke, are you *pregnant*?!" she demanded, hurt and angry that she'd had to find out about her (nonexistent) grandchild from an entertainment reporter. It took all day to stuff that bad genie back in the bottle.

But as I sifted guiltily through the scores of congratulatory e-mails, comments, and tweets from my cyber-tribe, I was reminded yet again of how familiar we've all become to one another, and how rewarding the exchange generally is. As a celebrity, it's a safe way for me to engage, let my hair down, and feel a part of, instead of apart from, the people I most identify with—other moms. (Even though it is a little weird when I emerge from a bathroom stall in some public place and a total stranger who's been following my tweets greets me with a too-cozy, "Oh, hey! How's Rain feeling? I know she was sick this morning!") For better or for worse, with social media, we're letting each other inside our real lives, in real time. Just how real is something I found out at two-thirty one memorable morning, when I was on the verge of mommy meltdown.

With my first two kids, I was an ardent believer in attachment parenting, including the concept of a family bed, which was not only a great bonding experience but also practical when I had my firstborn, since Neriah traveled everywhere with me when I was shooting *Wild On* and we would share a hotel bed. That was a decade ago, and I remember how I was thirsting for information, but didn't have the time to do any research in that neo-Google era. Sure, I had every baby book imaginable, but I was the pioneer among my friends in becoming a mother, so I didn't have any peers who could help me sort through all that expert advice in all those books, and tell me what really worked and what was hot air from someone with degrees out the wazoo but no real experience whatsoever in extracting raisins from a small nostril. If I'd had Internet access to Mommyville back then, I probably would have floated the family-bed idea first, and a zillion people who knew what they were talking about would have warned me that if you let your child into your bed, you will never get them out. And that if you have additional children, and add them to that bed, they, too, will never leave, and you will quite possibly find yourself someday sandwiched between eight thrashing feet and eight jabbing elbows, and that's not counting your husband's, because there was no room for him and he decamped to one of the kid's unused beds many zzzzzs ago. You know this because you can hear him snoring contentedly in the room down the hall, and if you could figure out how to extricate yourself from the middle of this child sandwich, you would march right in there and jostle him back to conscious- ness so you could innocently whisper, "Are you awake?" Not that I would ever, ever even dream of doing such a spiteful thing, but only because I can't dream, because *I can't sleep!* Truth be told, I haven't slept in ten years. If anyone ever pro- duces a reality show called *Zombie Mommies*, I'm a shoo-in.

But wait, that wasn't my meltdown. That came when I decided that I had to sleep-train my two youngest. Rain is tricky, since she favors the stealth maneuver of silently slip- ping into Mommy and Papa's bed sometime before dawn, when we're too exhausted to get up and take her back to her own room. Shaya, though, is a different story. David usually lies down with him in our bed while I'm reading Rain a bed- time story in her bed, and once Shaya is asleep, David puts him in his crib. Invariably, Shaya then wakes up screaming in the middle of the night, and won't stop until I bring him back to our bed, which I always do right away so he doesn't wake up his older sisters. Determined to break this exhausting cycle, I did my research and found the most successful method. When Shaya began to cry, I was supposed to go in after ten minutes, tell him it was night-night time and that I loved him, then leave again—no cuddling, holding, patting, or stroking. If he kept crying, I was to wait another fifteen minutes and repeat the drill, and keep repeating it at increasingly longer intervals, until he sobbed himself to sleep. Everyone said it would be hell for a few nights, but then the problem would be solved once and for all. I steeled myself for the worst, and Shaya quickly obliged.

That first night, I was ready to cave after maybe four minutes. I can't recall whether David was somehow sleeping through Shaya's despair or if he was out of town on a movie shoot—I just remember that it was two-thirty in the morning and I was dying inside as I sat in my own bed and listened to my baby cry. Desperate to distract myself, I opened up my iPhone and started tapping the keys. *Trying to sleep-train my youngest*, I tweeted into the lonely night. Shaya kept wailing. *I just want to go in there and get him!*

Before I knew it, return tweets started popping up on my screen:

You can get through this, you're doing great! a mom in the Midwest cheered me on.

Don't go in there, Brooke! He'll be fine, someone else promised.

I was stunned, and a little embarrassed. What was I doing? I just needed to vent, but I wasn't going to call my best friend and wake her—and her family—at absurd o'clock in the morning. So now I was having this intimate conversation with people I didn't even know. Who were up at two-thirty in the morning. Or maybe they were in Australia, and it was seven-thirty at night. Whoever and wherever, it was bizarre, but at the same time, very powerful. Like being embraced. I put the phone down and stared at it for a moment, wondering when it had downloaded a soul. Unnerved by both my public vulnerability and Shaya's ordeal, I padded into my son's room to do the next check-in, feeling even more miserable as he sobbed, "Maamaaaa, Maammmaaaaaa!" when I turned my back on him again. I wasn't sure I could take this much longer. I hungrily checked my TweetDeck again. Even more parents had sent words of encouragement. The next time I went to Shaya's room, I took the phone with me.

He's still crying, I told my unseen support group, *and now I'm sitting outside his door crying, too.*

Do not go in there!!! a father of five admonished me.

Others chimed in: *You're doing great . . . you're a good mother . . . it's hard, I know, I've been there, too . . . he's just testing you . . . it'll be over in 3 nights, I promise. . . .*

Shaya and I both made it through that god-awful night, though I have to confess that he ultimately won the war by figuring out that if he cries until he pukes, I'll have to rescue him. So no, he's still not sleep-trained. I know, I know: I'm weak. But I know my tweeties will forgive me and pop in again the next time I need them.

One of the things I love the most about social media is how it organically draws from all sorts of sources you wouldn't necessarily think of turning to for particular information or problem solving. Case in point: When I posted a blog on Modern Mom fretting about finding my couples groove again with David after we'd been apart for three months while he was working abroad, I received some sage advice from an army wife who had responded in my Comments section. Her marriage was built around her husband's deployments and home-comings, and she thoughtfully shared her wisdom about recon-necting. Granted, shooting a TV show is hardly comparable to a tour of combat duty, but she was too compassionate to trivi-alize my circumstances. I appreciated her suggestion that I ask David what he wanted for a homecoming meal, and what he was missing the most, and not to stage any big surprise parties or celebrations that would force him to immediately be on, when he probably really would just need to decompress a bit and ease slowly back into family life. I would have never thought of asking friends and relatives—including our par-ents—to hold off calling or visiting for a few days without Army Wife's input, and that turned out to be the smartest advice ever. David didn't have to spend his first few days tell-ing the same stories over and over to everyone who was eager to catch up, and we got some quiet alone time to sort of reshuf-fle ourselves again as a family.

Of course, for all the kindred spirits you'll find out there in cyberspace, there are bound to be haters, as well. I have to say that my followers show a lot more interest in my everyday mom challenges than in the celebrity aspect of my life. I get bagged on big-time for posting pictures of a beautiful sunset while vacationing in the Caribbean, but everyone loves it when I share a picture of my clown feet in David's size 12 sneakers. Opening my life for public viewing does have some risks, but so far they've been minimal. I let the authorities deal with the truly scary or potentially dangerous, and otherwise, I just let the garden-variety haters have their say—if being ugly is what makes their little worlds go round, that's their prob-lem, not mine. I know some bloggers prefer to sort through their comments and post only the positive, or quickly take down the negative ones, but I like the idea of a spirited open forum where debate and controversy are part of the mix. Besides, it's easy enough these days to run filters to delete posts with inappropriate language. What I don't do is waste my time reading nasty comments (my mom can't help herself, though, and works herself into a lather no matter how many times I tell her the drive-by insults don't bother me). When she was competing on *Dancing with the Stars*, poor Kate Gosselin was a magnet for celeb bashers, and since she hadn't come up through the trenches of Hollywood, she didn't yet have the layers of thick skin you need to survive in this business. She often came across on-screen or in print as defensive because she was following the hurtful feedback and cruel chatter, and she felt under attack. You just have to be your own best filter, and treat social media the way you would a real encounter: If the person is upsetting you, move on and don't look back. If firing back a zinger of your own will make you feel better, that's your choice, but you don't need me to tell you that people who bait you are hoping for a reaction. Remember, you've got the supremely satisfying option of quietly blocking them if they're a Twitter follower or defriending them if they're a Facebook frenemy. Nothing shuts down an attention seeker faster than no attention at all.

MINDING YOUR OWN BUSINESS

I've always been one of those women who loves to come up with ideas and dream about marketing them. Look at the number of women whose phenomenal success stories began with nothing more than a little notion, like the mom and her little girls who got out their crafts box and decided to decorate their Crocs one day, and ended up inventing Jibbitz, those insanely popular little charms that fit in the shoes' holes. Right now, Etsy.com is all the rage for people who want to sell their handmade crafts or vintage items; you can use it as sort of a small test-market for the funky hobo bags you've always dreamed of designing, or just to make extra cash for the holidays by selling the collection of church-lady hats you inherited from your great-aunt. The first time I launched my own business, I sort of jumped right in without enough research, and naïvely funded the costly start-up myself—rookie mistakes. The misbegotten venture was an Italian swimsuit line I designed in the late nineties. I soon discovered that I didn't have anywhere near the time, energy, or capital it would take to market the high-end line to the masses. I was disappointed, but not discouraged.

My next bright idea came after I had Rain, when her French grandmother expressed dismay that I wasn't binding my belly to get my figure back, as I told you about in chapter three. That all led to the creation of Tauts and the babooshbaby.com Web site. I started my mommy blog on the company Web site as kind of a lark at first, figuring it would help build a customer base, but I was soon hooked. Blogging is basically my online diary. It's deeply therapeutic for me. It forces me to reflect before I write, and to be honest with myself. I have to ponder what's relevant in my life, what I'm doing right, what I'm doing wrong. Have I connected with my kids enough? Am I teaching them valuable lessons? What kind of partner am I?

It's similar to keeping a journal, but it ups the ante. When you blog, you're really putting yourself out there in a vulnerable way. You're inviting conversation or comment and feedback. That can be scary, but it's also enlightening. There are times when I'm on the fence about some situation, or maybe I'm reacting more than I'm listening. If I know I'm going to write about that particular topic, I think it forces me to handle it better. It's sort of like fighting alone or fighting in public: The very act of blogging often makes me make better choices. Just having that opportunity to be able to talk about things going on in my life and to share with other women and get feedback from them, to learn together, is nothing short of amazing. Is it always warm and fuzzy? Hell, no! Is it always valuable? Hell, yes! Even getting less than desirable feedback opens my mind more, and makes me consider other possibilities and different ways to handle things. It's exciting to have this intimate access to other people's philosophies and opinions, where it's not just your good friends cheering you on and telling you what you need or want to hear. In the Internet world, people just tell it like it is. There are plenty of women out there, too, who chime in and get more involved in the comments than actually reading stuff, because they just want to get their voices heard. Social media is a great way to vent, and feel a sense of validation and release.

The reason I blog is because it helps keep me real. It helps keep me accountable. It's an exchange. I'm always trying new things, changing my ways, making adjustments here and there to the way I live and love. It's an ongoing learning process. Sometimes, when I'm writing about my kids, I realize things I may not have seen in the moment—that a daughter's backtalk came from insecurity, not insubordination, maybe. More than once, replaying a scene for my blog has shown me where I screwed up.

But my real tech turning point came when Lisa and I started fantasizing about creating a Web site that could become a trusted source of mom-to-mom information, sharing ideas, relevant news (like Amber Alerts or consumer recalls), great must-have products, and life experiences. We envisioned thousands of articles, original content, videos, celebrated experts, interesting bloggers, and everyday moms accessible whenever you needed them, on one hip site covering the everyday life of the modern woman. Lisa and I had been friends for years because our kids attended the same school and played with each other, but we'd never realized that we had similar entrepreneurial streaks. We ended up buying a site that became Modern Mom, and merged it with babooshbaby.com, which had outgrown my mother's condo and now offered not only the original Tauts but body wraps to enhance workouts for men and women, too, as well as an ever-growing array of pregnancy and post-pregnancy products.

One weekend when we were all together at the Rosenblatts' mountain cabin, Richard urged me to sign up for a free social network called Twitter. I had no idea what he was talking about. When he explained the then-new platform to me—brief comments not exceeding 140 characters, "tweeted" out to a flock of followers that would grow virally—I was skeptical.

"Why would I want to let people into my personal life for a play by play?" I asked. Did I really want to be that vulnerable?

"Trust me," Richard replied. "This is going to be big. Just do it."

I agreed to give it a try; I could always shut it down if it wasn't good for me.

Yeah, just like I can give up coffee if I really want to. So let's just get this out of the way as quickly as possible, in less than 140 characters:

Hi, my name is Brooke, and I'm a Twitterholic.

Hi, Brooke! (That was from the world's estimated 10 to 15 million active Twitter users as of this writing.)

Just about anything and everything shows up in my tweets, from pictures of the bling I'm trying to decide to wear on *DWTS* that night to bulletins about my mortifying mommy moments, like Shaya peeing on our office floor during his first week of potty training. Personally, I only follow about twenty friends on Twitter, along with CNN and a couple of inspirational sites. At this minute, if I look at my TweetDeck, my animal-loving pal Denise Richards is trying to find a home for an abused German shepherd, while Lisa Rinna is wondering if anyone has ever snuck something into the house so their husband wouldn't know (check the guest room closet, Harry!). Tiny Buddha is tweeting a great quote from John Lennon: "Life is what happens while you are making other plans." So with just one quick glance, I'm reminded that the world is brimming with compassion, humor, and wisdom.

Tweeting is also a great way to advertise your business. Whenever I tweet about a special deal at babooshbaby.com, our sales skyrocket. Unlike a lot of celebs, I don't sell my tweets (some tabloid regulars command five figures a tweet for plugging products and places), but that's a personal decision to protect the authenticity of my own brands and image.

Authenticity is paramount to me, whether it's the words coming out of my cool avatar's mouth on the Wii "Get Moving: Family Fitness" workout game I did with JumpStart, or the words flying across my computer screen as I recount my latest adventures and misadventures in Mommyville. I know it sounds like a postmodern contradiction, but if you want to thrive in the virtual world, you have to be real. There is no software, app, or program that can give you that. Authenticity was actually the topic I chose to talk about when I was invited to speak at Web 2.0. I've yukked it up with my fair share of famous talk-show hosts over the course of my TV career, but I have to confess that I was nervous about addressing the geek elite. My fears were quickly allayed by the warm welcome, though, as I settled onto the couch next to fellow panelist Mark Cuban and we started talking tech. It was pretty mind-blowing to realize I was looking out at an audience of hard-core techies and Internet wizards whose collective passion and intellect will no doubt create tools in my children's lifetime that I can't even imagine now.

But in the meantime, if anyone's got an app to get your kids to sleep in their own beds, please tweet me a link. . . .

PULLING THE PLUG

An acquaintance of mine recently described her relationship to the Internet this way: "Wikipedia is like my dad, Google is my mom, and ehow.com is my best friend." I laughed knowingly, but at the same time, I felt a guilty twinge: Was I getting too attached to technology?

I've always been diligent about rationing the kids' media time, whether it's TV, their favorite Wii games, or the computer. One afternoon, when I had no other option but to take my kids to Modern Mom with me while I worked for a few hours, I looked up from my computer screen and saw Rain happily watching a movie she'd downloaded on my iPad, while Sierra played one of the games that came free with my phone, and Neriah exchanged messages with a friend on her iPod Touch. *Yech*, was my first guilty gut reaction, followed immediately by, *Thank God they're occupied*. It's such a double-edged sword; setting—and maintaining—boundaries requires a determination that I admit I don't always have. I want my children to go to dance class, and play outside in the fresh air. They're only allowed on the computer for home-work during the week, though I do let them play games on my cell phone if we're stuck in the car for any length of time. It keeps them entertained, and the apps I've let them download all have some educational value. I know that being tech-savvy is a skill they'll need to succeed in school, and in the profes-sional world when they grow up. Still, I admit I was shocked when three-year-old Rain was by herself in the backseat one day with my phone and, when I couldn't turn around to help her, managed to hack into Sierra's account so she could play a game she liked. Neriah has been begging for her own cell phone lately, but I'm reluctant to cave in on that one. She's only ten, and she's never in any situation where she's not with an adult who has access to a cell if making a call is all that important. It's bad enough that she once tried to use her dad's phone to text me good night instead of calling me when she was staying at his place. I cut her off at the pass on that one. "No way," I said. "I want to hear your voice!" I could easily lose my family to technology if I didn't watch it.

But applying that same vigilance to myself is a lot tougher.

David usually likes to drive when we're going somewhere together, so it was odd when he began suggesting that he would ride shotgun for a change. When I'm in the passenger seat, I usually settle into multitasking mode, knocking off some business calls on my phone while scrolling through e-mails on my iPad, maybe squeezing in a few minutes to work on a blog or send out some tweets in between. With my hands on the wheel, and David chatting beside me, the lightbulb finally went off in my head: Hah! He just wants me to drive so he can separate me from my technology!

And who can blame him? Nobody wants to feel like a chauffeur while their mate sets up office and proceeds to shut them out for the next twenty minutes (make that ninety, if you're in L.A. traffic). It's as rude as one of those lunches where your tablemates never take their eyes off their CrackBerrys. I wasn't the only guilty party here; David is notorious for spending hours at a time on the phone, while my resentment slowly builds over being ignored. So we agreed to put down our respective devices and converse with each other when we're in the car. If I look out the window as we drive along the Pacific Coast Highway and spot a pod of dolphins leaping through the waves, it's honestly gratifying to share the moment with the man I love. I can always tweet it later. While he's on the phone.

Have you ever noticed how kids manipulate to get you away from the phone or computer or BlackBerry when you're busy and *just need five minutes, dammit*? Their little instincts know something about human connection that we brush aside by the time we're overwhelmed adults. You can lose intimacy. Sometimes I miss us playing word games in the car, or picking up the phone to hear that sweet message from a friend or loved one. Seriously, declaring periods of cyber-silence in our household wasn't such a hard sell with me. I knew already how refreshing it could be to pull the plug once in a while and let life unfold without all that electronic stimulation. When Sierra was a newborn, and Neriah was barely two, I was wrapping up my *Wild On* stint and ironing out the details of a new series E! had in the works for me. With two production teams suddenly wanting chunks of my time, plus photo shoots and other projects bouncing around, my phones seemed to be constantly ringing. Not a good thing with two babies in the house. One afternoon, I was in my office, going through the accumulated mountain of e-mails in my Not Read box while juggling way too many phone calls. Between work and new-mom hormones and fatigue, I was feeling bombarded. My German shepherd was sleeping at my feet, and he somehow got himself tangled up in my various cords. The doorbell rang, the dog bolted, and you know how you sometimes see a disaster happening in slow motion, like a cartoon, and you know what's about to happen, but for some reason you do nothing to stop it? I remember just sitting there and watching my laptop flip up into the air like a tiddlywink and smash onto the floor. And, just as clearly, I remember my first thought:

Well, thank God, they can't reach me that way now!

It felt so decadently, deliciously, good-as-tiramisu good that I then called the phone company and had them disconnect us. What can I say? It was just one of those diary-of-a-mad-housewife moments. I wasn't thinking, just reacting. Being unreachable was the next-best thing to sleep, which any new mom will tell you is nirvana plus Oz plus Utopia, Brigadoon, and Atlantis all rolled into one, it's so beyond the realm of possibility.

Unfortunately, in this case, one of the people who couldn't reach me was my then-husband, who came home from work all nervous and testy. (And that was before he found out that the blackout was self-imposed.)

David and I enjoyed a similar unorchestrated respite when we took our first family vacation ever last summer and spent a week in the Tuscan countryside, where I soon discovered that my laptop was just excess luggage. With no Internet service, and astronomical roaming charges if we dared to use our cell phones, we had no choice but to kick back and totally unwind. I lounged in the sunshine and devoured the first novel I'd read in years. My kids weren't as happy with the cold-turkey disconnect as I was, but after asking anxiously for their computer games a few times, they moved onto entertaining themselves, and actually got along better with each other than they ever had before. David and I reveled in each other's undivided attention when we were alone together, too. Not that we were ready to go Amish or anything, but maybe declaring a technology Sabbath at home once in a while would be an experiment worth trying—disconnect so we could reconnect. What a great idea! I couldn't wait to tweet it.

8

can you hear me now?

Onstage hosting Rock Star: INXS, *tuning in to baby Rain.*

*W*HEN IT COMES to communication, I think we should all aspire to the emotional intelligence of horses. I reached this conclusion watching my middle daughter, Sierra, learn to ride. Horseback riding lessons were the only thing she wanted for her eighth birthday, and flashing back to my own fond girlhood memories of riding on my father's ranch, I was thrilled to grant her wish. So, on a sunny spring afternoon, in the tawny hills above Malibu, I watched a trainer introduce Sierra to a gentle Arabian named Reggie. Despite my own love of horses, I have to admit that my protective instincts kicked in when I first saw my child's vulnerable little body perched atop such a powerful creature, but I was reassured by the instant connection they seemed to have. Week after week, I watched in fascination as they learned to communicate, girl to horse and horse to girl.

Riding a horse isn't a matter of just saying "giddyup" and steering the animal with the reins: It's obviously a lot more sophisticated and subtle than that. You have to signal your intentions with the slightest shift of weight or click of the tongue. You read each other and then find your common rhythm.

Aside from horses' natural beauty, one of the reasons we humans—girls in particular—are so drawn to them is because they possess this almost mystical sensitivity. As soon as you touch a horse, the animal will reflect whatever energy you're bringing to that moment—if you're confident, the horse will likely be relaxed and cooperative; if you're nervous, he will probably be skittish, too. It's communication stripped down to its basic form, without any of the BS or posturing.

As I watched my daughter learn how to effortlessly maneuver her horse, I found myself wishing that human communication could be so uncomplicated, so lovely and pure. A connection built entirely on trust. What does it take to achieve that? I've spent a small fortune on therapy over the years—some of it helpful, some not so much—and now I was wondering if a horse had the answers! Once I stopped laughing at myself, sitting there on the steps watching Sierra happily circle the riding ring, I decided there was actually something for me to learn here, too. I realized that a horse and rider work together to learn each other's language, and that fluency happens only when both are focused and connected. You can't canter up to a wall and hope to clear the jump without breaking your neck if you're thinking about whose turn it is to take the kids to the dentist, or stewing over the fight you had with your sister. You have to be in that moment 100 percent. Persuading a horse to do what you want—achieving that wonderful connection—really comes down to four core communication skills:

Clarity
Confidence
Consistency
Compassion

What if we made a conscious effort to apply those same qualities to our human interactions, as well?

Maybe, I thought, we'd make it over a helluva lot more walls.

SHUTTING UP, SHUTTING OUT

I grew up in a volatile, dysfunctional family. My mom and stepfather fought constantly and loudly. I spent a lot of time in my room with my headphones cranked up to drown them out. I've always dreaded conflict, and it was far easier for me to hide out, or even take on the role of peacemaker, than it was to confront anyone. Even from a young age, I could glean that there were always two sides to every story, and that the truth usually could be found somewhere in the middle. I made it my mission to figure out who was coming from where, and I felt genuine empathy for each combatant in any given skirmish. How I wish I could have bottled and saved that pure compassion of a child, because there sure are times as an adult when I could use a double dose.

Because I spent much of my childhood surrounded by a lot of aggressive energy, too much fighting, and very strong, egotistical men, I learned at a very young age to smooth over most situations, remove myself from the unbearable, and to try to see the good in even the very bad times. I became so accustomed to making everything okay in my mind, it became habitual in my young adulthood, and it squashed my ability to speak up, make changes, define my own desires, and fight for what I wanted. Being tolerant became the norm for me, and as I entered young adulthood, I'm afraid that I tolerated way too much. If something didn't give, I was on my way to becoming one of those spineless, decorative women I so despised in my father's life. My usual MO during an argument was to lock myself in the bathroom until my man called my mother to come coax me out. Running and hiding, both physically and emotionally, felt like the best option to me. Little did I realize then that it was the least effective choice.

Sad to say, for most of my life I didn't know what I wanted; I only knew how to be okay with whatever rolled my way. I would stay frozen for years in a bad relationship because okay was the best that I knew. I didn't know how to ask for what I wanted, I didn't have the voice to help me get what I wanted, and I had no example of what a healthy, functional relationship looked like. That's a scary place for a young woman to find herself in.

I spent most of my first marriage silent, accommodating and adjusting to what I thought I should be. I even befriended other doctors' wives in hopes of emulating them and getting it right. But "it" was my marriage, not a dance routine. I was committed to the idea of marriage more than I was committed to the marriage itself. There were no predetermined steps to memorize and then execute with well-rehearsed technique. Don't get me wrong—Garth never tried to restrict my freedom to be myself and pursue my dreams; in fact, I took the job hosting *Wild On* while pregnant with our first child, and continued traveling the world with Neriah in tow through her toddlerhood. Together, we traipsed through tropical jungles and bobbed on dolphin seas. But inside, the topography of my soul seemed blank and barren. And I couldn't find a way to express that. I think Garth and I had maybe three fights in our entire marriage. I remember once when he told me to shut up, and I did. For three days. I was mortified by his words; it didn't cross my mind to be indignant, and more important, to let him know it.

I realized after many years of therapy that I didn't have much of a voice, and that I had no concept of what a list of needs would even look like, much less how to get them met. In fact, it wasn't until I spent much time with a close friend and her lovely husband that I was able to see what a healthy, connected relationship looked like. The sad truth dawned on me then: I wasn't living my life; I was hosting it. I have to say, it was a brilliant performance, and if you were on the outside looking in, it was pretty darn picture-perfect. But I had a long way to go, and a lot of hard work ahead of me if I wanted the reality instead of the illusion.

Identifying what I need in a relationship and expressing it appropriately—whether it's romantic, professional, or platonic—is something I have to constantly work on. If I don't, the resentment quietly builds inside me until the pressure becomes too much, and the anger explodes. At that point, it's emotional shrapnel, hitting innocent bystanders as well as intended targets, causing unintended damage, inflicting pain, and doing very little to resolve the actual problem. The compassion I possessed so effortlessly as a child is sometimes hard to summon forth as an adult.

So, fast-forward through seven years of therapy, and I'm in the arms of the man I always wanted to be with. Problem is, my heart is shattered. I was surviving a divorce and all the guilt that comes with breaking apart your family. That hardly left me in a position to offer the best version of me to anyone. But, when love calls, you show up or you miss out! David and I forged ahead, but it was, and sometimes still is, tough going.

From the very beginning of our love affair, David and I found ourselves emotionally on different playing fields, and our styles of communication are vastly different. I'm the queen of denial, and David is the king of direct. There's no small talk with him, and his hunger to connect with me at his depth level can stress me out. He's adept at reading body language, and picks up on all the little nuances I'm not even consciously aware of. "What's wrong?" he will demand, often before I know anything is. My first impulse is to snap back, "Nothing, get off me!" and then try to shut it down as quickly as possible. But David knows how to seal off my usual emotional escape routes. I was not used to being with someone who was bound and determined to get to the bottom of my soul and explore all its chambers in the process. Let me also note that he is a Tunisian-French Jew, who is strong, macho, and egotistical. I am a French-Portuguese-Irish Jew who is admittedly stubborn, defiant, and shall we say attitudinal (or so I've been told). That's a lot of spice tossed into one dish. And while David and I both thrive on the passion, fire, and excitement of our unique concoction, those same ingredients contribute to some major blowouts, as well. I don't know how many times I've packed my bags in the heat of a fight with David and headed for the door, screaming that I was leaving him as he tried to block me. I'd usually jump in the car and head up the Pacific Coast Highway for a half hour or so, until I found some spot where I could just sit and contemplate the ocean until I calmed myself down or cried myself out. Then I would head back home, feeling upset and unsettled, wishing I had the tools to avoid the meltdowns.

The last time this scene started to play itself out, David stunned me when he didn't make his usual move to bar the door.

"If you really want to go, you should," he said quietly. "But I think you really want to stay and just don't know how to make it better."

Thank God he knows me oftentimes better than I know myself. The truth of his words hit home. It takes a concerted, loving effort sometimes to deal and face each other with open arms and unclenched fists. We both know how to push each other's buttons, and if you've seen the movie, rest assured that *Mr. and Mrs. Smith* had nothing on us, except the blood. The ironic thing is that what we complained about not getting from each other was invariably exactly what we both were not *giving*. It's a whole lot easier to focus on what you want instead of asking yourself whether you're giving those very same things. Four years and two children into our engagement, David and I were on the brink of splitting—not because we'd lost the passion in our relationship, but because we'd lost the compassion. It didn't help that my running shoes were always laced up and ready to go, either. It wouldn't have been the first time I'd broken an engagement. Or the second. Or the fifth.

Most people are too proud or too angry to ask for what they need, but I know that when David or I have found the courage to do that, even during our worst fights, it has opened doors.

We decided to go back to an exercise we'd done together early on in our partnership, where we wrote down all the things that were important to us and what we wanted in a mate (thank you, Tony Robbins—you shed a lot of light in my life!). We then asked ourselves how many of those things we were willing to be ourselves. That's when I really began to focus on giving what I wanted to receive: devotion, honesty, loyalty, romance, tenderness, commitment.

Take a few minutes to give yourself the compassion quiz: Are you listening, or just reacting? Are you complaining, or gently asking? Are you engaged in thoughtful conversation, or just silently rehearsing your lines and waiting your turn to speak? Do you want to win, or to understand? How often do we think about how we feel instead of how the other person is feeling? Funny how I don't do that with my kids, but I sure have been guilty of doing that with my man.

PUTTING YOURSELF IN TIME-OUT

Yes, I still take a tearful drive up the coast now and then, but most times it's preventive instead of reactive. Adults need to give themselves time-outs sometimes, too. It's healthy to take a break, to just say, "This is getting ugly, let's stop," and chill for a bit. Before packing your bags, try simply admitting to your partner what you are feeling, even if that means sharing the fact that you want to bolt but are choosing to stay, or that you feel lost. Stepping back is not the same as running away. If you happen to be one of those passion-driven people prone to Vesuvian eruptions, give yourself permission to vent privately (I can vouch for the discretion of cars and closets) before spewing publicly. You need a chance to check in with yourself and figure out what you really want and how to send that message in a way likely to get the response you need. I don't know that I buy into the pop-advice mentality that there's such a thing in love as fighting fairly, but I do think you can fight honestly, and try to save at least some of the fireworks for more worthy encounters (like makeup sex).

David and I are both too passionate and hot-blooded to fight logically. We have fantastic fights. Many of them are also spectacularly ridiculous fights. I do have to confess that I feel a little sorry for the guy sometimes, because he had the bad luck of hooking up with me right when I was undergoing an important epiphany in my emotional life, and truly discovering that I had a voice after thirty-five years of keeping quiet. I'm still in the beta-testing phase when it comes to sensible self-censorship, and plead guilty to sporadic outbursts of marital Tourette's. I can really work myself into a lather over nothing sometimes.

When your significant other is an actor, you have to cope with situations that feel real, but aren't. It drives me nuts when David has a role with a romantic scene. I don't consider myself the jealous type, but no one wants to see someone else's hands running down her man's nude back. Not long ago, he was in Canada filming a Lifetime movie, and at first I would teasingly ask him what he and his "girlfriend" had done that day as the cameras rolled. ("We went for a walk," he might say.) As filming went on, my playful tone grew ever so slightly sharper.

"Tell me about your love scenes, so I can be prepared," I demanded. (I still harbored some resentment from the first time I went to one of his premieres, having been assured there'd be nothing more than a kiss on-screen, only to be confronted with a big make-out scene. I felt sort of cheated on in a silly, avoidable kind of way.) This time, David kept insisting there were no big love scenes. I couldn't let it go, though. I can

actually handle a lot, but I need the respect of being prepared for it. That doesn't seem like too much to ask.

"Are you kissing today?" I wanted to know. David had told
me there was a scene involving a kiss.

"Just a peck," he reported back.

In hindsight, this same conversation could have had a completely different vibe, if I had just turned left instead of right.
We could have used that situation to our advantage and
steamed up the phone lines with lust instead of anger. But I
didn't follow my own cardinal rule of stopping to check in
with myself before (over)reacting when David announced,
"I'm doing a love scene with my girlfriend today."

He might as well have told me that Angelina Jolie had
strolled onto the set naked, wrapped herself around him and
implored, "Let's get out of here now, my private jet with a
waterbed is waiting for us."

"You lied to me!" was my instant accusation. How did the
story line change overnight from a simple peck to a (in my
mind) all-out orgy? It must have been in the script! He had to
have known all along, and he *chose to deceive me*! Who knew
what other secrets he was withholding from me, now that we
both knew how easy that was? I let him have it. This wasn't
about acting! This was an indictment of his entire moral character! Were public stonings legal in Canada? We were so done.
O-ver. There was no reason to discuss this any further. I
refused to take his calls or respond to his text messages. In
desperation, he tried to lo-jack me by sending messages
through my makeup artist, sucking poor Steve into domestic
warfare, when really he'd rather just glue on my eyelashes.
After fuming for hours, and mentally packing up the kids, I
deigned to listen to David's explanation.

"Brooke, chill out," he said. "There was no romantic scene because they had taken it out before to put in the peck, but when that didn't work, they put the romantic scene back in and that was the first I knew about it."

If this is the part where you expect me to tell you I felt chagrined, then just skip to the next chapter. Because I felt excited. Alive. Fighting dirty can have that effect on me, frankly. I'm an adrenaline junkie, and when it comes to romantic relationships, I'll take a fight over indifference any day of the week. (Definitely gotta work on a more functional turn-on, LOL!)

By now, we can all probably dutifully recite the cookie-cutter advice for constructive rather than destructive fighting: Don't dredge up old issues, don't accuse, don't push hot buttons, and so on. Makes perfect sense. In a perfect relationship, maybe, and if those were easily manufactured, Zappos would be offering them in an endless variety of shapes and sizes, with free next-day delivery. I'd be all over that. ("Hello, customer service? What's the exchange policy on the French Hottie after thirty days? Can I keep the free-kids-with-purchase?")

Seriously, I'd love it if Diplomatic Negotiator were my default setting, but it's not, and I can't become that any more than I can become the Dalai Lama, much as I'd like to. I can, however, work on becoming a better version of me. If you approach the challenge of improving your communication style as some kind of extreme emotional makeover—"I have to be x instead of y"—you'll only end up feeling frustrated and defeated. So why not take a step back, honestly assess who you are, and rock the style you have? If you're passive in the face of conflict, as I used to be, turn your inclination to remain silent into a plus: Use it to truly listen, instead of retreat. If you're inclined to mouth off, retrain yourself to be as quick and effusive with compliments and appreciation as you are with the zingers and put-downs.

Just as there are times when you should speak up, there are likewise times to shut up. Or at least sleep on it. I have my producer to thank for inadvertently defusing me before I set off World War III in my blended family. During my first season cohosting *Dancing with the Stars*, I was excited about my older girls coming to sit in the audience. My mom was going to pick them up from school and bring them straight to my dressing room before showtime. It was a Monday, and the girls had spent the weekend at their dad's, so I had brought a bag with a change of clothes for them with me.

I was doing last-minute prep with my hairdresser, makeup artist, and producer when my older daughter, Neriah, passed through security and came clicking down the CBS hallway in a pair of gold, three-inch stilettos. And a micro-minidress with no shorts or leggings underneath. Did I mention she was in fourth grade? Scarily enough, she was looking quite sexy, and everyone in the room did a double take. My eyes went straight to the shoes, and I bit off my words in that controlled, clipped voice you use when you're furious but are someplace where yelling like a wild banshee is socially unacceptable.

"What in the world are you wearing and Where. Did. You. Get. Those. Shoes?" I demanded. I knew full well where she had gotten them! They fit her perfectly, and since I didn't purchase them and her father certainly didn't, that left one suspect I was only too eager to charge with tramping out my ten-year-old: the stepmother.

"I can walk in them," Neriah smugly informed me.

"Yeah? Why don't you show me?" I challenged her. The gauntlet was down.

Neriah promptly stumbled a few steps across my dressing room floor like a fawn on stilts. Case closed. Now I could be triumphant as well as furious.

"Get. Them. Off."

My producer was signaling me that we were ten minutes to air, and I had no time to have it out with Neriah or speed-dial my ex's wife to lay into her, much as I wanted to. All I could do was hand Neriah the change of clothes (with shoes) I'd packed for her, take a deep breath, paste my best hostess smile on my face, and walk out in front of a live audience as if tonight's celebrity foxtrot was the only thing in the world on my mind.

When we got home that night, I was tired, and decided to let it go for the time being with Neriah. Nevertheless, I snapped a picture of the shoes and attached it to an e-mail I sent to her father. "Not sure where they came from, but think you might want to ask your wife," I informed him. "I think it's totally inappropriate and I wanted you to be aware of it." To his ever-lasting credit, Garth replied immediately and politely, agreeing the shoes were inappropriate and promising to look into it.

The next day, Neriah came to me apologetically.

"Mommy, you know, I really thought it was okay," she said. "I actually thought you'd really like them. I picked them out myself."

One of the things I admire most about children is how unfiltered they are, how they're able to say exactly what they're thinking. I had to remind myself now how black and white their world is, and to hear what Neriah was saying instead of merely reacting to what had happened. Now that I'd given myself some distance from the drama, I could appreciate that she genuinely did not understand what she had done wrong—

she thought quite innocently that the shoes were cute. And they were—for someone twice her age. I could see that it was a judgment call, and Neriah simply wasn't old enough to make that judgment. It didn't need to be a fight. We needed to have a conversation and I needed to explain it.

"Where did you get them?" I asked her again, gently this time.

"Well, actually they were my stepsister's, and her mom bought them for her a long time ago and she found them in her closet and wanted me to have them and they fit me." She thought they were special, and put them on for this special occasion. Her intention had been to honor me, not horrify me.

I thought for a moment about what I really wanted Neriah to carry away from our conversation, and it wasn't my irritation with the stepmom and -sister, who, though I hated to admit it, have as much right as I do to their own taste and judgment. The real message I needed to convey to my daughter was what was appropriate, and what wasn't, and why.

"You know, Neriah, they are really cute," I conceded. "In fact, I love them and want to wear them myself, but you know what? You're ten and it's just not appropriate. They're too high for you, and your dress was too short, and it's just not appropriate. If you want to play dress-up at home, that's okay, I get it."

I also got it that I had aimed my fury at Neriah in my dressing room when the target I really wanted to hit in that instant was her stepmother. I was glad that I had waited, and communicated my feelings to Neriah's father, instead. It was a parenting issue, not a power struggle. If I had given in to my angry impulse (which I probably would have, if I hadn't had to hurry onstage), I would have called the step and lit into her;

falsely accused, she no doubt would have gotten defensive, and then all sorts of other issues and resentments would have come up, and we would have had a full-blown feud on our hands instead of a simple misunderstanding that was easily smoothed over. It was a good lesson for me: Breathe, wait, and give situations a chance to present their details before you act.

BONDING WITH YOUR EX

A working divorce is as rewarding, in its own weird way, as a working marriage. Garth and I have to communicate now more than we ever did before, and we communicate far better as parents than we did as husband and wife. We decided, in the midst of our own agony over the split, that we absolutely had to take the high road for our kids, and that meant committing to one another as parents. I had failed to speak up during our marriage, but now it wasn't just important, but imperative, for me to communicate with him in a consistent, clear way. Our kids' happiness was at stake, and neither of us was willing to gamble with that.

To shift into neutral with an ex, the first thing you have to let go of is that overpowering need to be right. That's pure ego, and if you want to have a strong, appropriate relationship as parents, you need to start from the square marked "Humble," not the one called "Pride." You're partners in this, not competitors.

Despite some bumps along the way (we still know how to push each other's hot buttons), I'm proud of the civilized relationship my ex and I have managed to establish. We're genuinely raising our children together. We share in all their important decisions, attend their events together, and try to communicate with kindness about kid stuff on a daily basis. I actually think that, with the healing passage of time, we have built a decent friendship. So how the hell did two people so lousy at being married get so good at being divorced? Props go to my shrink in this case, and to a great book I was given called *Making Divorce Easier on Your Child—50 Effective Ways to Help Children Adjust*, by Nicholas Long and Rex L. Forehand. I likewise appreciated the advice I found in *Mom's House, Dad's House: Making Two Homes for Your Child*, by Isolina Ricci. I also read Roma Downey's very sweet book, *Love Is Family*, to my kids.

My shrink made me understand that sharing custody isn't about enduring the same bad relationship you had with your ex-husband until your kids turn eighteen. Successful coparenting demands that you wipe the slate clean and develop a new relationship with this person you lived with, breathed with, and knew as a mate. That can be tricky. Both parents have to acknowledge and commit to the fact that this new partnership is purely for the children. You have to be willing and able to communicate clearly, casually, respectfully, and constantly. For anyone who thinks that by getting a divorce you are getting rid of your partner, if you have kids, *think again*. I deal with my girls' dad more now than I ever did. We will be in each other's lives forever. Looking back, I realize that I basically grew up with Garth. I didn't stop playing the child until I became a mother myself. Despite our differences, I'm grateful for what Garth gave me.

I try to channel that gratitude when I'm dealing with him

now, and it's given me a good basis for open communication between us. The one thing most people want from one another is acknowledgment, pure and simple. Don't just convey the nuts-and-bolts information when you're exchanging the kids. Sincerely listen, discuss, and be willing to try your ex's suggestions—if his method for getting the procrastinator to stay on top of school projects works, it's win-win for everyone; if his new girlfriend thinks peanut-butter sandwiches cause brain damage, resist the urge to wonder aloud whether she was the test study. Try saying, "Interesting, I'll have to look into that," instead, and thank her for her concern. Remember that you always have three choices in a difficult conversation: deflect, engage, or escalate. When raising kids with your ex, it's absolutely vital to check in with each other regularly to make sure you're on the same page when it comes to big issues like discipline, Internet use, or when your teen can start dating. The point is to share your thoughts, not to criticize, second-guess, or be a helicopter ex. In the end, if you can't agree, get outside help and learn what negotiating or mediation tools work best for all of you—new partners included, since that's likely to be one of the sorest friction points.

If conversations with your ex tend to get fraught with emotion, try texting instead when you have to exchange simple info. It forces you to be brief and to the point, and the platform doesn't lend itself to dangerous overanalysis when you're feeling PMS-y. On the flip side, avoid e-mails when you're emotional about some perceived wrong. We all feel a lot bolder when we're typing instead of talking, and even if you're liberal with the emoticons, things can get misinterpreted or blown out of proportion no matter how many ;)s you put in there. Write it if it makes you feel better, but don't put a name in the address box, and remember to hit save instead of send. Let it sit there for a day; then reread it out loud to yourself before you do anything more. The delete button is your friend. If your ex hasn't mastered the art of self-censorship, a bit of distance may be your best defense.

It's much easier to actively coparent with an ex than to try to pretend you are all living separate lives. You really aren't, and you're still going to have to deal with lots of his crap when your kids bring it back to your house, and vice versa. In the end, life will be easier for everyone if you choose to keep a sense of humor rather than a scorecard.

naked truth When someone really sends me over the edge, I let my inner bitch write a venomous letter spelling out their every fault. (Never do this in e-mail, or you might accidentally hit send. Create a separate Word document. Then delete.)

LEARNING LANGUAGES

My four children all have their own communication styles, and I have to speak to them in their own languages to really get through. What I mastered with one has completely failed with others. Many's the day when I feel as if I'm speaking Norwegian in Nepal, and everyone is either staring at me with pity or ignoring me altogether. I may succeed with one, and feel as if I'll never get through to another. One day, I can feel like the All-Star Hall-of-Fame Mother of the Millennium, and by the next morning something will have happened to make me wish I could just burrow under the covers and never show my face again because I'm convinced I'm the worst mom in the history of the universe.

Rain, my youngest daughter, is an old soul. If she's starting to lose it, I can tell her, "Take a deep breath—I'm here for you," and she can often pull herself out of an impending melt-down. I sometimes have to remember that she's only three and not expect too much from her. Neriah is a noisy, fabulous whirlwind who needs a jolt of adrenaline—a stern command or threatened consequence—to get back on track. Sierra is my hypersensitive middle child—the tactics and tone that work with Neriah would make her crumble. Shaya, my baby boy, seems to be training me instead of the other way around: He spent his first two years playing hard-to-get, and I had to keep M&Ms in my pocket to pay for his kisses when I came home from work. He's a man who needs his space!

My kids actually teach me a lot about good communication. One of the things I love about young children is how unfiltered they are, how they're able to just blurt out what they feel when they're feeling it. They're also a merciless reflection of our own failings, giving us wake-up calls when we most need them. A friend still cringes when she tells the story of the day she was scolding her four-year-old niece for throwing a tantrum.

"I had her literally backed into a corner, and I was crouched down at her level, in her face, wagging my finger," she recalls. "I wasn't yelling, but I was angry, and speaking sharply. She kept putting her hands up over her ears, and I kept raising my voice. No way was I going to accept such disrespect! I was going to get through to her!" The sobbing four-year-old looked up at her angry aunt.

"You're scaring me!" she cried.

Suddenly, my friend understood. She wasn't delivering the message she meant to—that the child's behavior was unacceptable—she was acting like a bully, and she needed to be called out on it.

I had a similarly shattering experience not long ago when Neriah and I were going through a rough patch. She was only ten, but acting like a fifteen-year-old who'd just gotten dumped by her boyfriend on prom night and was hormonal and bratty and grounded. She was miserable, and seemed hell-bent on making everyone around her miserable, too. Every time I turned around, it felt like I was yelling at her and banishing her to her room. We were in a dangerous skid, and if I didn't find a way to steer us out of it, we were going over the cliff any minute.

Things came to a head one weekend when we were spending Memorial Day with friends at their lake house. Neriah had just gotten into trouble—again—when she looked at me with undisguised pain in her beautiful eyes.

"You think I'm a bad kid," she said, tears falling. "All you ever do is tell me what mistakes I'm making. You're always yelling and telling me all the bad things about me."

I was stunned, and started to cry, too.

"Oh, my gosh, I do not think you're a bad kid!" I protested. "You're a good kid! I think you have so many great qualities."

"You do?" Neriah implored.

"I think you're responsible, I think you're smart, I think you're beautiful, I think you're a great student. You help me with so many things," I replied. "I just focus attention on the things you do wrong because I have to teach you."

It was such a painful conversation, but as much as it filled me with guilt and sorrow, I was heartened that we were finally communicating instead of just smashing into and bouncing off each other like hot atoms. I was going to have to make some changes if I wanted to get through to her. The messages I was sending certainly weren't the ones I intended. I needed to remember that everything I say to her is shaping her, that she takes every negative thing in. And for her to think she was a bad kid, well, shame on me.

One of my hot buttons with Neriah is materialism, and it's a trait I really want to head off at the pass as she careens toward teendom. She'll be a perfect child if there's a material reward at the end. How could I get the behavior without the manipulation?

I started by reprimanding myself, not her. I'm the one who has to take responsibility for not exposing her enough to alternative ways to feel gratified or fulfilled. She's wildly artistic, so why wasn't I taking her to the theater now and then? Why wasn't I recruiting David's mom, who's an amazing artist, to come over some Sunday afternoon and give us a painting lesson out in the garden? I needed to remember the power of positive reinforcement. Being negative all the time was squishing Neriah's self-confidence, and it wasn't having an effect at all on the behavior I was trying to correct.

I firmly believe that it's more important for me to be my children's parent than their friend, and I wasn't about to throw discipline and consequences out the window. But I needed to make every effort to reward them with positive feedback, to compliment and encourage them, to focus as much attention on my children's positive qualities as I do the challenging ones. It was time to start leading by example rather than exclamation point, and check my impulse to yell first and think later. If I wanted my children to be kind and thoughtful and considerate and generous, then I needed to be those things to them. Was I telling Neriah five great things about her every day? No, but I sure was telling her five bad things, and she was absorbing those like a sponge. That had to stop.

What we don't say to one another can be just as ugly as the words that do tumble from our lips. It's a useful, and humbling, exercise in self-awareness to lock yourself in the bathroom for a few minutes during a calm moment, and just make the face you feel yourself customarily making when you're scowling your disapproval at your tween, or shooting daggers at your spouse. See yourself, literally, as they do.

Sometimes I feel spread so thin, dividing myself among four children, a mate, my mom, my friends, and a slew of projects on the work front. And since I share custody with my older girls' father, I only have them half the week. Even though we stay in touch on their daddy days, we can still sort of lose our places in our own story together, and it takes patience I admit I don't always have on tap to fully reconnect. I always make the time for special events like school field trips, parties, and performances, but I also try to carve out one-on-one time with each child at some point during the week, whether it's taking a riding lesson with Sierra or banging on pots and pans with Shaya for twenty minutes during his preschool music class. At night, I rotate beds, and climb in for fifteen minutes or so with each child, just to cuddle and talk softly about whatever's on their mind or heart. Doesn't matter whether it's silly or soulful, I just crave that ritual rebonding.

Today, I'm a woman who knows what I want. I know what I need, and I know how to ask for all of those things. Better yet, I'm getting a handle on how to create those things in my life. Life's gotten a lot easier since I taught myself to communicate my feelings as I feel them, with sensible censorship, and to say something along the lines of, "I'm not getting what you mean and it feels kind of bad. Can you try explaining it to me?" instead of sitting there and silently seething. I acknowledge my own responsibility to teach my partner my language, and accept that he can't read my mind, no matter how many romantic movies pretend that true soul mates can. Life is a reality show, not a fairy tale. True tenderness is taking the time and making the effort to teach others our language, and master theirs, and to be humble enough to ask for translation when we don't understand, instead of guessing haphazardly.

I've seen this same drama play out time and time again on the set of *Dancing with the Stars*, as celebrities and their professional partners struggle to find a common language. I could totally identify with Jennifer Grey when she walked out of rehearsal on Derek Hough because his shortness with her was making it harder for her to learn the routine. I fully understand the stress of competing; been there, done that. I was proud to see Derek immediately correct course with Jennifer, and explain that he was frustrated, not angry. They quickly found their groove again. Things didn't work out so well, however, for Michael Bolton and his professional partner, Chelsea Hightower. When she failed to connect with the superstar singer during one rehearsal, she gave her struggling student a dismissive, "Whatever." Bolton called her out on it. "Whatever" wasn't the way to teach him. But then he must have overcompensated for their spat, and become too eager to please, because he agreed to open a routine to "Hound Dog" by trotting out of a doghouse on all fours with a big bone in his mouth—a bit of choreography that was so beneath him it was excruciating to watch. The judges shredded him, with Bruno declaring it the worst jive in the show's history. Bolton was eliminated, but spoke up publicly about his rude treatment, demanding an apology. None was forthcoming (it's a judge's job to criticize) but fate offered Bolton a classier exit strategy: when Susan Boyle dropped out of a scheduled performance on the results show the following week, Bolton graciously returned to our stage to sing in her place on a moment's notice. His rendition of Leonard Cohen's haunting "Hallelujah" was an absolute showstopper.

When you have confidence, you can communicate in a vulnerable way. You can be heard and not be afraid to share something because of what the other person might think; you can tell someone how you feel, compliment them, praise them without second-guessing how they're going to receive it. It opens you up to spontaneously send your younger sibling a note for no reason other than to share a memory you just recalled, or to tell someone that you're crazy in love with him when you feel that emotion, instead of waiting for the "right" time, or holding back out of fear of rejection. It feels as good to speak and share honestly as it does to hear those moments from my loved ones. I realize that it's all an exchange, and my relationships work best when it's pitch and catch.

intervention:
sibling rivalry

SIERRA AND NERIAH are at that age when they seem
to be constantly fighting! I'd need to wear stripes and
become a full-time referee if I tried to intervene every
time. They need to learn to settle their own differences, but when they get really hateful, I separate
them and make them write down five things they like
about each other. Then I read them aloud. I also apply
some reverse psychology to reinforce the sibling
bond by forbidding them to have any contact for a
while, telling them: "Now you've lost each other."

ALL CLEAR

If you ask people what they value most in a relationship,
they'll probably say honesty. No arguments there. But what
about clarity and consistency? I think those traits are grossly
undervalued in our day-to-day communication. I probably
wouldn't have gotten so peeved at the nanny and finally fired
her if I'd just addressed my issues as they came up, so she
would know right away that me racing home to accommodate her workout schedule was not the relationship I was
overpaying her for, thank you very much, and good luck with
those glutes. (Yeah, I'm all swagger now, but I was a total
chicken in real time, putting off the inevitable as long as I
could—I dread firing people! My best advice on that front is

a less-is-more approach. Simply saying "This is not working out any longer" is direct but not rude.)

My late stepfather, Armen, taught me a lot about the value of consistency. Armen was not a warm-and-fuzzy, share-your-feel-ings kind of guy. But he was consistent, predictable, and there for me every time. And because I learned his language, I under-stood that those unemotional traits were his way of expressing love, and I loved him for that stability he gave us. He was also brutally honest, which is both good and bad, but I loved know-ing that what you see is what you get, and there was no beating around the bush. It's no wonder I hooked up with David.

For women, the language of girlfriends is our native tongue, our home country, a members-only lounge with its own set of rules. I think every woman needs another woman to count on. One you can run to when you feel lost, one who picks up the phone at two a.m., one who says you and your *four* kids can move in if need be, one who tells you yes, your ass looks fat in those jeans, one who tells you the truth even though you want her to lie, and one who reaches out to help you even when you don't have the heart to ask. I've always been best friends with my man, but let's be candid: A guy can never share the unspoken language of girlfriends. David comes pretty close—we cook together, he loves fashion, and he's as passionate about child rearing as I am, *but* I am not dishing about cellulite over lunch with him, nor am I fessing up about the libido waves.

I love how my girlfriends and I can lose touch, and then simply resume, no explanations or analysis or apologies needed. Women just share a different sort of bond. I recon-nected not long ago with one of my best friends from pre-kid days. She's a really flaky girl, and I was a flaky girl, too, back when we first got to know each other. Life's demands have changed me in the interim, but she's still much the same. If you make plans to meet for coffee, or invite her over, there's a fifty-fifty shot she'll show up or bother to call to tell you she's not going to.

"How can you have a friend like that who's so unreliable?" David wants to know. It drives him nuts, but not me.

"I love her and expect that of her" is the only answer I can offer. I enjoy having her in my life, and we're happy to carry on the way we do. I'm willing to roll with the flakiness, and, in fact, appreciate her unique charm. Communicating with someone isn't a matter of teaching them how to behave, or what to say. It's understanding who they are, and feeling understood in return; listening to what they have to say, and being heard in return. An exchange of gifts.

through others' eyes

AS AN EXERCISE to measure how you're perceived, my pal Joanne Bradford, a branding genius and the chief revenue officer of Demand Media, suggests e-mailing ten friends and asking them each to think of four words to describe you. At first, I was flattered by all the positive reinforcement: I was "devoted," "down-to-earth," "a great mom," "entrepreneurial." . . . Then I noticed something missing: Hey! What about "hot"? Sheesh, I didn't even get a lukewarm "stylish"! I never went to the office in sweats again.

The secret language of mothers is especially rich, because we can connect with each other even if we're total strangers, with nothing more than a sympathetic glance during a kindergartner's meltdown in the cereal aisle. My single girlfriends may be sweetly empathetic, but only my mom friends truly get it when I say I'm beat, and they can tell by inflection alone whether I'm in a state of contented fatigue or crazed exhaustion. We know we can't fix it for each other, and we don't try, but a little commiseration goes a long way. When they say, "Don't worry. It'll be okay," it's a promise, not a platitude, because I know they've been there and done that. I thank God every day for the sisterhood of motherhood.

thanksgiving year-round

LOTS OF FAMILIES make it a tradition to go around the table at Thanksgiving and have everyone say what they're grateful for. Why save such a sweet way to connect for the holidays? Do daily appreciations at dinnertime, or even once a week over a leisurely Saturday breakfast. Have each family member choose a different person each time, and share one thing they appreciate or admire about them.

MEANWHILE, BACK AT THE RANCH

After watching Sierra for a while, I decided to sign up for horseback riding lessons, too. I already knew the fundamentals of riding, and after so many years away from it, I felt this kind of peaceful joy settle over me as I yielded to muscle memory, and the emotional intelligence of the horse now taking measure of me. Together we would test our boundaries in the riding ring, going around in careful circles, before we ventured out across the canyon, with its rocky trails, its untamed beauty and hidden surprises.

During my first lesson, I was taught once again how to assert myself by sitting straight and remaining calm, exuding a quiet, reassuring confidence. I learned to steer with the slightest pressure and shift of weight, and to find my balance as we synchronized our rhythms and hit our stride. I was reminded how to reward with a soothing tone and kind pat. To discipline with a strong command and clear expectations. Our connection felt certain, strong, true, and good.

And then the instructor told me to drop my hands to my side and ride without reins. At first, I was dubious, and a little scared, but once I did, I learned the most important lesson this horse had to offer me about human relationships and the nature of communication: It's not about control, it's about trust. And it's only with trust that we can keep moving forward.

malibu mood

We throw a big family party to decorate our tree every year, then let the kids sleep under it one night.

"DON'T THINK I didn't notice the TV is gone."

That was one of the big downsides of staying in touch with David via Skype while he was shooting a television show in Africa: He could catch occasional glimpses of my stealth redecorating back on the home front. Now that he'd noticed the TV missing from its spot at the foot of our bed, I briefly considered trying to cover my tracks by telling him we'd been robbed . . . but what kind of burglars leave all the jewelry untouched and stop to build you a girly vanity table on their way out? I took the chicken's way out, instead: "Sorry, babe. Connection's bad. Love you. Bye!" David would be home soon enough to see what I'd done to our nest. The missing TV was just the beginning.

Anyone who's known me for ten minutes will tell you that I'm obsessed with ambience, whether it's choosing the perfect music and wineglasses for an elegant cocktail party or selecting which scented candle to light while I soak in a warm bubble bath. (Hint: Both answers depend a lot on what kind of company I'm expecting!)

When I want to create a certain mood, the first thing I do is set a goal. I know that probably sounds totally anal, but just hear me out. Anticipation is half the fun, and if you first ask yourself what your ideal outcome would be—I want my guy to feel thoroughly seduced or my houseguests to feel as if they are vacationing on the Mediterranean—then you have a better chance of turning your fantasy into reality. That's the point, isn't it? But setting the mood shouldn't be limited to special occasions, sexy rendezvous, or holiday get-togethers. Your house, your office, even your car all have their own vibes, and as far as I'm concerned, no space is too small or inconsequential to merit a little TLC.

How do I want to feel in this space?

What do I need to do to feel that way?

Just taking a few seconds to ponder those simple questions has prompted some big changes for me.

Having my man on another continent for three months gave me plenty of time to contemplate the places we occupy together, not just physically but emotionally, as well. When we first got together, David and I poured every bit of our hearts, souls, and savings into building this house together. But two years after moving in, I still felt slightly unsettled. It wasn't enough, I concluded, to have our surroundings merely reflect our mutual taste. (Luckily, we both gravitate toward a cozy Old World chic, reflecting both David's French upbringing and my penchant for romance.) Missing David, I had begun wandering through the rooms we shared with eyes freshly opened. What came into focus were all those spaces within spaces that we so often ignore or overlook because we're so fixated on the grander scheme of things. Isn't life like that? There are too many things we let slip under the radar, and go forever unnoticed. Now I began to zero in on all the places I had never enjoyed in our home—all the places where David and I could be enjoying each other.

Granted, having the TV right at the foot of our bed had always been a bone of contention; I hate, hate, *hated* it, especially when David was watching one of his *Ultimate Fighting Challenge* marathons. It felt like jeering fans and sweaty steroid gladiators had invaded our most private sanctuary. I have a strong aversion to negative energy at night, even the news. Moving that TV to a more discreet corner was a no-brainer. But as I looked around the room, I saw that my work had just begun. We had never fully exploited the romantic potential between those four walls, and it was time to ratchet the mood up a few notches, from pleasant enough to positively hot. I wanted this to be a place where my partner and I could connect on every level. Case in point: We had spent considerable time and effort tracking down the beautiful fireplace salvaged from an old French chateau, but then what had we done? We had parked an antique chaise left over from David's bachelor pad in front of it; after all the attention we had lavished on the fireplace, that chair screamed "afterthought." I had tried re-covering it, but the face-lift didn't take, and the piece was still a misfit, not to mention the scandalous energy it exuded. Admittedly, I have often used the latter in fantasy, but for the most part, the bachelor chaise was grossly out of place. Problem was, the chair wasn't big enough for two to cuddle up together, and neither of us ended up enjoying it alone. So it became the consummate clutter collector, a place to toss a purse or drop a jacket. Without David there to object, I banished this relic to another room for the time being, and reconsidered the prime real estate it had occupied. How did I imagine us there? A sofa to snuggle on seemed redundant—after all, our bed beckoned just three steps away. The more I thought about it, the more one particular fantasy began to take shape: I kept picturing us simply sitting there face-to-face, enjoying adult conversation while a fire crackled cozily beside us. That space needed to be a place to just talk.

Next, I pondered the balcony. When the house was quiet, I loved to stand out there just inhaling the jasmine on the evening breeze while I listened to the Malibu symphony of crickets, tree frogs, and birds settling in for the night. *Why don't we ever make love out here?* I asked myself now. A space needs to clearly signal its intentions, and if my balcony had naughty ones, the patio chairs were not worthy accomplices. If it was passion alfresco I craved, I was going to have to rethink the mood that balcony was channeling. With that in mind, I ordered a rustic Bali-like bed for the balcony, along with two proper chairs for the fireplace, chairs that invited you to sit upright, have a conversation, drink a glass of wine, and connect with another person. What the Bali bed invited us to do is between me and the symphony.

But I still wasn't done with my mood adjustments. I know couples who want their bedroom to convey a kind of rough-and-raunchy mood, and others who find a certain inspiration in the cool, contemporary aesthetic of an ultrahip hotel. David and I both had originally envisioned our master suite as a lush, sensual retreat. Put your head on my pillow, and you'll be looking up at a cinched-satin starburst canopy. Remembering the romantic nights we had once spent in a hotel on St. Bart's, where gauzy drapes cocooning the bed had billowed in the warm breeze, I decided to re-create that sensuous mood by hanging some sheer curtains around our bed at home. That simple touch of enclosing the bed also coincidentally fed my recurring fantasy of being an Arabian princess dangerously captivated by a man.

Finally, I targeted the master bath, and rewarded myself for all my efforts by replacing the built-in bench that no one used with a fabulous vanity table. I had originally chosen not to fight that battle when David had insisted on the ridiculous cushioned bench, but since he never once lounged there after a shower the way he had imagined he might, I felt entitled to give my fantasy for that corner a whirl.

Mission complete, I couldn't wait for David to get home and feel the difference. That would be the true test—not how it all looked, but how it all felt—because the décor is pointless if it doesn't instantly summon the vibe you're after. Setting a mood is all about capturing that feeling, and being able to preserve it so you can enjoy it again and again.

RECAPTURING A MOMENT

David and I have only spent a handful of nights apart from the kids since we had Rain in 2007, so it's no surprise that we cherish any chance we have to rewind those memories, the way those filmy curtains around our bed carry us back to St. Bart's again. You know how certain songs on the radio can instantly flood you with memory, then sweep you back to a particular time and place? You can also re-create emotion by essentially restaging whatever originally evoked it. It's like leaving sensory bookmarks throughout the chapters of your life, so you can quickly flip through the pages and land on your favorite passages to enjoy them whenever you feel like it. I discovered the trick to it the first time David and I ditched the kids for a road trip up the California coast and into the Napa Valley, where some friends were getting married one postcard-perfect weekend.

The first morning we were there, we treated ourselves to breakfast on a rustic terrace at the gorgeous Auberge de Soleil inn. Sitting outside in the fresh morning air, gazing out over the sun-drenched vineyards, we both felt that wonderful sense of peace that comes with true relaxation. The simple wooden table was adorned with flowers in a pretty little pot, crisp linens, and polished silver. Jellies and marmalade shimmered in their tiny glass jars next to the ceramic crock of butter, and it took a lot of willpower to keep my hands out of the inviting basket full of fresh muffins and bread. The attention to detail was what you would expect at any nice restaurant. But they had somehow done more than merely set the table; they had set a mood, and we slipped into it effortlessly. As we sipped our coffee from china cups and enjoyed this gentle reverie, I had one of those ideas so obvious you wonder why a cartoon lightning bolt doesn't appear above your head.

"We're doing this when we get home," I announced to David. We already had a little wooden table and chairs sitting unused out back, but now I envisioned a different setting for them. "Let's put that table and two chairs in the rose garden," I suggested. "Just two chairs. Not four, not six, just one for you and one for me. We'll take fifteen minutes each day to set ourselves up right and have coffee together, and just have a conversation and start our day like this." We would have nice porcelain cups with matching saucers, not clunky mismatched mugs. We would sit down and actually savor our java. We were usually in such a rush in the morning that, by the time I was heading out the door, I was always either having to knock back my last sips of tepid coffee like a tequila shot or reheat the mug in the microwave for the third or fourth time, then take it to go. Morning "conversation" was pretty much limited to hasty who-what-when-where exchanges of the day's schedule of appointments, errands, obligations, and so on.

It didn't have to be that way, I admitted to myself on that terrace in Napa. We could create our own version of what we were enjoying so much that Saturday morning. Even if it was just twelve minutes, it would be worth it. Back home, I immediately put the plan into action, setting up a pretty coffee tray the night before. Of course, plenty of mornings still slip out from under us in the chaos of family life, and the weather doesn't always cooperate, but we do try to make our garden breakfast à deux a priority, and when we manage to pull it off, the effort is more than worth it. It feels great to venture into the world feeling serene and connected to my soul mate, instead of hurtling out the door like a human cannonball flying across the circus tent. (Though the circus theme would explain all the noisy little people forever piling into my car. . . .)

Speaking of the Mommy Mobile, consider the possibility that sometimes you can make the biggest difference in the mood a particular space conjures with a simple change of attitude instead of appearance. Take my SUV, for example. Or, I guess I should say, take my children's SUV, since the only reason I have a few square inches in it at all is because no one else is big enough to reach the gas pedal or get a driver's license yet. (Don't think I am not counting those days.) The front is usually an office on wheels, with my phone, laptop, and satchel full of work riding shotgun, and a cup of coffee in the cup holder. (We pause now for a brief commercial break: If automakers can put a warmer in the seats, why can't they make the cup holder do the same thing?? I'm just sayin'. . . .) The backseat and cargo area? Complete and utter chaos, with two toddlers in car seats, plus two big girls with their backpacks and assorted school projects, not to mention a stray friend or two occasionally squished in between. The vibe back there is generally somewhere between amusement park and street riot. When I'm ferrying four kids to various schools, lessons, sleepovers, or events, you'll see me in my full-throttle adrenaline zone, trying my damnedest to manage squabbling siblings while answering my phone (yes, hands-free, and I signed Oprah's no-texting-while-driving pledge!), and paying attention to the road. My epiphany came one frazzled day after I had dropped everyone off at what I hoped were the right schools. I found myself stuck in L.A.'s maddening traffic on the way to work. No surprise there. Music was pulsing from the radio while I waited for another business call that would no doubt get interrupted by a dropped signal on my cell phone. My mind was racing, my nerves were fried, and I realized that I was maintaining that frantic Mommy Mobile mood even though the kids weren't with me anymore. We all know there are precious few minutes in any given day when any mother—especially one with a job outside the home—actually finds herself alone. And here I was, squandering my solitude! I immediately switched off the music and cell phone, took some deep, cleansing breaths, and let the traffic around me become white noise. Now, my car becomes my secret Zen zone when I'm alone. Making my surroundings match the mood I want has proven to be a healthy mini stress-buster when I really need one. (Still want the heated cup holder, though. . . .)

STAR POWER

On the set of *Dancing with the Stars*, the dressing room I was assigned turned out to have the exact opposite problem of my hyperactive Mommy Mobile: This personal space had no vibe at all. The area consists of two small rooms bridged by a bathroom in between. One room is where I have my hair and makeup done, and the other is a little sitting area with a pale blue sofa, a chair, and a coffee table. A TV monitor is mounted overhead. A couple of weeks into my first season as cohost, I decided that it was time to put my stamp on my dreary quarters, especially the hair and makeup room, where the glam squad and I spend so many long hours. Not only was that room aggressively ugly (the walls were a shade of pale slime one of my hair guys had dubbed "*Exorcist* Green"); it wasn't even very functional. The makeup table looked like a clunky kitchen cart that had run away from a cooking show. Crowded next to it was an unwieldy round card table that served as the parking lot for my hairdresser's equipment and products. Then there was a lonely stool wedged so close to the door that anyone daring to sit in it risked a split lip should my producer or cohost, Tom Bergeron, fling the door open without warning.

My desk, or what passed for one, was a wobbly TV tray. None of the pieces fit together, and everyone was always bumping into each other. Overall, there was just this haphazard air to the place. My makeover space needed a makeover!

I knew I needed a vibe with a lot of energy to keep everyone's pace up on show night, and given the nature of our work, something funky, edgy, and creative was in order. I was leaning toward teal on the walls, with a shaggy white area rug on the floor and a big gilded Venetian mirror I had at home to add the right dash of glitz. My dear friend Cyvia didn't give me time to procrastinate. This was an ugly emergency. As soon as I uttered the words, "I hate this room," she jumped right online and started shopping. As I mentioned earlier, I settled on Tiffany blue for one wall, and a heathery silver for the other. And since Tiffany made me think of my icon, Audrey Hepburn, I hunted down a mounted print of her in *Breakfast at Tiffany's* to hang on the wall for inspiration—love her! The other wall is an ever-changing collage of fashion-magazine tears featuring great hairstyles and makeup looks to inspire my artists. We found a lovely remnant of silver sateen up in Wardrobe, and I had a seamstress turn it into an elegant pleated slipcover for the runaway kitchen cart. A fluffy white beanbag added some fun, easily movable seating. A small shelf went up for two of my bare necessities in life—a phone and a scented candle. I was good to go. The room not only looked different, I felt different in it. It set the tone I needed to get myself into the mood for *DWTS*—old Hollywood class with just enough edge to be hip, fun, and modern.

All that was missing was the perfect inspirational quote to post on my cute new corkboard. I tried Google searches and an open appeal to my Twitter followers, but nothing was really grabbing me. Then one day, my celebrity stylist was making his usual last-minute adjustments before I go on air. Justin Ducoty is one of those legendary talents in the industry—he's responsible for my look down to the last diamond. That particular day, the gorgeous dress he'd pulled for me happened to have a lot of underslips and tulle that kept riding up and wrinkling. Justin smoothed things out. Just before I headed for the stage, he rushed up to me with an urgent question. "How do you feel on the inside?" he wanted to know.

I assured him all was well. We both laughed. He'd gotten his answer.

And I'd gotten my quote, which remained on my wall all season long to remind us all to check in and stay connected.

COLOR YOUR WORLD

If you ask me, color plays an underrated role in our day-to-day lives. As women, we're all keenly aware of how color affects us when we're choosing what clothes to wear—you know you'll feel sultry when you put on a flattering dress in black or red, or that you'll feel sweet and demure in ice pink, or happy in lemon yellow. But how often have you applied the same logic and given the same attention to the rooms you occupy 24/7? Did you really mean to live your life in beige? I have nothing against neutrals, but make them serve a purpose, as the quiet backdrop for a favorite piece of art, for example. And don't condemn yourself to eternal beigedom. Soft grays, greens, and even heathers can serve as neutrals, too. In my house, I've come to appreciate earth tones for their therapeutic value. Walking into our downstairs playroom used to be overwhelming. It was a mosh pit in primary colors, festooned with toys and paraphernalia for four active kids who happen to span different age groups. It was sensory overload. It dawned on me that the natural impulse to decorate a playroom in bright, childish colors was terribly misguided. They didn't need that extra color stimulation! Earth tones created a cozy but calmer vibe. The room was still fun and interesting for them, but they didn't go as crazy. All I did was the visual equivalent of shifting from Lucky Charms to Lucky Charms with 25 percent less sugar.

It's true that we generally think of "setting the mood" as a purely adult indulgence, but I think our children deserve the same consideration, if not more, since they're ruled more by emotion to begin with. My eldest, Neriah, used to love to take baths with me when she was little, and she especially loved it when I would put on soft classical music and illuminate the bathroom with candles and dissolve lavender bath salts in the water. "This is what I do to relax," I told her. We dubbed the ritual "Mommy's romantic bath." As she grew older, she adopted the practice on her own. Now, as a ten-year-old engulfed in tweendom's never-ending dramas, Neriah will sometimes come ask me if she can "get in a romantic bath and just relax for a while." I bring her the little bath gels and lotions from hotels when I travel, and I've even shown her how to float flower petals in the water. I figure if it works for me, it'll work for her. And it does: Creating a peaceful environment helps kids unwind and calm their bodies down. Even in our bustling kitchen, I try to set the quieter mood just before dinnertime, by dimming the lights a bit and switching whatever music I have playing in the background to an international blend or classical easy listening—the same playlist I use when I'm lucky enough to book a massage.

I can't imagine my life without music, and I love to make playlists for every mood and occasion, from let's-get-raunchy to brunch with the in-laws. (And thankfully, I haven't mixed those two up yet! My mother-in-law's no prude, but I'm not so sure she'd appreciate "Shakin' It 4 Daddy" with her mimosa.)

brooke's playlist of artists, albums, and songs to calm a chaotic house

"Diamonds & Pearls"

Bossa N' Roses

buddha-bar

Café del Mar

India.Arie

Corneille

Colbie Caillat

Joss Stone

Kem

Sade

Sara Bareilles

Bossa N' Marley

Oliver Peoples 4

WILD KINGDOM

Mood can transport you, and whether it's music or scented candles in a travel tin, you can transport mood virtually anywhere, too.

All my nesting work in anticipation of David's return home to Malibu from the game preserve in South Africa was suddenly put on hold when I got a call from his producers. David had just won a big challenge, and the prize was to bring his family to South Africa for a seventy-two-hour visit. Needless to say, this was a once-in-a-lifetime opportunity, and I wanted it to be magical.

I knew from the weekly Skype conversations we were permitted that conditions weren't merely primitive—they were hellish. "It feels like jail," David told me. Lack of privacy was an understatement. He had to share his living quarters with ten people. Six were sleeping in the same room with him, on mattresses lined up along the floor. I had agreed to the producers' demands that we spend the first night of our visit in a family tent on the reserve. We'd have to use the property's sole bathroom, an outhouse across the field, which meant dodging piles of ostrich shit in my flip-flops. In the dark. One misstep definitely would have been a major mood killer (except, presumably, for the male ostrich, but he wasn't the one I was flying halfway across the world to seduce). The only shower was a shared hose used for all personal and household washing. From the grim snippets I'd been told, I knew I needed to bring a slice of heaven with me to Africa for poor David. I needed to carry the essence of home with me. I made a list and set about with my hunting and gathering.

First stop was the cigar shop in Malibu. David loves to sit in our backyard after a great meal, cappuccino in hand, and smoke a beautiful Cuban cigar. My father (step) smoked a pipe, and I will never forget the sweet smell of his tobacco. I never mind the smell of a stinky cigar—it's quite sexy, actually, in a dirty sort of way. And the sense memory brings me back to a special childhood place.

Knowing the importance of beautiful, intimate lighting, I packed some of our favorite Kai candles, with their heady scent reminiscent of gardenias and rain. And what's candle-light without a great bottle of wine? Wine has become one of our passions since building our home. Only problem is, we drink too much of it to ever fill our gorgeous vintage brick-and-cedar wine cellar. Now I chose two big, voluptuous reds, wrapped them in a traveling wine case, and crossed my fingers they would make the journey intact.

Next on the agenda was a trip to the neighborhood candy shop, which has all the old-school yummies. Rain was only too happy to fill a basket with her daddy's weaknesses—Milk Duds, Whoppers, Laffy Taffy, and Tootsie Rolls. From there, it was on to David's favorite men's boutique, where I splurged on a few new shirts and a pair of sunglasses. Absence makes the Am-Ex card grow fonder, it seems!

Considering I was the package he was most looking for-ward to, I then had to dress myself. Lingerie seemed too obvi-ous on this trip, but I made sure that all my bras and panties just happened to be matching lace and the sexiest pull from my collection. The info he had shared with me about the bugs there led me to believe that I was more likely to be sporting footy pajamas than my usual, but just in case, everything I packed was inspired by the pages of a VS catalog.

Music always dictates the mood for David and me, and it was probably the most important element of all for making my romantic fantasy come true. In his isolation, I knew David had been inspired to work on some new songs, and being deprived of music, as a singer and songwriter, had to be driving him crazy. I packed my iPod and a battery-operated dock. Since David had been gone, my attention to music had turned inward, as well. I had discovered a whole new collection of artists through Pandora.com, whose search engine analyzes your taste in music and offers new suggestions accordingly. I had compiled a pretty impressive catalog during all those celibate nights. Even today, it's fascinating to go back and listen to the music I was drawn to during that first month David was away. Much of it was lyrically very deep, serious, and hopelessly romantic. Some of it was lonely and tragic, but it all had an intense vibe of desperate love. That was the beginning of a playlist I came to call DEEP. Songs like "Gravity," "Soldier of Love," and "Let Me Love You" all sang to my soul, and I could not wait to share these new treasures with my man.

So with songs, sweets, sexy notions, great smokes, fine wine, and all the fixings to set the most romantic mood ever, off I went on the craziest, most whirlwind adventure of my life—a thirty-eight-hour trip (one way) with Shaya and Rain in tow, to hook up with my man for a few precious hours on an air-mattress. What can I say? Desperate times call for desperate measures, and I wasn't going to let reason stand in my way, no matter how many people told me I was nuts to drop everything and take two toddlers halfway around the world for a weekend. Ah, what I wouldn't do for love! I fully expected a Partner of the Year plaque waiting for me when I got home.

When we at last arrived at the reserve and I laid eyes on the mail-order family tent, I wondered if I had packed enough wine to get into the mood. I wondered if my candles would burn it down. I wondered if killer mosquitoes and unidentified creepy-crawlers had a thing for Milk Duds, and whether Cuban cigar smoke would act as a bug repellant. Then I wondered what Rain and Shaya would think of my lace G-string in such close quarters, and I hoped they wouldn't request *High School Musical* on my iPod dock, because Troy and Gabriella had not made the cut on my DEEP list.

Surveying the tent, I was admittedly disappointed that it wasn't the rustic but spacious tribal honeymoon hut I had imagined, but after our grueling journey and four weeks of celibacy, my opinion of the pop-up Sports Chalet special was starting to come around. As was a family of goats. A family of goats who were loudly and rudely determined to climb into (or, failing that, onto) our tent. They were obviously as curious as I was about what would possibly take place in the middle of a game reserve, in the wannabe-romantic family pop-up tent, with TV cameras posted everywhere but inside.

The good news was that the kids were wiped out, and fell fast asleep moments after their little heads hit their air mattress. It wasn't going to be the first time David and I snuck in some TLC while the little ones were just whispers away. I removed our microphone pacs, lit our candles, and uncorked the wine. There was no stemware, but drinking Chateau Margaux right out of the bottle like a couple of hoodlums somehow complemented the rough scene. Then I put on my sexiest playlist.

There is something very spiritual about the African air, the darkness, the sounds of nature, and the animalistic energy.

The zebras began stampeding all around us outside the tent, like an urgent primal drumbeat to the music playing within. I had been up for at least twenty-four hours straight by then, but I felt suffused with this mood that was so strangely, intoxicatingly tender and wild. I felt new. I didn't know what to do first, and the power of our kiss was almost too much to handle. What I had brought with me, and what I found already there, seemed to collide in a sensual explosion. The soft perfume of the candles and the loamy scent of earth beneath us; the seductive songs and the pounding hooves; even the crude, heavy feel of the wine bottle against our lips followed by the warm, sophisticated mouthful of Bordeaux. Our reunion was everything I had hoped for, and much, much more.

At first glance, that dreaded tent had looked like a bad scene from *National Lampoon's Vacation,* but I managed to transform it into the most romantic love nest Malibu and Africa had ever seen! I prayed that the rest of the reserve didn't experience us that night, and I wondered if our pheromones had anything to do with the animal action huddled around our tent. I don't think the crazed goats were eavesdropping because they were Kem fans. I no longer cared; by then, the wild audience was part of the ambience. I wanted us to live inside that sweet, excruciating mood forever.

Maybe I'd have to look into some zebra print for the bedroom when I got home. . . .

a bed of roses

WHEN I WAS pregnant with Rain, David wanted to throw a big beautiful party to celebrate. The whole idea was contrary to Jewish tradition, and sounded way over the top, but it was his first child, and I knew he was excited. Our house wasn't finished yet, but a generous friend offered his Bel Air mansion. When we arrived, the tableau took my breath away. The house was filled with white roses and white orchids, and the tables were draped in snowy linens, with crystal goblets reflecting the flicker of candlelight. More candles floated in the pool, shimmering against the water. It was ethereal, like a vision of Heaven, the first name we had chosen for our unborn daughter. David asked me to come for a stroll through the magnificent flower garden. When we reached a gazebo, David pulled out a video camera and asked me to say something to the baby inside me. *Corny!* I thought, but managed something awkward, like "We can't wait for you to get here!" "Your turn," David then said, handing me the camera. I watched, speechless, as he bent down on one knee and pulled out a tiny ring box. Inside was a stunning diamond eternity band. He slipped the ring on my finger and proposed to me with these words: "I want to spend my life with you." To this day, we set the mood for romance with white roses.

✿10

hall pass to the wild side

Naked in New York: The boys and I always get crazy and snap a souvenir shot sans clothes on my hotel terrace. Brrr!!

*B*ACK IN MY bachelorette days, I used to run with a posse of gorgeous girlfriends who, like me, happened to make their living as lingerie models. We were foxy little twentysomethings, and we thought we were all that and a can of whipped cream when it came to sensuality. After all, we were the half-naked vixens shooting sultry looks at you as you flipped through the pages of a Frederick's of Hollywood catalog. If that wasn't hot, what was?

We were about to find out, courtesy of the one married girl in our group.

She was a Playmate—sexy, beautiful, and wed to a hunky man who kissed the ground she walked on. We were all single and looking for Mr. Right, and since she was the first in our group to tie the knot, I guess we all kind of looked up to her a little bit.

One night, when her husband was out of town, this friend invited the gang over to her house. There were five of us. The wine was flowing, the mood was great, and she sat us all down on this plush sectional couch in her living room. There was a big upholstered coffee table in the center. Our hostess dimmed the lights and lit some candles.

"Okay, girls, I'm going to show you what I do for my man," she announced.

We glanced at each other nervously. *Is she for real?* But we were a bit tipsy by then, and frankly, too fascinated to refuse. She nodded toward the sound system and issued her instructions: "When I give the word, hit 'play.'"

Off she went, and we exchanged anxious, *what-the-hell-are-we-in-for?* looks. The Playmate was definitely feeling her Chardonnay—and did I mention that she was an exhibitionist even when she was stone-cold sober, and we all knew that she was kinda crazy, and the sky was the limit? So we all sat there like a bunch of little puppy dogs, and when we heard her call out, "I'm ready," we hit the music.

Our friend appeared at the top of the stairs in a classy black wraparound dress and heels. She slinked ever so slowly down the steps, jumped up onto the coffee table, and proceeded to do a striptease performance like you've never seen in a movie or imagined in your life. Suffice to say it was scandalous, and we all sat there dumbfounded. She turned her full attention on each of us, one by one, as if we were VIPs in a members-only club. We were so aroused, and so uncomfortable, and so freaked out! It was a trip and a half. I remember vividly what was going through my mind:

Holy shit, how did she come up with this choreography and this number and where'd she get the guts to perform it?

Not that I was naïve, but I found myself thinking incredulously: *Is this what some women do for their men, has somebody done this for my man, I need to be doing this for my man, no WONDER she's got the man!*

It was sheer voyeurism, and no, it didn't devolve into a girl orgy by any means. It was more like an uninhibited tutorial. We all gaped at our friend in pure amazement, and by the time her little show was over, we had placed her on an even higher pedestal in our minds. *That* was sexy. We thought she had it all, but we realized now that she was kinda giving it all, too.

That night woke up a lot of things in me, and it obviously unnerved the other girls, as well, because we hastily convened a powwow the very next day. We had all been assuming we were sexy enough, and were confident that we were pleasing our men, but we sure weren't doing what she was doing. We reached a consensus: We needed to pull it together, step it up a few notches. We ought to be pulling out some of those moves and trying them on our mates. And I have to admit, the whole experience did set my competitive juices flowing. I couldn't bear the thought that another woman was giving more sexy than I was. Game on.

Easier said than done, though. For me, this was a real challenge. Yes, I could pose in front of a photographer and crew in racy lingerie for eight hours a day on a catalog shoot, but that was work, and there was an emotional disconnect. Playing the seductress in the privacy of my own bedroom for someone I was attracted to was a whole 'nother story. I wasn't a prude, but I definitely wasn't a performer, either. I had once bailed out of a bikini contest when I saw other girls parading around in thongs. I may have had the freakiest of intentions about surprising my man with a one-woman show, but I doubted I would have been able to summon the nerve to even venture out of the bathroom had I put on the ensemble the Playmate was wearing that unforgettable evening. I certainly wouldn't have had the guts to choreograph an entire number, light the candles, hit play, and let him sit there like a king while I delivered the performance of a lifetime. It just wasn't my thing. But what a treat for her man! Now I knew I had a lot to strive for.

Exploring your outer limits is unquestionably one of the most exciting parts of being a woman. Sometimes, it feels like we have all these separate identities neatly compartmentalized in one efficient yet always exhausted body: There's the nurturing mother, the devoted partner, the competent worker, and, finally, the woman within—your own private dancer. And she's usually not allowed out until all those other identities have fulfilled their duties and signed off on the overtime.

So give her the spotlight once in a while! She's more than earned it.

If you're not ready to whip out the feather boas or leather bustiers just yet, there are fun ways to coax your private dancer out of the shadows. Start by treating yourself to one of the burlesque how-to videos you can easily shop for online, or even better, take your man on a date to enjoy a live show. Make a few mental notes about the moves that seem to grab his attention the most. You can pick up and polish a routine like the pros by taking one of the burlesque classes available all over the country now—or try strippercize and pole dancing if that's more your vibe. Lots of studios even offer in-home instruction and props if you want to get a bunch of girlfriends together and make a party of it. I love the old-school seduction of burlesque, myself; it's often as much about what you leave on as what you remove. Innuendo becomes foreplay. Peeling off a single glove with a saucy stare can be far more seductive than stripping down to tasseled pasties and doing a dirty lap dance.

All relationships need a dash of the unexpected now and

then, a little something to jazz up the routine and tease the imagination. Doesn't everyone deserve a hall pass to the wild side?

CROCODILES, THE FIRST LADY, AND MY ASS IN A SLING

I have to confess that I'm a born adrenaline junkie. I'm one of those girls who just enjoys a kiss of danger now and then. I wasn't a troublemaker growing up, but I've been known to gleefully test the boundaries. My parents were super strict, and as a teenager, I used pillows to build a fake sleeping body under my covers every night, then I would climb out my bedroom window, cross the yard, and scale a six-foot wooden fence so I could sneak off with my friends. I'd creep back before the sun rose, and be up in time for school, with no one the wiser. The only time I ever got caught was when a jealous classmate ratted me out. Even that didn't put an end to my midnight escapes—I just waited out the parental storm, and resumed operations. I was a good kid, with great grades, and my folks weren't the type to have a rebellious teen kidnapped by an afternoon talk show and shipped off to fascist boot camp, so the risk was fairly minimal.

After I graduated from high school, my stepdad enforced his ironclad responsibility rule: At eighteen, you either moved out or got a job and paid rent. I followed my boyfriend to Scottsdale, and gave myself two months to find work. One afternoon, I walked into the most popular bar serving the University of Arizona campus and asked to speak to the managers. They were a couple of young, cute Italian guys, and if they suspected I was underage, they never said so out loud.

"I need a job," I said.

"Sorry. We're not hiring," they replied.

"But I need work," I implored. What I lacked in experience, I made up for in persistence.

They ended up deciding to give me a chance. The head bartender trained me, and it didn't take long for me to work my way up to shot girl, which was like hitting the tip jackpot. Meanwhile, I kept booking what modeling gigs I could land—Arizona and Milan have exactly nothing in common—and I entered bikini contests to supplement my income with prize money. When I won Miss Hawaiian Tropic Tan, it came with an acting scholarship in California. I took my dog, packed my bags, and drove across the desert to Los Angeles. I was nineteen, and I didn't have a job, friends, or a place to stay waiting for me. My parents knew better than to try to talk me out of it, and, in fact, encouraged me to find my path and pursue it. "You can always come home," my stepdad promised as he hugged me tight, "so never live your life in 'what if.'" His words became my mantra, a reminder to embrace every opportunity, and to look for adventures instead of obstacles.

Ironically, I would have to say that one of my favorite sources of inspiration has always been one of the most sensible, staid, and decidedly unglamorous women in modern history: Eleanor Roosevelt. With her schoolmarmish face and debutante upbringing, you'd never suspect the late First Lady possessed such a zest for life, but her words prove otherwise. You've probably come across this famous Eleanor quote on some coffee mug or greeting card, but it truly is worth taking to heart. Here's what she said:

"Do something every day that scares you."

That attitude, plus my ever-multiplying wardrobe of bikinis, proved to be just the ticket for the young, slightly insane producers of *Wild On*. The acting scholarship had turned out to be a scam, but I was able to establish myself as a swimsuit and lingerie model on my own. When I answered the E! audition call, I was so young and naïve, I signed on without a second glance— no agents, lawyers, or hazard insurance policies involved. I'd already ridden motorcycles, jumped out of airplanes, and had a torrid affair with a German male model who spoke no English, so I considered myself one very cool little cucumber. Hey, I didn't even fear fear itself. Just spiders, but these guys weren't asking me to star in a remake of *Charlotte's Web*.

No, they were asking me to do an open-water dolphin dive off Australia in waters frequented by great white sharks. I never bothered to ask whether they'd done this before, or if they had researched it at all. We set down anchor, and they helpfully fired off some shock waves to deter any lurking man-eaters before I descended into the middle of the deep blue sea. For all I knew, Mr. and Mrs. Jaws and their friends had become so accustomed to divers using the shock wave trick that they all now merely regarded it as a dinner bell, and I was about to become the entrée. Swallowed up by the sea, hearing only the whoosh of my own breath, I felt tiny and insignificant. I looked around for the promised dolphins, but none were in sight. Suddenly, I sensed an eerie, large mass lurking somewhere above me. My heart raced. The water grew cold and dark, and I felt a huge shadow pass over me. *Please, please, please*, I silently prayed. Whatever it was, it was enormous! Definitely not a dolphin. A whale, maybe. But . . . omnivore or plankton connoisseur? Did I really want to know? The shadow slid past, sunlight breaking through the water again, and I realized, half a heart attack too late, that it was just our drifting dive boat. At last, some dolphins arrived for their camera call, and I was flooded with this euphoric lightness as these beautiful creatures circled curiously around me. Finally, I swam to the surface and climbed back aboard the boat. How had joy replaced terror so quickly? It amazed me that the place I was in had changed from menacing to magical in a matter of minutes. I never would have experienced the presence of dolphins if I hadn't overcome the possibility of sharks.

Whenever I took a risk, I came away with a stronger sense of self, and what used to frighten me now fulfilled me, feeding my spirit in ways I never imagined. When we filmed in Belize, I was sent snorkeling through an infamous reef known as "Shark Ray Alley," for the giant stingrays and nurse sharks who live there. This time, I carried along fish to feed them, and felt like part of the underwater neighborhood as friendly, five-foot sharks came by for a handout. The graceful rays were fascinating to watch as they floated past on velvet wings. The bolder ones would approach and latch gently on to me, giving me sea hickeys.

Far less friendly was the eight-foot crocodile I was supposed to distract while an accomplice stole eggs from her nest on another episode.

"Let's go into the croc pen," was how that encounter began. The egg thief making this suggestion was a bizarre, bearded Australian guy named Malcolm, with missing teeth, a straw hat, and the kind of amazing leathered face you'd expect to see in a *National Geographic* portrait gallery. Common sense was not a trait he telegraphed right off the bat, and I was uncharacteristically skeptical about this particular scenario the *Wild On* crew had dreamed up. (They were young and off the hook, and it was kind of like repeatedly putting your well-being in the hands of a frat house during a never-ending rush week.)

"Are you serious?" I asked Malcolm.

"Yeah, yeah," he insisted. At least, I think that's what he said. The accent and lack of teeth made understanding him something of a challenge.

"I could seriously die in there," I said, before following him through the fence. (What can I say? The *Wild On* gig basically turned my whole life into one big double dare.)

We marched into the smelly pen, and Malcolm handed me a five-foot stick, which, I quickly calculated, was (a) just a stick, and (b) a good three feet shorter than the two crocodiles giving me the evil eye from the muddy pond. Malcolm tied an old pair of white pants to the end of the stick, promising me that this would subdue a charging croc if I waved it in front of its face. I was dubious about this white-flag defense—is "truce" even in a crocodile's vocabulary? Did they sign the Geneva Convention?—but I had no choice but to play the hand I'd been dealt. I was just glad I still had a hand.

Malcolm headed straight for the crocodile nest to swipe a bucketful of eggs, and sure enough, an enraged mama croc lunged out of the water with a murderous growl and headed our way. Well, my way, technically, since I was all that stood between her and the egg snatcher.

"Oh God, oh God, oh God," I said. (I did a lot of spontaneous praying on *Wild On*.) I waved the pants-on-a-stick, which the croc latched on to, and then let go. We repeated the drill a few more times until Malcolm had harvested all the eggs. I felt giddy as we walked away. I was tougher than I thought. Fierce, even.

By the time we filmed in New Zealand, I was feeling down-right invincible. There, I got the adrenaline fix of a lifetime courtesy of some guy who had built his own rocket ship and tethered it to the top of his house, where he would launch it so it could circle around like . . . well, like a runaway rocket ship. There was no liability waiver to sign—I mean, why bother? I put on a helmet, climbed in, and hit the throttle. There were enough g-forces going on that reviewing footage of that particular stunt gives me a good idea of what I would look like with a really bad face-lift. Major Tom meets Joan Rivers—scary!!

Weirdly enough, it was one of the safer stunts on the New Zealand itinerary that finally tripped me up. I was supposed to do the famed Nevis bungee jump over a rocky canyon in Queensland. Heights usually don't bother me—I used to love to skydive until my then-husband, Garth, begged me to stop after I became a mother—and I didn't expect to have the reaction I did once I was in the sling and suited up for the highest bungee jump in the Southern Hemisphere. We were in this cable car, which was rocking madly in the wind. I went out on the jump ledge and was peering over, but the thought of plunging down 440 feet in an eight-second fall and then being whipped back up by a giant rubber band was not appealing to me. At all. Where are the bragging rights in that? And what if I hurt my back? The indemnity list of possible mishaps included "uterus prolapse." I know I could have talked myself into jumping, but I decided to listen to that inner voice saying "nope," instead.

"I can't," I admitted on camera. "This is insane. Nobody can say I don't take chances, but . . . no. No way." I went back inside the cable car and began unbuckling myself.

"I'm a chicken," I announced. "A big chicken. Maybe I'm a smart chicken. Chickens are not so bad."

This is the part of the story where you're expecting to hear that they later discovered a big rip in the bungee cord or a faulty latch on the safety harness, but I said "chicken," not "psychic," and I'll never know what gave me such cold feet that day. I just recognized, and respected, the difference between excitement and dread. And I knew that, in the end, it wasn't the TV crew or the local guides or the whims of the wind that I had to trust. It was me.

Just the nature of the show no doubt gave *Wild On* viewers the impression I was some footloose, wild party girl. But as a matter of fact, I was pregnant with my first baby when I signed on, and Neriah and I were a package deal. If she didn't go, I didn't go, and she never missed an episode. Her passport had forty stamps in it by the time she was two years old. I'd film my scenes at the world's wildest spring break, then retreat to my hotel room to feed the baby and get some sleep. Nowadays, Neriah gets a kick out of watching the old clips, but her younger sister, Sierra, is bewildered by my lust for adventure. "Mommy, why are you such a risk taker?" she once demanded.

"Because," I answered, "I want to experience life and wring it out."

Motherhood is a different kind of adventure, and it can scare me every single day, but I know for a fact that the rewards are richer when you embrace the challenges and throw yourself into them with abandon. Conquer, don't cower: That's my motto. Even if the only crocodiles I've got my eye on these days are size 7 platforms with a spike heel.

PRIVATE DANCER

I don't know what I'm afraid of. I'm in the bathroom, in lacy lingerie and stilettos, and I don't want to come out. My mind is replaying the private burlesque my Playmate pal staged in her living room, a man I love is lying in bed, wondering what my big surprise is, and despite the tequila shots we knocked back earlier, I still can't even summon the nerve to turn the doorknob. What's up with that?

At their core, most women I know, especially the moms, are fearless. We tap into our reservoirs of courage more out of necessity, though, than desire. To raise and protect our children, we struggle mightily to mask our vulnerabilities; the lioness instinctively knows not to show weakness. Just look around at the popular image of women in America today, whether they're corporate or political leaders, or teen vampires on the movie screen, or models selling cocktail dresses in the pages of your favorite magazine: Fierce has become the new feminine. There's much to celebrate about that, don't get me wrong, but some-times, something, some*one*, gets drowned out in the roar.

I'm talking about your deepest, most intimate secret self, the one you probably consider the truest one of all. Your private dancer.

There's a big stretch of road between risk and risqué, and what I've learned—yet have to remind myself again and again—is that being unafraid and being uninhibited are two very different things. Being unafraid is when I step out of a small plane with a parachute on my back, anticipating the exhilaration of my free fall before I tug the rip cord and then float through silent sky back to earth. Being uninhibited is stepping outside that bathroom, and outside my own comfort zone, and finally, outside myself, and allowing myself to let go and trust and free-fall into my lover's arms. The second scene is harder for me to pull off than the first.

When David and I finally got together more than a decade after our hot fling in Mexico, I was both flattered by and fearful of his determination to peel back all the layers so he could truly understand and fully know me. Maybe it's being in an industry ruled by imagination, or our exposure to acting classes and exercises, but role-playing was an important facet of our relationship from the beginning. And it's always come more naturally to David than it has to me.

I can remember the first time we went lingerie shopping together at Agent Provocateur. I was swooning over a flowing La Perla–like gown in sumptuous ivory silk, and he was wanting to have them ring up the stripper G-string. I was as baffled as I was intrigued—David's taste is usually very classic and refined. We hit the same comical impasse at home sometimes, when things would get frisky and he would urge me to go into my closet and put on something stupid and Britney-ish, like a plaid skirt and knee socks.

"I don't *have* anything like that in there!" I would protest. (That was then . . .)

Trashy lingerie, silly outfits—what he was envisioning wasn't me at all! Which, I've slowly come to realize, is the whole point.

It's not that he wanted this "other" woman, or secretly yearned for me to be more like "her." What he wanted was for me to abandon myself, to feel uninhibited enough and safe enough to just let go and play. Especially when we first became a couple, when I was newly divorced and buckling under the pain of all that baggage. "I want for you to be able to completely detach and experience bliss," David said. "I want you to completely forget everything else for a while, escape and be free."

Sex had always been hot between the two of us—I'm pretty

sure our first child, Rain, was conceived in the back of a Hummer on an L.A. side street because we just couldn't wait to get home. Lust wasn't really the issue here. As I matured as a woman, and hit my sexual prime, I could see a whole new level of my sexuality to explore, but being able to reach that place was going to take time and patience. The goal was no longer purely physical release (not to downplay that!). To abandon your inhibitions, I discovered, you have to let go of yourself. But that seemed to go against the very conviction I held strongest as a woman: Be true to yourself. How could I reconcile that?

naked truth
As a young model, I was once living at the Ritz-Carlton while in transition, and I happened to be in a very steamy relationship, when my mom decided to come visit. My man and I started sneaking off to the laundry room, ice room, or other random places when lust overcame us. One night, we took the stairwell up to the rooftop. There was a helicopter landing pad, with this big red bull's-eye right in the center. The view was amazing, with the marina shimmering below us and the lights of the L.A. skyline in the distance. And then there was that bull's-eye. We could see the security cameras, but just the idea of watching someone watching us turned me on. It was all so risky and so scary and so inviting. . . . What can I say? We were just carefree and young and restless. It was hot. Very, very hot.

When the subject of why men enjoy the dress-up game so much came up in a conversation with a friend not long ago, I had to laugh when she turned the tables on David and asked him if he would wear something dumb if I asked him to.

"Of course," he said.

"What if Brooke said it would be a turn-on if you dressed up in a French maid's costume?" she teased.

"Done," he said.

Obviously, I never want to see my man tricked out in a frilly apron and feather duster (well, hold on a minute—can we just lose the apron, LOL?). The image did not thrill me. But his willingness definitely changed my POV and made me aspire to the same freedom and abandonment he felt. Maybe being true to myself meant trusting myself—and my lover—enough to let go.

PICTURES AT AN EXHIBITION

Before David and I began living together, I rented a house built by an artist in Mandeville Canyon. It was hauntingly beautiful, all brick and open beams and soaring ceilings, with a moody Old World vibe. It looked and felt like a set for one of those old black-and-white movies where fate and propriety conspire to keep lovers apart until the yearning becomes unbearable. Although—or perhaps even because—David and I embrace a casual, beach-town lifestyle, there is something we both find deeply romantic about formality. I think it's the whole idea of an elegant, very proper façade concealing a core that's primal and untamed. The Mandeville house seemed to be inviting us to explore that notion, and did we ever have fun doing just that! This particular hall pass to the wild side just happened to come on engraved stationery with a wax seal.

I can't recall exactly how this fantasy game began, but it's safe to say that David is usually the instigator when it comes to directing a steamy scene. I just know I was starving for some romance at that time in my life, so that's what I played out. The basic plot was that I was the beautiful, sophisticated owner of an art gallery, and David was a mysterious, wealthy businessman who had come to look. Against the back wall of our living room was this old armoire, which concealed the sound system. It was filled with classical CDs—Mozart, Bach, all this very dramatic, moody music. In the corner of the room, a tiny bar was tucked away behind two little doors. I remember that the bar itself was this gorgeous piece of very masculine, rough-hewn wood. There was something so incongruous, so unexpectedly beautiful, about seeing a hand-blown crystal wineglass sitting so delicately atop that rugged surface.

David and I dressed to the nines for this favorite little passion play. I would put on some classic, feminine dress with stockings and heels, tasteful jewelry, and a spritz of Dune, the Christian Dior perfume I was wearing the night David and I met in Mexico. David would be perfectly groomed in a fine shirt and linen trousers. When he arrived at my "gallery," there would already be candles flickering and music playing. We would chat, and I would naturally invite him to have a drink at the sexy little bar. I would pour us each a snifter of amaretto on the rocks. We would then walk around the gallery and pretend to study the artwork as we continued our polite conversation. Secretly, though, our lust would be mounting like the chords of the Bach fugue playing in the background, until we could no longer contain ourselves.

It's a silly story, I know, but sharing it is worth the embarrassment to drive home the underlying point: True passion demands a playful mind as much as a willing body. When the objective is pure abandonment, you have to be open enough, and experimental enough, to allow yourself to go there, to be playful without worrying about what he's thinking, or how you look, or whether you're doing it "right." Overcoming your natural reserve may take some effort, but it's worth it to experience that thrill of slipping out from under the weight of everyday life. Go anywhere your mind allows you to go, and let your body follow.

Just use your imagination. (And a good perfume.)

naked truth When we were building our house, I wanted David and me to have our own private sex dungeon. Someplace to be just man and woman, letting our imaginations and inhibitions run wild. The room would have a hidden door with an old-fashioned lock, and only I would hold the key. I envisioned a dark chamber with a little chandelier or candelabra, lots of plush pillows, and walls covered in a deep burgundy fabric. Of course, there would be surround-sound and a wide-screen TV. Which is probably what gave David the idea to turn the space into a family media room, instead. Pass the popcorn, please.

11

getting it (back) on

David and I nuzzle in St. Bart's, our favorite romantic getaway.

*W*HEN DAVID CAME across an old unde-
veloped roll of film labeled "Skydiv-
ing," I was immediately intrigued. I used to love jumping out
of airplanes, but had given it up after having my first child
because it just felt too risky once there were small people who
were counting on me to come home in one piece. Motherhood
felt like a free fall often enough, anyway.

"So did you try it?" I asked David, who had deemed the film
too ancient to process.

"Yeah, I went with this girl and some friends years ago," he
reminisced. My first time had been on a group date, too. Like
David, my memory of the experience was vivid, but I had long
since forgotten the names and faces of the people who'd jumped
with me. I guess time had just deleted all the unnecessary
details. As we compared notes, it turned out that David and I
had even parachuted over the same empty California desert.

It didn't take us much longer to figure out that we had actually done it together and were, in fact, each other's totally for-
gettable date! How was that even possible? How could we end
up as absolute soul mates eighteen years later, when we didn't

even recall sharing such an extraordinary adventure as reck-less twentysomethings?

"It's because we weren't ready for each other then," David believes.

Exactly how, why, and when we connect with one another has been a timeless source of fascination for scientists and poets alike. Whether it's kismet, coincidence, or the perfect collision of pheromones and fantasy, true intimacy is one of life's most extraordinary gifts, and I feel blessed to have found it. But I'm also keenly aware that the bond David and I have, no matter how strong it is, is always going to be tested. You can fall in and out of love, and in and out of lust, countless times with your one and only. Our relationship reminds me of the ocean—constant yet ever-changing, waves crashing against the rocks one moment, then rippling softly in the sunlight the next. We swim through it and sail across it, dive beneath it and soar above it, but no matter how much we explore, the ocean is still too vast and deep to ever fully understand. So we take comfort in what knowledge we can have, and find beauty in the mystery that remains.

I've always found the term "hopeless romantic" to be such a contradiction. No question about it, I'm a romantic through and through, but it isn't an absence of hope that makes me so, it's an abundance of it. Romance is all about possibility and promise. If you want to find it, you have to believe in it and pursue it. And once it first blossoms, you'd better nurture it if you want to keep it flowering.

Full disclosure: When I say I'm a romantic, I have to qualify that a bit and explain that I'm more of what you might call a thoroughly modern romantic—there's just enough rebel in me to give any purists out there the vapors. I'm the mommy who reads fairy tales to her little girls but tweaks the endings. I hate the idea of my daughters growing up believing that Mr. Perfect is going to just come galloping up, sweep them off their feet, and *voila!* everyone lives happily ever after. I look at my three-year-old daughter's innocent face and imagine how crushed she would be to buy into that myth and then realize as a young woman that she'd been duped, and I think, *She's not going down like that!* So I make the fairy-tale prince take his dream girl back to the castle to meet his family, and then they spend some quality time getting to know each other before proceeding to get married and have a wonderful life together. No more speed-dating and instant weddings! And why do all the beautiful maidens always have to wait for some guy they barely know to rescue them from bullying, false imprisonment, or comas induced by produce they should have washed first? So, as you can see, it's not like I'm entirely devoid of skepticism here. Given all that, however, the romantic in me has a startling true confession:

I believe in love at first sight. Absolutely, positively, and without a single doubt.

I joke a lot about first spotting David because of the hideous jacket he was wearing when we were both out on the dance floor at that Mexican beach resort for the charity event. Hard to believe now that we were both barely even drinking age. But it wasn't mere lust (or tequila) that brought us together. I recall the exact moment when we first glanced at each other and our eyes locked. His were deep and green and gorgeous. Even though it was eighteen years ago now, my heart captured every single detail about that night, and I still get a little rush replaying the scene for myself. I remember the breeze, the balmy night, the music, the scent of salt water and warm skin. But most of all, I remember this never-before feeling deep in the pit of my stomach, before David and I had even uttered a word to each other. It wasn't *wow*, it was *whoa*. If you've ever experienced it, you'll know exactly what I mean; if you haven't yet, there's no way to clearly explain it. There was just this chemical connection, this magic that I felt, and he felt it, too. We had our sizzling fling in Mexico, then returned to L.A. and pretty much went our separate ways. We stayed in touch very casually, remained friends, and dated here and there, off and on, but we never really gave each other a chance. "Right guy, wrong time," is how I've always glibly explained it. Privately, though, I still sometimes wonder why we didn't plunge headlong into a full-blown relationship. Or at least stop dating starlets (him) and bad boys (me). Was it because that instant connection was so strong that it scared us? Could I not trust my gut reaction, or did I not trust him? That fearful voice that lives inside all of us and calls out when we get close to what we want was chattering away inside my head: *Too hot, he'll cheat, he'll leave you, too much work, he'll hurt you, HOT but RUN!!!* Good thing my body didn't listen. But the bottom line is, I wasn't ready and he sure as hell wasn't ready. We both had a lot of changing and growing and life experience we needed to have before we were ever going to make it. David was healing from a serious relationship that had just ended painfully, and I was enjoying the footloose and fancy-free single life. If David and I had tried to become a real couple back then, we would have failed miserably. It took thirteen years for us to get the timing right.

So in truth, our love story isn't about connection after all. It's about reconnection.

And it's the ability to reconnect that keeps us together.

show and tell

> I HAD DEREK Hough and his partner Joanna Krupa try this to stay connected when they were stressing out during their semifinals on *DWTS*. The exercise works well in romantic partnerships, too, and it's simple and straightforward: Imitate each other in your worst moments. Sometimes we just don't realize how we act until we see it played out. When you're done, name each other's best qualities. And maintain eye contact while you're doing it!

THE PURSUIT OF HAPPINESS

Life just happened. After Mexico, David started to pursue his singing career in Europe, and eventually moved back to his native France. We fell out of touch, each of us left to wonder what might have been. I ended up marrying a good man who was a great catch by any standard—Garth was intelligent, successful, and supportive of my career aspirations. We welcomed two beautiful daughters, and I changed the ending of their fairy tales because maybe, deep down, I knew I had changed my own.

By the time fate finally worked things out and reunited us for good, David and I tried to settle into the reality of love

without surrendering the fantasy. There are spaces in any relationship. Sometimes, we may find ourselves separated physically for months or weeks at a time, and although we miss
each other, we grow too accustomed to being alone. Other
times, we somehow get emotionally detached and have to
work our way back to the sweet spot, that good place, that I
think of as home.

When I imagine our lives together, I dream of growing older
together the way Aunt Margo and Uncle John have. They were
shotgun-wedding high school sweethearts who were never
supposed to make it for the long haul, but here they are, retir-
ees enjoying life to the hilt after raising four happy and successful children. The last time I visited, Aunt Margo girlishly
admitted that she still gets excited when she hears her husband's car pulling into the driveway. Uncle John obviously
delights in her presence, as well, the way he's always pulling
her close for a slow dance in the kitchen, or singing sappy love
songs to her. "You are my shining star," he croons to her, and
anyone can see that he means it. They catch up with each other
over a cocktail while watching the sun set. I've always enjoyed
basking in the warmth of their family, but I study Aunt Margo
and Uncle John in a different way now that I'm a grown
woman longing to hold on to love the way they have. And
what I notice most about them is that they have managed to
create and maintain their own separate, private relationship
within the wider borders of their family life. They're basically
having an affair with each other, within their own marriage.

There's a reason it's called "maintaining a relationship."
Keeping a partnership strong and healthy takes effort, and you
have to make that effort even when you're not feeling like it,

same as you make yourself go to the gym or hit the jogging path in an effort to keep your body in shape. It's something I work on continuously. You have to strive to keep the lines of communication open, so you can have that exchange of love and intimacy and closeness that makes you partners. Without that, you find yourself just going through the dull motions—passing each other in the hall with barely a grunt of acknowledgment, sharing meals without any real conversation, and interacting with each other mainly for the exchange of responsibilities with the kids. Before you know it, you're living parallel lives. It's such an easy trap to fall into, and I've had to pull myself out of it many times.

I've discovered that two key elements help keep the flame burning between David and me: ritual and surprise. That's the yin and yang, for us, the balance of sweetness and spice that offers a kind of comforting reassurance of love on the one hand, and a thrilling rediscovery of it on the other.

The biggest complaint I hear from women—and one I share myself—is a lack of time and energy to tend to our partnerships the way we'd like to, or know that we should. This is where ritual comes in: If you can find small ways to touch base with each other and just ingrain them as routine, it becomes an unconscious effort. You literally get in the habit of staying connected. No one can make a commitment to stay close no matter what—it's natural for relationships to crest and fall, shift and settle. But you can make a commitment to always acknowledge that bond, no matter how fragile it may seem at times. I apply the same technique I used to win the mirror-ball trophy on *Dancing with the Stars*, and to realize the dreams on my bucket list: I visualize myself getting what I want. Visualizing the life I imagined for David and our family when we first fell in love inspires me to keep actively pursuing that dream. Those efforts pay off in the present, too.

Some of the rituals David and I have created obviously may not work for everyone, but as I've said all along, I don't believe in one-size-fits-all templates for life. There is no single "right" way, and the best we can do is brainstorm with each other and cherry-pick from our common wealth of ideas and experiences. Right from the start in our relationship, David implemented what we call the three-hour rule: We never let three hours pass without speaking to or hearing from each other. There have been exceptions—big ones—when work put us in different time zones or out of e-mail range, but for the most part we're able to stick to our pattern. It doesn't have to be a long conversation; it can be a three-second voice mail saying, "Hey, babe, still tingling from this morning," or "Just wanted you to know I'm thinking about you."

It's fun and easy to create little couple rituals. Maybe it's something as simple as a walk every Sunday morning, holding hands (even if you spent Saturday night screaming at each other), or sneaking a midnight bowl of cereal together once a week. Or you could have a same-time-next-year date to mark the change of seasons, like planting a vegetable garden side by side each spring, or making a big pot of homemade soup together on the first chilly weekend of autumn. Something ordinary that becomes special because you make it belong to you, like the secret smile you exchange when the song you first made love to comes on the radio.

The idea isn't to touch base ("Are you picking up Sam after practice or am I?"), but to touch hearts ("I remember you, I remember us").

If ritual grounds us, then surprise is what lets us take flight.

We all probably have to have at least a hint of a control freak deep inside to raise a family and keep everyone on track, and if you're like me, just dancing through that day-to-day chaos can make you a tad wary of surprises. As moms, the word "surprise" alone tends to take on a whole new meaning, and it's usually along the lines of Magic Marker murals on the dining room wall or toddlers who give themselves a safety-scissor mullet or little blue "yes" lines on pregnancy tests.

But surprise is essential to romance, just to jostle us out of predictability and complacency, and add a little fizz to the whole crazy cocktail. When you think of something unexpected to do solely to delight your partner, you're reconnecting because you're choosing to put thought and effort into your relationship, and you're sending a clear signal: No matter how crazy busy we get, you still matter.

Just today, David and I conspired to meet at home and sneak upstairs after lunchtime. We claimed we had an important conference call for business, then locked the doors and forbade anyone to come disturb us. Then we did, in fact, confer. It was pretty thrilling and refreshing to be able to confer like that right in the middle of the afternoon, when we both weren't too exhausted, or rushing at the beginning of the morning trying to squeeze in a "conference" before starting our chaotic days.

My favorite tawdry tale of reconnection is probably David's homecoming from the three-month stint filming on that African game reserve.

I knew it would be super important to reconnect as a couple before diving back into Familyville after such a long separation. And between jet lag and the rugged conditions he had been coping with for the past few months, I wanted to give

David a chance to decompress a little first. His flight was due in on a Saturday, which meant I'd have to rush to the airport straight from our weekly production meeting at *Dancing with the Stars*. My game plan was to whisk David away for an overnight hotel rendezvous before taking him home, so I booked us a romantic oceanfront room a few miles from LAX and set everything up ahead of time. I filled the room with white roses (our favorite—remember that David proposed to me in the gazebo of a friend's formal flower garden). I brought in scented candles from home and a bottle of our favorite wine.

I'd also bought gorgeous new lingerie for the reunion, and was planning on wearing it beneath a pretty floral dress and heels, hoping to channel the classic, feminine Brigitte Bardot look that David loves.

As I described all this to a couple of friends over dinner a few days before David was due back, though, both husband and wife looked at me and scoffed.

"Are you kidding?" the wife demanded. "Your man's been gone three months and you're going to go all Estee Lauder on him? Really? Why don't you buy some hot, sexy black lingerie, throw on a trench coat, go pick up your man hooker-style and really do it?" Her husband quickly chimed in, recalling a young friend's account of his girlfriend picking him up in similar slutty style once, and how it had rocked his world. "I'll never forget that story," he concluded wistfully. I decided then and there to take their advice.

Come Saturday afternoon, I finished my *DWTS* meeting, then ducked into my dressing room to strip down to my sexy black lingerie and garter. I tied on a khaki trench coat, then slipped on a pair of killer Jimmy Choos and clicked down the hallway as fast as I safely could, praying no network execs would spot me and decide to stop and chat. The whole trench-coat gambit was risky as hell, because we're talking Southern California, not New York City in the middle of winter, and in a sea of people wearing T-shirts and flip-flops, I was bound to stand out like . . . Well, I guess that was the point. When the car pulled up to Arrivals, though, David was already waiting outside, thank God, so at least I didn't have to get out and treat the paparazzi to an eyeful. Of course, I already had the seduction playlist I'd made playing on the car stereo.

It was so exciting to see each other, and the trench coat added this very sexy aura of mystery, though David pretty quickly surmised what was—or more specifically, wasn't—on underneath. We couldn't get to the hotel fast enough. Once there, though, we decided to go to the bar and have a drink and torture ourselves a little longer, until the anticipation was almost unbearable. I carefully crossed my legs to hide what I was revealing. Two very dirty martinis later, we went upstairs and had our reunion. Estee Lauder would have been scandalized. I had planned on breakfast in bed, then a day to wander around Santa Monica by ourselves to just catch up and settle back into being "us" again, but David was up before dawn, and dying to see the kids. I felt a selfish twinge, wanting more time, but we had absolutely wrung out the evening and the wee hours of the morning, no quibble there, so it was coffee and muffins to go at eight a.m., and back to Malibu. The children had colored a big welcome home sign for David, and they nearly bowled him over with glee when he came through the door. More than anything that connects us, the children make our bond tangible, and seeing David in his role as father never fails to fill me with joy and gratitude. Those are the moments when I know that this man is not just in my life; he is my life.

Decadent hotel trysts aside, David and I are both shamelessly corny, and we get our kicks out of surprising each other with high school crush gestures, like lipstick hearts drawn on the bathroom mirror or mash notes left on the car windshield. When I track down a bottle of the now discontinued perfume I was wearing when we first met (Dune, by Christian Dior)— the scent he equates with falling in love with me—a secret spritz on his favorite T-shirt before he packs it for a trip will remind him of me, of us, when we're far apart. Sly humor is always appreciated, too, like the time David took me out to breakfast on the terrace of a local hotel, and I suddenly realized that we were overlooking the quiet side street—not to mention the exact parking space—where we had once pulled over in a frenzy of lust one night and, I'm pretty sure, conceived our first child together in the back of my Hummer.

Cars seem to play a recurring role in our romance. (No big surprise there, since I was an aspiring mechanic when I was a little girl, and David and I share a passion for quality horsepower.) When we first moved in together, David still had the first set of wheels he had ever owned—a Jeep he had bought at sixteen, and dreamed of giving to a son of his own someday. He considered the truck vintage, but I considered it more of a twenty-year-old eyesore sitting in our driveway. I knew he loved it the way you love your oldest, most threadbare jeans— the ones so retro they're cool again, and even when they become unwearable, you can't bear to toss them out because they've just hung in there so long and have been through so much with you. I totally get that kind of sentimental attachment to possessions that everyone else in the world considers replaceable. Anyway, that heap of a Jeep had always been David's baby. Until he had a human one, and had to concede that the whole car-seat-but-no-roof thing was not feasible. We opted for a more family-friendly ride, but the Jeep still sat in the driveway.

One afternoon when I came home, it wasn't there. I idly wondered if David had taken it for a nostalgic cruise along the Pacific Coast Highway, but when I got inside, David was there waiting for me. "Come out back. I want to show you something," he urged me. I silently hoped it wasn't a landslide: We had had to scrape together every spare dime we had to finish building the house, and we hadn't been able to afford to put in all the landscaping yet. We dreamed of having beautiful, terraced gardens someday, but so far, there was just dirt, and our imaginations were the only thing flowering on the terraced hillside. "Look," David said now.

I found myself gazing at pots full of beautiful roses. There were hundreds of rosebushes, blooms in every possible hue, their intoxicating scent perfuming the breeze. It took my breath away. "How did you do this?" I managed to stammer.

It turned out that a gardener had been admiring David's old Jeep. His son needed a car, but the gardener didn't have the cash to buy him one. David ended up bartering with him for roses. His sacrifice was so unexpected; the sheer tenderness of it touches me deeply to this day. It's no coincidence, years later, that one of my most gratifying pastimes is to work in my rose garden. The roses have become an affirmation of David's love for me, and even a single stem in a bud vase on my vanity is a powerful reminder of how much we mean to each other.

YOU'VE LOST THAT LOVIN' FEELING . . .

I was having lunch with some girlfriends when the subject of how to get the sex you're not getting came up. So to speak. Half of my table could relate, while the other half reported the opposite problem, and fantasized about their mates being sent on extended, preferably foreign, business trips involving lots of cold showers.

So why are some women wanting more and others wanting less? I used to think that hitting my thirties would automatically transport me to that much-ballyhooed "sexual prime." After sprinkling in two babies, though, that was hardly the case. I've done the full loop-de-loop on the hormonal roller coaster, wanting it all the time during pregnancy and then not at all after delivery. Or I'll be feeling all sensual and lush and womanly, only to have my man's new-daddy hormones kick in and refuse to regard me as anything but a Madonna figure (and I don't mean the one in the raunchy cone bra).

It's sad and disappointing to be a sexual woman and then practically lose your mojo overnight. Happy to report that, even after sprinkling in two more babies, I'm enjoying my sexual groove now. That's not to say the fire doesn't wane on occasion. If you're trying to reignite the passion in your relationship, or keep the blaze burning, there are plenty of things you can do about it. The first step is to take stock: Is your life so hectic you can't slow down long enough to even think about sex, let alone do it? Fatigue is the root of all evil. I cannot tell you how many times I have had the freakiest of intentions, only to end up passing out and enjoying my own fantasy in la-la land.

Couples are rarely on the same sex clock, and that holds doubly true for busy parents. Men and women are hardly ever in sync emotionally and physically, even in the courtship phase: One is always in pursuit. Fortunately for most of us, this dynamic shifts all the time, so you may be the horn-dog one week (or for nine months, if pregnancy does to your libido what it did to mine with the first one), and your man may claim the title the next. Keeps things interesting, to say the least! But what happens when you lose interest altogether? And more important, how do you get it back?

Let's start with the most common culprit: No one ever prepares you for the impact of pregnancy and parenthood on your sex life. And by impact, I'm thinking, *knocked senseless by a sizeable meteorite that came hurtling out of nowhere.* Especially if you're a first-timer, you can't be blamed if you start to wonder whether you're having a baby or a nervous breakdown when the hormones take over. You're just not yourself. I turned into this depraved little sex monkey when I was pregnant with Neriah—consumed by lust so out of control I actually went to the doctor to see if there was any way to adjust my dials. (He laughed and said his own pregnant wife was having the exact *opposite* symptom.) Here's the really sick, inexplicable part: At the same time your body may be flushed with constant desire, there's a good chance you'll also start hating everything about your husband. Every woman I know has turned on her man at some point during pregnancy. You'll suddenly loathe the way he chews his food, or despise the sound he makes when he breathes, or resent the sheer nerve of him to blithely go about his business while you're waiting to explode. This, too, shall pass. Meanwhile, hide the steak knives.

Once the baby arrives, of course, there is no return to the old normal, because this amazing, beautiful, helpless, needy creature is your new normal. When my sex drive went AWOL after I had Rain, I was scared: *Really? Is that it for me? What about my sexual prime???* After all, I was just settling into my new dream life with this man I adored, our relationship was in a great place, and we had enjoyed an exciting love life until now. I wanted it back! I made an appointment with my ob-gyn, wondering whether my testosterone levels were off or something. I was crushed when all the tests came back fine; I had hoped for a quick fix. I wasn't alone.

When I joined *The Doctors* as their resident mommy correspondent, I remember going to visit a mommy-and-me class to interview the women there. "So what did you least expect, what have been your hardest challenges?" I asked. Out poured this torrent of frustration and anxiety: There were women who'd lost their sex drives altogether, and ones who wanted to resume lovemaking, but were hurt by their husband's tentativeness and image of them now as a mother instead of a lover; some hadn't lost their baby weight and felt undesirable; others were just plain too tired. Even the women in the group who had been quiet grew animated with our discussion. "Omigod, I'm going through the same thing!" "Really? I thought it was just me!" "I was wondering if I don't love him anymore!" Just sharing their concerns with each other was clearly helping on some level. Until Brooke Shields wrote her fearless memoir, *Down Came the Rain*, no one ever talked publicly about postpartum depression, but virtually every mother I know has gone through some version of the baby blues. Feeling like you're going through it alone is even worse.

After my firstborn, I would cry at the drop of a hat, and wanted to curl up in a little ball with my baby and make the rest of the world go away. Including my poor husband. When it started to happen again after Rain, I was less willing to just silently wait it out. I was frankly worried: I was in this relationship with a man I considered my soul mate, and suddenly I didn't want him around me! But I was also a little wiser this time around. I knew that a woman in this predicament has to compassionately give herself a chance to roll through her hormones and be very patient with herself; it's really time to be your own friend. I also knew that it was more important than ever to keep the emotional intimacy of my relationship strong when the physical connection was weak. When I was younger and didn't have so much at stake, I would call it quits as soon as the infatuation wore off and I started to feel like I had fallen out of love. But now I know I'm with the right person, and I have a stronger sense of resolve when we start flatlining. I don't want to accept the pleasant-but-parallel-lives option, and I'm willing to invest the effort needed to avoid that. It's a sense of destiny, not duty, that makes me stay.

Whether it's baby-related or not, the first thing you need to do when you've lost that lovin' feeling is to reconnect with yourself as a woman, with your own sensuality. Remember the woman behind the scenes, and who she was before you became a mother. She's still there. Coax her out. So you don't feel in shape or in the mood for sexy lingerie? Buy yourself a flowing, silky nightgown, instead, and appreciate the whisper of smooth satin against your skin. Treat yourself to a new perfume or scented lotion. Paint your toenails, take your hair out of a bun, and stop whining about not having enough time to pay attention to yourself. There's *never* enough time, and if you're waiting for the earth to magically slow down on its axis and give you an extra three hours a week so you can shave your legs and deep-condition your hair, you're going to end up looking like King Kong in an Amy Winehouse wig. Carve out small, manageable chunks of time for yourself, and zero in on one part of you to pamper every day or two: Slather on the conditioner and pop on a shower cap to let it soak in while you fold a load of laundry. Take a bath with your baby, and when you're rubbing lotion on her afterward, do yourself the same favor. Do something for yourself every day to feel like a woman. Feeling feminine gives you confidence, and nothing is sexier than confidence.

And just because you and your man aren't having sex together for the time being doesn't mean you can't do sexy things together. Hold hands in the car. Order in pizza and watch old movies in bed. Spoon together and whisper bedtime stories to each other in the dark, describing a different fantasy every night. Declare a no-chores weekend. Stay connected by scheduling regular date nights, even if the date is dinner for two at the kitchen table after the kids are down for the evening. Light a candle, get out the nice plates, and even microwaved nachos can look romantic. Food is a passion David and I share, so we feel connected when we can get in the kitchen and cook together. We'd both love to find other pastimes we could share as a couple, too. It's kind of tough, because he's hyperathletic and competitive. I'm no wuss, but I've seen him play volleyball, and I'd rather not have to leave the beach on a gurney, thanks anyway. Reconnecting with your mate should never involve paramedics.

love potions

- lychee fruit
- ginger
- conch
- uni (Especially if it's picked up right out of the ocean in Sardinia by a sexy man who feeds it to me right off the spear! Not sure if it was that visual experience or the sea urchin itself that turned me on so much.)
- damiana—love elixir of the Aztecs; try the liqueur in a margarita
- oysters
- almonds—said to make men more potent . . . nature's little fertility treatment
- chocolate-covered frozen bananas—is it the chocolate or the performance of eating one that's the bigger turn-on?

If you're feeling distant and disconnected, sometimes it helps to take yourself back to the starting point psychologically. Reenact the things you did instinctively when you first connected: Make eye contact, and not just when speaking; let him catch you studying him. Daydream, conjure up a fantasy about him. If you're out with other couples and the mood is fun and mellow, play talk-show host and playfully ask your friends what they find sexy about each other. When someone idly posed that question to us not long ago, I was swept away when David revealed that just that evening, when I put on my dress, it had

sexy art and science

SEDUCTIVE FRAGRANCES

Kama Sutra oil

pheromones like musk oils

Danya Decker Acacia candle

Kai body lotion

BOOKS

The Story of O

The Kama Sutra

Love Letters: An Anthology of Passion, by Michelle Lovric

HOTTEST MOVIE SCENES

The Notebook (boat in the rain)

Last Tango in Paris (fur coat boot scene)

9 1/2 Weeks (blindfolded feeding)

Body Heat

Revenge

Indecent Proposal (in the kitchen)

MUSIC

Robin Thicke, "Lost Without You"

Maxwell, *Urban Hang Suite* album

Morcheeba, "Undress Me Now"

Keith Sweat, "Make It Last Forever"

Sade, "Sweetest Taboo" and "By Your Side"

Brian McKnight, "Everytime You Go Away" and "Back Seat Getting Down"

Tina Arena, "Victoria's Secret"

D'Angelo, "Brown Sugar"

Kem, "Heaven"

fallen in a way that drew his eye to a small curve he had never noticed before. "And I just thought, *Wow, I am so f'ing happy*," he said. Needless to say, a public declaration like that made me feel beloved, and drew me that much closer to him.

Speaking your mind without fear of judgment or criticism is vital in any serious relationship, and David and I try to check in with each other emotionally now and then to keep the lines of communication open. Just ask each other simple, honest questions with no hidden agendas: *Is there anything you're missing? Anything you want that you don't have? Anything that you're wishing for that maybe you want me to do that I'm not doing? Is there anything you're not getting that I need to give you, that I can give you? Let me hear your wishes.* It takes a lot of strength to have a very vulnerable, nondefensive conversation like that, but why wouldn't you want to know those things about the person you love, and to have him know them about you? You're setting yourselves up for success, not tallying shortcomings.

One of the most powerful ways to reconnect with your loved one is through the written word. David and I rediscovered this old-school art when David's movie projects forced us apart for long stretches of time. Putting pen to linen paper and letting the words flow feels so intimate, because you're likely waiting to do so when you have some quiet time to yourself, when you can focus and reflect. Your lover, though far away, gets your undivided attention, and you'll find yourself able to speak from your heart without embarrassment. When you're on the receiving end, you're just as likely to seek a quiet, private place to pore over his words, and allow yourself the luxury of being able to really contemplate what's being expressed. Just seeing a loved one's handwriting is so personal and sentimental, and a letter always feels meaningful.

If I'm e-mailing, my messages to David tend to be more newsy and superficial—I'll certainly sign off by telling him I love him, but in between, he's likely to hear about Shaya's latest bit of mischief, or what happened at my rehearsal that day, or which household appliance has decided to go on strike. If I'm writing out my thoughts in longhand on stationery, though, it just feels more formal, and I'm going to go deeper. The love letters David and I exchange that way become keepsakes of the memories we've shared, our dreams of what we want to do together, of our most vulnerable feelings at that moment in our lives. We both save them.

When David and I hit our roughest patch ever, and were teetering on the edge of a breakup, he landed the role in South Africa. For three months, we had only sporadic, brief telephone connections, and he had no computer access. But old-fashioned airmail worked fine, so we communicated mainly by handwritten letter. I felt a rush whenever an envelope was waiting for me in the mailbox at home, and I can remember studying his penmanship so I could decipher whether he was sad, or stressed, or doing okay. When I was missing him, I would take out his letters and just reread his thoughts, and feel connected as I drank in his emotions. Apart, and in writing, we found our sweet spot again, and we ended up holding tighter to what we had instead of letting go. Sometimes, I would struggle to find the words to send him. One of my favorite quotes is one I still use now and then, as a silent mantra to myself, when I need to find my way back to us:

"I followed my heart. It led me to you."

In the end, that's the greatest truth we hold on this incredible journey we share as mothers, as lovers, as women, our one certain compass, certain to lead us safely home no matter how lost or alone we sometimes feel. Our hearts. Love is what allows us to close our eyes and listen to the music, to dance when we stumble, and lift each other up, spin wildly, laugh joyfully and never let go.